Your First Year Teaching Computer Science

A Practical Guide to Success for New Computer Science Teachers

Chris Gregg

ALINEA

Alinea Learning
Boston

ALINEA

Alinea Learning
Boston, Massachusetts
Published in the United States of America by Alinea Learning,
an imprint and division of Alinea Knowledge, LLC, Boston.

Education is not the filling of a pail, but the lighting of a fire.

— William Butler Yeats

I never teach my pupils, I only attempt to provide the conditions in which they can learn.

— Albert Einstein

Computers can do all the left hemisphere processing better and faster than the human brain. So what's left for the human brain is global thinking, creative thinking, intuitive-problem solving, seeing the whole picture. All of that can not be done by the computer.

— Betty Edwards

Teaching is the one profession that creates all other professions.

— Anonymous

CONTENTS

Terms   vii

Acknowledgments   ix

About the Author   xiii

I   MOTIVATION   1

1   WHAT HAVE I GOTTEN MYSELF INTO?   3

2   WHAT I WISH I KNEW BEFORE STARTING   13

II   NUTS AND BOLTS   25

3   KNOW YOUR STUDENTS   27

4   KNOW YOUR SUBJECT   45

5   KNOW YOUR TOOLS   55

6   PLANNING YOUR COURSE   71

7   CREATING AWESOME ASSIGNMENTS   91

8   LECTURES   139

9   GRADING (AND THE ROLE OF TEACHING ASSISTANTS)   175

10   ONLINE RESOURCES   203

III   IMPROVING YOUR CRAFT   215

11   OBSERVING OTHERS TEACH, AND REFLECTING ON YOUR OWN TEACHING   217

12   HANDLING FEEDBACK   229

13   STAYING CURRENT ON, AND CONTRIBUTING TO CS EDUCATION RESEARCH   241

IV   INFLUENCING STUDENTS (AND OTHERS)   255

14   INTERACTING WITH STUDENTS: HOLDING OFFICE HOURS, MEETING INDIVIDUALLY WITH STUDENTS, ADVISING COMPUTER SCIENCE MAJORS, AND WRITING RECOMMENDATION LETTERS   257

15 PRIORITIZING YOUR TIME, AND WHEN TO JUST SAY NO287

Epilogue   297

Appendices   301
A   TEACHING ONLINE   303

TERMS

As this book attempts to be school and educational-level agnostic, there are a number of generic terms that I have used to encompass many educational institutions. For example, if you see the term "instructor" and you are a professor, think "professor," and if you are a secondary school teacher, think "teacher."

ACM The Association of Computing Machinery.

CS0 The ACM designation for a "precursor" computing course that focus on computing skills and/or computational thinking. CS0 courses are not traditionally part of a computer science curriculum for majors.

CS1 The ACM designation for the first introductory computer science course in a college or university curriculum. CS1 courses usually focus on teaching programming skills to students with no prior programming experience.

CS2 The ACM designation for the second course in a computer science curriculum. CS2 is often a data structures course.

INSTRUCTOR Professor, lecturer, teacher, instructor, etc. This is the lead person responsible for the course.

LMS Learning Management System. Often this online service is provided school-wide to instructors and students, and there are many varieties (e.g., *Blackboard*, *Canvas*, *Moodle*, and *Sakai*). LMS sites can host gradebooks, rosters, forums, etc.

TA Teaching Assistant. Sometimes called a Teaching Fellow, Course Assistant, or Section Leader, and often advanced undergraduates or graduate students who help with the course by grading, teaching sections, holding office hours, etc.

TERM This can refer to a quarter, semester, year, etc. Whatever fits your own school's model is what you should think when you see 'term'.

I can no other answer make,
but, thanks, and thanks.

— William Shakespeare

ACKNOWLEDGMENTS

THE NUMBER OF TEACHERS, relatives, friends, and acquaintances who have helped inform my own teaching is an uncountably infinite set. However, I wouldn't be a teacher if it wasn't for my mother, also a teacher, who modeled compassionate, thoughtful teaching every day as she and my father raised my sister and me. My sister, Tory Kuester, is another model – though younger, I always admired (and still admire!) her hard work that always seems effortless. I am also grateful for my wife Rachel's love and support as I've drafted this book.

My grade school, middle school, and high school teachers prepared me as much to be a teacher as they did to be a learner. My teachers that stand out: Ms. Harter (4th grade), Mr. Rabideau (5th grade), Ms. Caldwell (7th grade), Ms. Barbi (9th grade), Mr. Denno (10th grade), Mr. Campbell (10th grade), Ms. Pingel (11th grade), Mr. Pingel (11th grade), Mr. DeVinney (12th grade), Ms. Smeltzer (12th grade), and Ms. Forster (12th grade).

When I was getting my Master of Education at the Harvard Graduate School of Education, Kay Merseth and Vicki Jacobs provided a tremendous foundation for good pedagogy and teaching philosophy, and Eric Toshalis gave me insights into teaching and observing teachers that I use every day in the classroom. My student-teaching cooperating teachers, Victor Melehov and Stacy Kissel at Brookline High School showed me very different (but effective) ways to teach physics, and Stacy remains one of my best friends.

Also at Brookline, I was greatly influenced by Ed Wiser, Allyson Mizoguchi, Liz Crane, Lexi Murphy, John Andrews, Danielle Rabina, Margaret Selzter, Aubrey Love, and Emily McGinnis (among many others).

In Ph.D. school at UVA, my advisor, Kim Hazelwood, along with Joanne Dugan and Kevin Skadron, gave me the opportunity to teach a large class at the collegiate level, and I am grateful for that experience. Aaron Bloomfield, Mark Sherriff, and Tom Horton also gave me outstanding teaching guidance while I was at UVA, as did Luther Tychonievich, Michael Boyer, and Ray Buse.

Carla Brodley and Ben Hescott gave me my first post-grad school collegiate teaching opportunity at Tufts, and they are both incredible educators. I would not have made it past day one at Tufts if it wasn't for Bruce Molay and his pedagogical mastery, and I am also grateful for the support, guidance, and friendship I had at Tufts from Ben Shapiro, Ming Chow, Mark Sheldon, Sam Guyer, Soha Hassoun, Norman Ramsey, and Kathleen Fisher.

One of the reasons I moved to Stanford was to be part of a vibrant teaching cadre with CS education as a focus, and I am grateful to be part of the Educational Affairs group, filled with amazing lecturers, teaching professors, and administrators. Mehran Sahami, Eric Roberts, Jay Borenstein, Jerry Cain, Michael Chang, Cynthia Lee, Nick Parlante, Chris Piech, Keith Schwarz, Marty Stepp, Nick Troccoli, Lisa Yan, Patrick Young, and Julie Zelenski are all phenomenal teachers and I continue to learn from them every day. Claire Stager, Meredith Hutchin, and Danielle Hoversten (among others) make Educational Affairs tick largely from behind the scenes, but their support is both critical and outstanding. I have also enjoyed teaching with Professor Phil Levis, and have enjoyed talking about CS teaching with Pat Hanrahan, John Osterhout, Kayvon Fatahalian, and Mary Wooters, as well. As department chairs, both Alex Aiken and John Mitchell have always supported the Educational Affairs mission without fail.

Finally, the many thousands of students, teaching assistants, and section leaders I have had over the years, with ages ranging from nine to sixty, have been the real reason I continue to teach. I learn as much from my students as they (hopefully) do from me, and their energy, enthusiasm, and perspective impresses me every day.

My mission in life is not merely to survive, but to thrive; and to do so with some passion, some compassion, some humor, and some style.

— Maya Angelou

ABOUT THE AUTHOR

CHRIS GREGG IS A LECTURER in the Stanford Computer Science department. His primary focus is at the introductory computer science level, teaching many courses in the Stanford computer science core curriculum. He has also taught courses in teaching computer science, and he is the director of the Stanford Computer Science Education Certificate program. He has been named to the School of Engineering's Tau Beta Pi Teaching Honor Roll twice.

Chris grew up in the tiny town of Skaneateles in Central New York, and he received his undergraduate degree in Electrical Engineering from Johns Hopkins University. After college, he joined the Navy as a cryptologist, and he spent seven years on active duty followed by another fifteen years in the Navy Reserves, retiring as a Commander. While on active duty, Chris started out stationed in San Diego, CA, and sailed on a number of ships across many oceans. He then spent two years living in Gerringong, New South Wales, Australia on exchange with the Royal Australian Navy where he learned to surf, and perhaps surprisingly, survived.

After his active duty Navy stint, Chris decided to follow in his mother's footsteps to become a teacher, and he pursued and received a Master of Education degree from Harvard University with a focus on teaching high school physics. He taught physics and computer science at Brookline High School in Brookline, MA, and physics at Pacific Collegiate School in Santa Cruz, CA. While at Pacific Collegiate School, Chris wont the High School Teacher of the Year award.

Eventually, Chris decided to pursue a Ph.D., and he received his doctorate in Computer Engineering from the University of Virginia. While there, he won the All-University Graduate Teaching Award in Math, Science and Engineering. He subsequently spent a year recalled to the Navy in Djbouti, Africa, where he served as the Information Operations Chief for the Combined Joint Task Force–Horn of Africa.

Following his discharge from active duty recall, Chris began teaching as a lecturer in the Tufts Department of Computer Science where he taught introductory courses, a wearable devices course, and the Senior Design Project course.

After a couple of years at Tufts, Chris decided that he wanted to be back in California, and took his current position at Stanford. He loves the job and can't imagine a better place to work. He, his wife Rachel, their infant daughter Celeste, and their two whippets, Jupiter and Juno live amongst the redwood trees in Felton, CA.

Part I

MOTIVATION

WHAT HAVE I GOTTEN MYSELF INTO?

THINK BACK UPON your first computer science course. You may or may not have already had some background in programming, but try and recall your first day in a classroom-style computer science course. How did the instructor open the first day? Maybe it was with a welcome and a brief outline of the course, and maybe there was a (probably boring) discussion about administrative details, and about when the midterm and final exam dates were. Or maybe the instructor launched into some actual course material, to give you a feel for what you were about to learn during the term. Possibly, the instructor gave you a motivational speech about how amazing computer science is, and how much you were going to learn about *thinking*, instead of just about *programming*.

Whatever it was, did you happen to think about what the instructor had to do to prepare for that first day? I would guess that you probably didn't think about it, nor were you expected to consider it at all – you were the target audience, there to be taught, and not the teacher. If you're reading this book, then you have just jumped over to the teacher role, and now *you* are going to be the one who has to plan that first day: the introductory welcome, the (hopefully not boring) administrative material, the introduction to the course content, and that motivational speech about how wonderful the world of computer science is. Hopefully, that thought brings you images of joy, about how you're going to be the one molding all of those young minds, and about how much your students are going to love your class. Likely, though, if you pause to think about it for a few more seconds, a bead of sweat might begin forming on your brow, and you might start to catalog all of the things you are going to have to do, and not just for that first day. You might be thinking to yourself, "What have

I gotten myself into?!" and no one is going to fault you for that question. There *is* a lot to think about when getting ready to teach a course, and it can be overwhelming to consider in great detail. Hopefully you have found this book before the first day of class, so you have time to plan (or you have planned already).[1] This book describes those nuts and bolts (see Part II) that go into planning a computer science course, and it provides recommendations and strategies for improving your teaching (Part III), especially in your formative teaching years. The last part of the book (Part IV) considers a broader perspective on your role as a teacher, advisor, and faculty member, and suggests ways to make your computer science instruction more meaningful than simply teaching a bunch of technical topics. Indeed, much of the material covered in this book is applicable to any number of subjects, but this book will focus on preparing you to teach a computer science course. But first, we motivate!

Teaching is one of the most rewarding, fun, and engaging vocations, and you should be genuinely excited about what you are about to do. You will in fact mold those young minds, and you will also learn a great deal yourself – as the Phil Collins lyrics in Disney's *Tarzan* state, "In learning you will teach // And in teaching you will learn".[2] You may think you know all there is about your subject, but I guarantee that come the end of the term you will have an even more thorough understanding than you ever imagined. Before and during the term, as you prepare your material to teach it, you will have to think about it in more detail than you have in the past – you will be predicting the types of questions the students will ask,[3] and you will be synthesizing the topic to fit into the hour per class you have to teach it. You will

---

1 If not – well, you can do it! It is an oft-repeated saying that you only need to be one day ahead of your students, though it is generally followed by a hearty chuckle and a knowing nod that it isn't quite that easy. But, the odds are good that you know the material yourself pretty well, and you can get through the term. You might want to jump to Part II to get some tips on planning.

2 *Son of Man* by Phil Collins.

3 though you will get many questions during the term that you didn't expect!

also be creating section problems and exam problems that test the material, and you will be thinking of real-life examples that demonstrate why learning the course content isn't simply about regurgitating it on the exam.

Your own background will, of course, color your own teaching of your course material, and how you teach in general. During your own education, you have had dozens of teachers in all subjects, some of whom you loved, and some of whom you did not. Go ahead and make a list of all the teachers you remember – not just the fabulous ones, but the merely good ones, and also the ones you didn't particularly care for. You likely did not analyze *why* you liked or didn't like their teaching (or personalities, or grading schemes, etc.) then, but you can probably come up with some reasons now.[4] Analyze those reasons, and start thinking about who you might want to emulate. Also ponder the type of teacher you *don't* want to be, so you can recognize the signs if you do end up veering in that direction. You will grow into your own style over time, but you undoubtedly have some ideas of how you want to teach already, and you are most likely already imitating some of your past teachers to some extent. You can only benefit from clarifying what those teachers did that you now do or want to do with your own teaching.

One thing to keep in mind about those fabulous teachers in your past – you may not be able to emulate all of them, for lots of reasons, and that is okay. One of my favorite computer science professors was a master at live-coding – he didn't need notes, and he could immediately code up a function to do just about anything, and it was marvelous. I, on the other hand, had better know exactly what I'm going to type if I'm coding in front of a class. I get a bit nervous when live-coding, and I can't always think straight in the heat of the moment. So, even though I would love to be able to live-code like that professor, it isn't going to

---

4 And for the really great ones, make contact again and tell them that! When your own students come back to you some day to tell you how much you inspired them, you will appreciate it more than you can imagine.

happen. You will find your own style, and you certainly don't have to emulate everything that your own great teachers did in their classrooms.

In addition to your teaching style, you will have your own ideas about what to teach in your class that is important. This may already be decided for you to some extent – there is a high probability that the course or courses you are slated to teach has or have been taught before, and you may already have a syllabus, textbook, and labs and assignments ready to use. This is a good thing! It is far harder to teach a brand new course than a course that has already been set up and tested by others, and although you may want to make some changes to the curriculum[5] as you plan for the course, having the bulk of the course already built is incredibly helpful. If you are teaching at a college or university that has a Computer Science department and you are slated to teach a CS0, CS1, or a CS2 course (or, really, any course already in the curriculum), try your best to locate the materials used in prior versions of the course. Depending on where you are teaching, this material may be excellent or it may be mediocre, but in either case you will be able to utilize it as a framework at the very least.

Even with a fully-prepared curriculum, you will be responsible for delivering the lectures, and you get to decide how each class goes. You may decide to deliver your courses "naked," with only a marker and a whiteboard (and likely a set of notes), you may decide that you want to produce (or use) a slide deck (e.g., PowerPoint, Keynote, Google Docs, Beamer, etc.), and you may or may not use other classroom technology such as clickers or phone/online instant response systems. You may also be in a situation where your courses can (or must) be recorded. These are all choices that will be based on your own educational background, and potentially what you have read in education literature[6], or what you have seen other people do (and they may also

---

5 if you are allowed – some schools have strict requirements for the material taught in some courses, particularly in the introductory course sequence
6 or in this book!

be based on institutional requirements, such as recording the lectures). Planning lectures–even with already-prepared slides–is a time-consuming job, especially if you need to refresh your own understanding of the material (which is often the case when you are taking over a course). See Chapter 8 for a discussion about lecture style and preparation.

While lecture planning takes time, designing outstanding assignments can take an even greater (and a surprising) amount of time. Assignments are, arguably, the time when students learn the most (despite your amazing teaching skills), and good assignments should be designed to challenge students in the material while at the same time be engaging (so the students enjoy doing them) and also be gradable so students can be assessed on their knowledge. According to Eric Roberts, Professor *Emeritus* at Stanford, a good CS assignment for a CS1 course can take upwards of 100 hours (!) to create. Don't let this number scare you too much – the computer science world embraces sharing good materials (with attribution, of course), and there are many places to look to find terrific assignments that you may be able to modify to suit the needs of your class.[7] You may remember great assignments from your own coursework, and feel free to reach out to your old professors to ask about borrowing those assignments for your own class. Additionally, by studying and assigning well-designed assignments, you will be prepared to craft your own as you improve your own teaching and course preparation. Chapter 7 describes strategies on how to make awesome assignments.

One thing you must always keep in mind when designing your courses is your audience. Who are your students? What are you expecting their background to be? When writing your lectures and making your assignments, you want to design them as best you can to challenge students but to also be within the grasp of the hardworking student who wants to learn the material. Where you teach can affect this, as can the general population of your

---

7 For example, SIGCSE's Nifty Assignments, is a great place to start.

students. There are obviously a lot of subtleties to determining who your audience is, and you will certainly have a wide swath of students with different abilities and motivation. You should assume that students will work diligently even if you presume some will not, and you should calibrate your material accordingly. As a new teacher at a new school, you will have to adjust your own understanding of the students as you teach, and the first couple of courses you teach may require a good deal of re-calibration mid-term. If you are new to a school, make sure you ask your colleagues about their students, and try to poll as many people as you can. Chapter 3 discusses the art of knowing your students.

Assessing students is another hard goal as a teacher – not only do you want challenging and engaging assignments, but the students need feedback on the assignments. The feedback should be constructive so they know what they can improve on, but it also (in general) needs to have a grade assessment because most schools require that students receive grades on their performance in a course. Additionally, grading should be fair so students are satisfied that they have been assessed correctly. Also nice (though not always possible) is for the grading to be completed reasonably efficiently. With enrollments in computer science booming, classes can be large or humongous.[8] You may decide to hold exams in your class, as well, and exams (unlike many assignments) must be created new each term, as questions from prior term exams are certainly available to students.[9]

Exploding class sizes may be one of the reasons you have the job that made you pick up this book. Computer science professors, lecturers, and teachers at the high school level are in huge demand right now, and it is because so many students want to study computer science. Indeed, hiring cannot keep up, and class

---

8 U.C. Berkeley's 61A introductory programming course routinely has more than 2000 students each semester these days.

9 Cheating on assignments is another large concern. See Chapter 9 for some strategies to limit (and/or catch) cheating on assignments.

sizes will undoubtedly continue to rise at many institutions.[10] One potential benefit to larger enrollments is that this produces a larger pool of potential Teaching Assistants (TAs) for your course, particularly if your school or department is willing to hire undergraduate TAs. Depending on where you teach, you may be able to hire many TAs. Introductory courses at Stanford can hire upwards of fifty Section Leaders (Stanford's name for undergraduate TAs) per course, and the Section Leading program, which runs itself with student leadership, is a model for how to successfully create a robust undergraduate TA pool. However, managing (and even getting to know) fifty TAs is itself challenging – did you think when you took your job teaching computer science that you might have to manage fifty people at once? If the TAs are expected to lead recitation sections or labs, you will also want to ensure that there is training for those positions in place, too. You may, of course, not have the luxury of many TAs, and managing the limited resources you have is an important skill, as well. With limited grading resources, you will need to make your assignment grading even more streamlined. Chapter 9 describes strategies for grading and ideas for utilizing your potential teaching assistants to the maximum.

One additional consideration when teaching large class is that there will be proportionally more special cases you have to deal with. A colleague of mine likes to say that with a class of four hundred students, there is at least one student with a legitimate special case problem every other day. Students have real-world problems that often have nothing at all to do with the specifics of your course: in the most serious cases, students have family emergencies, physical illnesses, and mental health problems. In the more routine cases students have sporting events, symphony

---

10 Or, limits will be put in place. Sadly, research shows that limiting enrollment affects underrepresented minorities, women, and first generation students the most. Furthermore, limiting the number of students does not help the bigger picture that colleges and universities already have a hard time producing enough graduates to meet the demand in industry.

practice, and other class conflicts. Depending on your TA situation, you may be able to delegate handling the routine cases, and you can have class policy that covers many of them. You will have to deal with the serious cases yourself (in terms of your class – hopefully there are school resources that can help), as you can't delegate that to other students. You should be prepared to handle special cases before your class starts.

One category of special case that is worth mentioning is that of the students who have classroom accommodations, which may include being able to have a designated note-taker in class, to being able to get extensions on assignments, to the more common case of being allowed more time on exams (50% more time is typical). There are a number of federal statutes (if you are in the United States) that cover disabilities, including *The Americans with Disabilities Act Amendment* (2009), *The Americans with Disabilities Act* (1990), and *Section 504 of the Rehabilitation Act* (1973). Schools must provide students a way to be assessed on potential accommodations, and you as an instructor must ensure that your students who have accommodations get them. This means, for instance, that you must find rooms and proctors for students who need extra time on their exams, and this can be challenging, and time consuming. Again, the number of students with accommodations often scales linearly with the number of students in a class, and a course with 400 students could easily have twenty or more students with individual accommodations.

Once the calendar planning, lecture planning, assignment planning, lecture delivering, office hour holding, grading, managing and training TAs, and handling special cases is done, you are done, right? Not so fast. You may have to deal with *Incomplete* grades, where students don't complete the material during the term and need to finish it up afterward, you may need to deal with students who cheated, and you will undoubtedly get queries about why students got the grade in the course that they did. You may also have to advise students majoring in computer science, you will have to write recommendation letters to college or graduate school, and you will certainly get asked by students for tips on how to ace their interview at *Top Tech Company*. But, while some of these duties may be annoying (e.g., dealing with cheaters), many of them can be enjoyable, such as advising, or providing interview tips. It should go without saying that at some level you should actually enjoy being around students, for you will be around a lot of them once your teaching career begins.

To get back to the question posed by the title of this chapter, "What have I gotten myself into?", you have absolutely gotten yourself into a job that is challenging. Hopefully this chapter has given you an idea of what you can expect in that regard. But, you have also gotten yourself into a job that has a plethora of benefits you are going to love. You get to teach students about a field that you yourself probably enjoy. You get to talk about cool ideas every day, and you get to introduce other people to those cool ideas, which is a great feeling. Good teaching takes a tremendous amount of creativity, and that keeps your own mind sharp. You will grow your own understanding of the material by teaching it, guaranteed. Indeed, most teachers came into the field because they love learning, and that absolutely continues when you become a teacher. What have you gotten yourself into? You have gotten yourself into a field that you will be proud to be a part of, and that will be rewarding beyond what you can imagine.

It's the Little Conversations that Matter

Sometimes we forget some of the conversations we have with students that change their lives, but they do happen. I received the following email from a graduating CS student, Erica, one of the strongest students in the school: *"On the first day of comp15 (almost 3 years ago!), I was on the fence about majoring in CS (mostly because I was intimidated). I was on the waitlist for the course, but since I wasn't a declared major, I may not have gotten in to the class. However, if I remember correctly, you ended up volunteering to teach an extra lab so that everyone who wanted to take the class could get in. If not for that, I'd probably be a somewhat-bored Biopsychology major. (I really can't picture myself majoring in anything other than CS.) You taught the first lab of the course, and after I finished the lab you asked me if I was a CS major. I said something like, 'uhh I think so, but I'm not sure yet.' I remember that you responded, 'people like you are the reason I wanted to let everyone in to the course.' I remember that situation whenever I teach the same lab (2 times per semester * 5 semesters = 10 times now), and what students might be 'little Ericas' considering CS but unsure. I would never have had the confidence to apply to be a TA if you hadn't explicitly asked me to. And, being a comp15 TA has been one of the highlights of my time at Tufts."*

I didn't know that I played a pivotal role in Erica's decision to become a CS major, but I'm glad that the few short conversations I had with her to encourage her paid off.

2

WHAT I WISH I KNEW BEFORE STARTING

In order to get where you are today, you have been through close to or more than twenty years of school. You *know* school, and you know what it is like to be a student. You likely have been a Teaching Assistant, and you may have already taught courses yourself. But, if you are reading this book, you are probably in a new job, and probably at a new school. There are some safety nets that you might have relied on in other situations (e.g., a fully-prepared curriculum, or someone else who was the instructor-of-record). Chapter 1 gave an overview of some of the things you can expect as a new teacher in computer science, but this chapter will delve into some of the more specific things you may face that you aren't necessarily expecting. This is not meant to be a comprehensive list, and it is certainly subjective.

If you take anything away from this chapter let it be the fact that you *can't* prepare for every detail of the term ahead of you, and you will have to face issues that you've never faced before and that you have not prepared yourself for. Take heart that every teacher has had the same experience, and that you *can* deal with unforeseen issues as they arise. You should also recognize that there are many people available to help you out as you go through your first course – everyone wants you to succeed, and almost everyone is willing to give you a honeymoon period to get acclimated – in other words, if you do make mistakes, people (including your students!) will understand. Your colleagues will support you, as will your department chair. Your students will also support you, especially if you are honest with them about this being your first experience teaching their course. All schools also have support staff, from administrative assistants, to counselors, to student deans, who can point you in the right direction when you have questions about your students (see Chapter 3 about knowing your students).

All of the topics covered in this chapter are expanded upon in other chapters in the book. I have referenced the appropriate chapter where necessary.

TIME

During your first term teaching, you will, at some point, utter the phrase, *Where did the time go?* Like a gas to its container, the number of things you have to do when teaching easily expands to fill your day. You might spend an extra two hours crafting that lecture you are excited about, or you might have a long meeting with a struggling student. Grading may take more time than you expect, or you might decide to write that grading script that will *eventually* save you time.[1] Hopefully, you want to have a good life/work balance, and the *life* part needs some time, too.

In other words – you're going to be busy. This comes as a surprise to too many novice teachers, especially if they are given a reduced course load during their first term. They think, *this is going to be great! I will have so much time!* When I was in my student-teaching year as a prospective high school physics teacher, there was a brand new teacher at the school who was transitioning careers from industry as an engineer into teaching. He had a new baby at home, and he had decided that he wanted to teach because he thought (as we found out later), *teachers come in at 8:00am and get to go home at 3:00pm.* He had the common (and incorrect) notion that teachers have an easy job with regular hours, and he had no idea about the amount of planning, grading, meetings, etc. that he was about to undertake. He lasted three weeks on the job.

Too many teachers face early burn-out because they don't expect to spend the amount of time on their work. They also may

---

1 See this XKCD comic for tips on calculating whether that script will ever save you time.

not plan effectively enough, which is something you should strive to do. One critical part of the planning process is to understand that you will have to work long hours, and you may have to take work home, or spend extra time at school. However, this does not need to be an oppressive thought: you hopefully love what you do, and you are willing to put in the time to do it right. And the fact is that as you become more experienced, you will be able to streamline your work, and you will have prepared materials to use, especially as you teach the same classes multiple times. Just know that it isn't as simple as walking in the classroom, teaching the students, and telling the TAs to grade all the work.

Once you realize that you will be time-constrained, you need to prioritize your daily activities. Being prepared for class is critical, as is preparing good assignments and exam materials. Holding office hours is necessary, and answering some emails in a timely manner is important, as well. If you are in a research position, then you must also prioritize those activities, and you may have other priorities that are job-specific but unrelated to teaching. Regardless, you should have a list of priorities, and you should stick to it. You often can take some extra time for grading, though it is best if you are in a position to give feedback to students to do so before their next assignment is due. If you have TAs, set the expectation for getting grading done when the course begins, and hold them to the plan. See Chapter 9 for tips on grading and utilizing your TAs effectively.

Be sure to set aside enough time to prepare your lectures and other materials. This is best begun (especially for a new course) in the weeks before the course starts, but it is particularly difficult to plan all your lectures out ahead of time the first time you teach a course. You will find that if you try and plan out all of your lectures exactly before the course starts, you will have to do some significant re-planning based on how the course is going. See Chapter 8 for detailed guidance on planning your lectures, and Chapter 7 for information about creating assignments.

If you are teaching large classes, beware that as classes get bigger, you will have to spend more time dealing with individual student issues. As discussed in Chapter 1, the number of individual student concerns scales with class size. This is, again, where good TA resources can be critical, as can a good chain-of-command structure to handle student issues. If you find yourself dealing with too many student issues yourself, try to fall back on your TAs for some assistance.

Although it may seem that you need twenty-five hours in a day to teach during your first term, you can handle the work, but you should be prepared for the feeling of continually being out of time. Plan well, and fall back on your prioritized list of things-to-do when you feel in a crunch. Sometimes, too, you will need to guard your time – see Chapter 15 for a discussion about when you should say *no* to a request.

LOGISTICAL MATTERS AND ADMINISTRATIVE POLICIES

Every school and department has different policies and traditions, and if you are at a new school you may be surprised at some of the differences than what you are used to. For example, I have been at schools where midterm exams are always given during class-time, and other schools where they are scheduled outside of class. This example can seem minor, but if you are used to one way and don't know about the difference, then you risk being unprepared. Students will expect policies that are similar from courses they have already taken, too, and while you can change them, knowing what students are expecting is important, as well. As a further example regarding exams: at Stanford, the school's Honor Code forbids instructors from being inside the classroom to proctor exams. I have never seen this at any other school, and until someone told me, I had no idea about the rule. You will find out about your own set of school-specific policies as you go through your first term or year, but you can help by asking good questions (see below) to ferret out the important policies ahead of time.

I have yet to work at a school where classroom policies and normal procedures are given to new instructors. The new instructor is simply supposed to figure them out, and while this usually works, you should probably sit down with a veteran in your department and ask some targeted questions. For example:

1. Are there key documents I should read that detail policies for the school or department?

2. Is there a standard course website template? What needs to go onto the website? Is there a standard syllabus template? How do I request that a website gets made for my class?

3. How do I make a request to the bookstore to have textbooks for my students to purchase? Are there procedures for students to purchase other materials (e.g., clickers) for class?

4. How does TA hiring work? How many hours are TAs supposed to put towards my class? How do TAs get paid, and do I have to do anything to approve their hours?

5. How are exams delivered? Are there any specific policies or traditions regarding midterm and final exams? Where can I find the exam times for my courses? Who schedules the rooms for exams? What is the policy for students who have overlapping exams? Are there any departmental guidelines for regrade requests on exams?

6. How does the department handle cheating? Who do I report cheating to? Do I need to handle cheating myself, or is there an office I can go through? Am I even allowed to handle cheating cases myself?

7. How do students alert me of their accommodations? Do students take exams through an office of accessibility, or do I need to set up rooms and proctoring for them?

8. Are there attendance policies?

9. Am I allowed to record my classes and post them online?

10. How many hours a week should I have office hours?

11. What system is used for grading? Where can I find the end-of-term grading deadlines?

12. Where are rosters located? Do the rosters have images?

13. Are there policies for students taking courses Pass/Fail (sometimes called Credit/No credit)? Are students allowed to audit my courses and not get a grade? If so, what are the policies for auditors?

14. How do *incomplete* grades work?

15. What resources are available for students if they have mental health issues? Are there emergency contact numbers? What is my responsibility if a student tells me about a mental health issue they are having?

16. Are there specific Integrated Development Environments (IDEs) that students are used to? Are there departmental computer systems that students can log into? If so, how do the students get their accounts? Can I install software onto departmental or school machines?

17. What software tools do faculty use to make classes more efficient (e.g., autograders, online/digital feedback, etc.)? (See Chapter 5 for information about tools).

18. Do students have access to non-free software (e.g., MATLAB, Mathematica)? Will students primarily have one type of operating system or another? Do all students have laptops?

19. Is there anything else I should know about teaching at this school, and in this department?

There will be many more policies and traditions that are not reflected in the above questions, and do not be surprised when you find out about them.

DIFFICULTY OF MATERIAL AND HETEROGENEOUS CLASSROOMS

Given that you are about to teach a computer science course, it is a good assumption that you have an aptitude for CS, and that you have taken a number of CS courses on your own. You may even be an expert with a Ph.D. in Computer Science.[2] This puts you in a great position to teach an awesome class, but you may have a skewed perspective on how hard the material will be for your students. Particularly if you are teaching a CS1 or CS2 course, you will undoubtedly have a wide range of students, and you should be aware of the heterogeneous nature of your audience. This is regardless of where you teach, by the way – you can be at a top 10 university or at any other school, and you will have some students who will struggle greatly with your material, and others who will find it a breeze.

As someone with a strong aptitude and a comprehensive CS background, you may relate best to the students who find the material easy. However, those students are not the ones who need you the most! On the contrary, the students that have a hard time learning CS are the ones who need support above all others. You need to be prepared to help those students, and you also need to be patient and understanding when they have a difficult time with your course material. Those are the students who will flock to your office hours and who will pepper the online question and answer forum with questions, and those are the ones who will

---

2 You may also be coming into computer science from another field, e.g., mathematics, other engineering, etc., and your own CS background may be relatively shallow. Fear not! Chapter 4 discusses knowing your subject. You probably wouldn't be teaching the course if you weren't interested in it, and that in itself gives you a good advantage.

need the most clear instructions for the assignments and the exam questions.

Contrary to your own experiences (potentially), computer science is not an easy subject for a wide spectrum of students. That said, many of those students will still enjoy the material, and many will also work extremely hard to do well. Some will even become computer science majors, and they will thrive in the field, despite their own difficulties. Be sure to support the students who work hard but find the material difficult – congratulate them on small wins, and encourage them to continue to put in the effort. You will rarely have to counsel students *out* of computer science, but you will often need to keep encouraging the ones who have a drive to do well but take more time to learn the material.

UNDERREPRESENTED STUDENTS

Computer Science has seen exploding enrollments recently, and although CS is still over-represented by white males, the number of underrepresented students has grown significantly, as well. The number of women, underrepresented minorities, LGBTQ+, first-generation college students, and other underrepresented students has increased, but you should understand that those students may have some apprehension about being in your classes, particularly if they do not feel like they fit in.

This is not to say that you should treat any of your students differently. However, you may want to consider reaching out to underrepresented students as a check-in during the term, or simply to show them that you know they are there. This does not need to be over-the-top, and can simply be an encouraging word about their performance in class, or an offer to talk about how the course is going, or about majoring in CS, or just to simply talk CS. You might be surprised at how far a small personal comment goes to giving students confidence that they are in the right place, and they they are welcomed in computer science.

SPECIAL CASES

One of the most surprising things I found when I was in my first year of teaching was the number of *special case* situations I faced with individual students. As mentioned in Chapter 1, the number of students with special cases grows with increasing enrollments, and in a large class, you will have to deal with students with unique situations more than you might think.

Some instructors craft detailed course policy and attempt to stick to it as often as is possible. For example, your assignment late-day policy might be to allow students to take three late days during the term without penalty, and after those three late days are used up, assignments are penalized when they are late. If you are clear about the policy and apply it for all students, regardless of the situation (e.g., sickness, family emergency, athletic events, etc.), that can potentially work, and it will hopefully be seen as fair by the students. However, it can seem unsympathetic to penalize students for events beyond their control. Refusing extra late days to a student who has been in the hospital for a week after appendicitis is a big decision, and one I would not make. My own policy has been to simply treat special cases individually, and make a decision based on the specific facts at hand. With illnesses or family emergencies, I am generally in the compassionate camp, and I will give the students minor extensions as necessary to compensate for the situations that are out of their control. I set specific limits, though. For example, if a student misses a week for an illness, I will usually suggest a plan for getting back into the regular schedule as soon as is possible. I want to avoid having the student continually behind on future assignments, so we work out a deal where the student can make up the work and still catch back up in a reasonable amount of time. If that isn't feasible, another option is to postpone the specific assignment due date until the end of the term, with the potential that the student receives an incomplete grade until they can hand it in.

Illnesses and emergencies often have a straightforward solution, as in the previous paragraph. However, there are other situations which get more difficult. They also are harder to craft policy for, or to prepare to deal with ahead of time, as they are often unique.[3] These cases usually come up at the end of the term, with students you have either never seen before, or who stopped producing work and/or attending class at some point in the term. The student is usually going to either fail the course, or get another grade they do not want. They will show up in your office (or, more likely, will send you a detailed email) to request special dispensation. Once you talk to the student (and you should do this in person if possible) to find out what the situation is, you have to make an assessment. Sometimes it is an easy decision – the student did not put in the work, and the mitigating circumstances that they relate to you do not meet the bar for special treatment. Students who claim to have had a difficult term will have reasons, but if those reasons were within their control (e.g., the student fell behind early, but did not attempt to get help), it is straightforward to argue that the student should have prioritized the course more. If the reasons are borderline (e.g., the student had mental health issues but did not address them), then this is a harder decision. You may want to reach out to a school counselor dean of students (or other suitable student-advocate), especially if the student did say that they were in contact with someone about the issues. However, in the end: if the student reaches out at the very end of the term and does not have a reasonable argument for special consideration, it is best to give the student the earned grade, while encouraging them to try and rectify similar situations in the future early on in the term.

---

3 Though, once you have been teaching for many years, you will start to see similarities.

FINAL THOUGHTS

The longer you teach, and especially the longer you teach at a particular school, the more you will know about teaching, students, and your school. You will face many surprises, and many situations you have not prepared for, and once you have dealt with a particular circumstance, you should reflect on it, and maybe take down notes on how you handled it, and how you might handle it differently in the future. Try not to get too frustrated with these surprises – hopefully in this chapter I have given you many things to think about before you begin teaching, but as I said in the opening paragraph: you cannot expect everything. Take each situation as a challenge, and as a learning experience, and you will find yourself more knowledgeable and less easy to surprise in the future.

Part II

NUTS AND BOLTS

KNOW YOUR STUDENTS

3

Do YOU REMEMBER that one teacher you had in high school or college that always gave too much work, and also always seemed to think that their class was the most important course and that you should prioritize it over all your other classes? As the work for the class piled up, you wanted to say, *Hold on! I'm taking four other classes, and you're giving me enough work to take up all my time!* You were possibly also on a sports team, or in a band, or on a dance team, yet your teacher didn't care (or know) about any of that. A lot of teachers can be like that, with a myopic attitude towards their own course, without considering that their students have full schedules and more to do than simply the one course.

Now think of that other teacher or professor you had, who jumped into material for the course and presumed you already had advanced knowledge that was necessary to understand the new topic. You re-checked the course prerequisites, and none of those courses had taught what the professor expected. You therefore had to either scramble to go learn that material on your own, or you ended up either doing poorly in the course, or withdrawing from it.

In both examples above, the teacher in question did not know their students, in different ways. The teacher who gave you too much work didn't realize (or care) that you were juggling an entire set of courses and activities, and the teacher who taught too advanced material without having prerequisites had no idea what you already knew.

As a teacher, you should strive to understand your students and to know their backgrounds and current abilities. Obviously, you cannot know exact details about students before the course begins (though for smaller classes you could take the time to get to know them after it starts). But, you should be able to make some educated guesses about your students before they enter your class, and prepare the course with that in mind. Furthermore, you should run the course with an understanding of what your students are going through. Guess what? When you are giving your midterm exam, your students probably have three other courses that also have a midterm exam during that week, and everyone benefits if you recognize that fact. That is not to say that you necessarily need to *do* anything in particular by knowing this, but it may color how hard you make an exam, or how you deal with students who will inevitably ask you about an accommodation because of it.

HOW DO YOU KNOW YOUR STUDENTS?

The first step to understanding your students is to simply put yourself into their shoes, and recall what it was like when you were in school. Before enrolling in a computer engineering Ph.D. program, I taught high school physics for seven years. When I became a full-time student again myself, I quickly remembered what it was like to take multiple hard classes all at once, and it made me realize that maybe I hadn't thought enough about that when I had been teaching high school. When I started teaching computer science while still a graduate student, I had a much better appreciation for this fact, and I made sure to consider it when planning and running the courses.

The second step to understanding your students is to explicitly ask them about themselves. As part of the first (or, as computer scientists often say, *zeroth*) assignment, have the students fill out a short survey to find out who they are. Figure 1 is the survey I have given out on the first day of my CS2 course.[1] In addition to questions about students, I also have them test their tools by run-

---

1 This particular form was created jointly with Chris Piech for CS 106B at Stanford, and has been influenced by a number of other lecturers in the Stanford Computer Science Department.

ning a program (in this case, a program that hashes their name) and learning how to use the debugger. I also ensure that they acknowledge reading the honor code handout.

Notice on the survey I ask the students some personal information about themselves: *What is your preferred name (what do you like to be called)?* and *What is your gender?* I use the information so that I can address them properly, both in person and via email.[2] I also ask the questions related to their studies: *What is your class year?*, *What is your (intended) major?*, and *What introductory CS course have you taken?* With a big class, the academic background tends to be diverse, but it is helpful to know the range of knowledge the students have, and what specific courses they have as a prerequisite. At Stanford, students end up in the CS2 course from a variety of other courses.

I use the last five questions on my survey to get a more in-depth picture of the students and their reasons for taking the course: *Why are you taking the course?*, *What are you most looking forward to in the class?*, *Are you worried about anything in the class?*, and *Is there anything else that you would like the course staff to know about you?* I use these questions for a number of reasons. First, they give me a good indication of the general mentality of the students towards the course. Are they excited about the course? Are they apprehensive? Second, I use the questions to address any issues at the beginning of the course, such as accommodations the student might list (e.g., information about extra time on exams, or policies on sporting team absences). While most students won't have much to say to the final question[3], I have found that some students will reply with important information that will help me make their experience in the course better.

In recent terms, I have decided to reply personally to *every* student's survey. For a class of 300+ students, this has been time consuming, but well-worth it. In order to cut down on the overall

---

2 I also use the gender information to inform me about the gender breakdown in the course.

3 though many say amusing things, such as "I have three pet rabbits!"

CS106B Spring 2018 Assignment 0

* Required

What is your SUNetID? (e.g. cgregg) *

Your answer

What is your preferred name (what do you like to be called)? *

Your answer

What is the hash value of your preferred name? *
Run the example program distributed as part of Assignment 0

Your answer

What is the mystery number you found by using the debugger? *

Your answer

What is your class year at Stanford / other? *

○ Freshman

○ Sophomore

○ Junior

○ Senior

○ Graduate, non-professional school

○ Professional School (Law, Medicine, Business, Education)

○ Other:

What is your gender? *

○ Female

○ Male

○ Non Binary

○ Prefer not to specify

○ Other:

What is your (intended) major? *

○ Computer Science

○ CS-related (but not CS) major (e.g., Symbolic Systems, Math & Computational Science, Electrical Engineering)

○ Other Engineering (not CS, not EE)

○ Humanities (e.g., Philosophy, English, History, Music, Arts, etc.)

○ Social Science (e.g., Economics, Political Science, Psychology, etc.)

○ Physical Sciences (e.g., Biology/HumBio, Chemistry, Physics, etc.)

○ Undeclared (don't know yet)

○ Professional school (Law, Medicine, Business, Education)

○ Other:

I have read an understand the Honor Code document located here: ... *

○ Yes

What introductory CS course have you taken? (choose most recent if you've taken more than one) *

○ CS 106A (Java)

○ CS 106AJ (Javascript)

○ CS 106AP (Python)

○ AP Computer Science in high school

○ Other C or C++ based introductory course

○ Other non-C or C++ based introductory course

○ Self-taught

○ I haven't taken any programming courses, and am not self-taught

○ Other:

Why are you taking CS106B? (Choose all appropriate) *

☐ Required for my (intended) major

☐ Required for my (intended) minor

☐ Exploring Computer Science as a potential major

☐ To satisfy a General Education or Ways of Thinking/Ways of Doing requirement

☐ For fun and enlightenment

☐ Retaking the course

☐ Other:

What are you most looking forward to in this class? *

Your answer

Are you worried about anything in this class? *

Your answer

Is there anything that you would like the course staff to know about you? *
This could be something fun, or something related to your educational needs, or whatever you'd like.

Your answer

SUBMIT

Never submit passwords through Google Forms.

This form was created inside of Stanford Computer Science and Electrical Engineering Departments. Report Abuse · Terms of Service · Additional Terms

Google Forms

Figure 1: An example survey that can be part of the first assignment in a course.

time to reply to the students, I wrote a Python script to scrape the student information from the survey data and populate a set of quasi-form letters to send out. I go through each response and add a line or two that specifically refers to the students' comments, and then have another script that sends the emails in bulk.[4] I tend to get a handful of replies, but many of the replies indicate a pleasant surprise that I would write personal emails to three hundred students, and this helps to start the course off on the right foot. With large classes, students can be apprehensive about reaching out to the instructor, and the emails break the ice so they feel more willing to contact you if they want to. On a related note: it is a good idea to set certain rules for emailing you directly, especially for large classes. My policy is to have students first email their Section Leader with concerns about grading and other administrative issues, and then we escalate the problem to the head TA, and then to me, and this is spelled out in the course syllabus.

Another way to get to know your students–and this should not be too surprising–is to talk to them directly! As a lecturer for a large class, you may have limited engagement time with your students, but if you arrive to lecture ten to fifteen minutes early, you should have time to set up for lecture and then mingle a bit with the students. I normally walk about the lecture hall saying "hi" to the students who arrive early, and I ask them how the latest assignment is going, how the last exam went, whether they are majoring in computer science, etc. When I hear a lot of comments such as "the last assignment took a really long time!" I have another bit of information about my students and the course that is worthwhile.

Although it is difficult to remember hundreds of names as you walk around, you will start to get to know the students that you talk to before the lectures, and be sure to always ask their names (and keep a list, if you need it!). Many students appreciate this gesture, as well, and once again, they are more likely to approach

---

4 See the website for this book for the scripts.

you about the course, or about computer science in general if you meet them, even briefly.

Many instructors start to get to know their students through office hours. This is hit or miss – with more than a few students in attendance, office hours can get busy, and you will often want to focus directly on course-related material. But, you should try to use any interaction with the students to learn a bit more about them, and about how the class is going.

Asking a bit more specifically about how students are doing outside of your class can be critical when you are meeting with a student because they are having academic difficulties in your course. Whenever you discuss academic troubles with students in your office, you should also consider asking how they are doing in their other classes, or what else is going on extra-curricularly. It may be that your class is one of many that they are struggling with, and you can suggest that they reach out to someone at the school who can help with strategies to improve. Keep in mind that some students will also share medical issues or mental health issues they are having – you should understand your own school's policies for handling such cases, and you should also be particularly careful to keep student information confidential. You should have a plan for what you will do if a student does relate information about mental health issues, which you should not attempt to deal with on your own. Most schools have a counseling hotline that you can call, or that you can suggest that the student calls. Again, *know your school's policies about mental health issues, and have a concrete plan to deal with situations involving your students.*

FIND OUT ABOUT THE PERCEPTION OF YOUR COURSE BEFORE YOU TEACH IT

If you are teaching a class that has been taught in your school before, you should not only get prior course syllabi and materials (as mentioned in Chapter 1), but you should also ask about the general perception that students have for the course. Is it known to be a particularly easy or difficult course? Do students plan their schedule around your course, making sure to round out their schedules for the term with easier courses? Do students consider it a *weed out* course? The more you know about how students already perceive your course, the better you can plan.

Be sure to ask faculty who have taught the course before what the student perception of the course is. They will be able to give you the history of the course, where it fits into the curriculum, and the types of students who take the course. During the first term you teach it, you should probably try to keep the course at roughly the same difficulty level as it has been taught in the past, although this is up to you. If the course is known to be easy and you want to make it more rigorous, by all means do so.[5] But, in fairness to students taking your class, you do need to keep them apprised of the amount of work you expect, and if students are looking for an easy course, you should steer them elsewhere.

Make sure you thoroughly understand what is covered in any prerequisites for your course. You might consider giving an assessment at the beginning of the term that ensures students know the material. The assessment is as much for the students as it is for you – even if you don't use the assessment to limit enrollment, you are putting the students on notice that they will need to know the material for the course. Also ensure that any prerequisites are actually necessary – you don't want to limit students taking your course if possible. If your school has prerequisites but does not enforce them, you should recognize this and either use an assessment or be very clear to students that they need to know the material to do well in your course.

SPECIFIC THOUGHTS ON CS1

If you are teaching CS1, there are some specific things you should know about your students. Often, a CS1 course does not have

---

5 And you may have been hired to give the course a bit more *oomph*.

prerequisites, and may even highlight the fact that "no prior programming experience is necessary." Do not be surprised, however, if a large proportion of your students *do* have some prior programming experience, either self-taught or from a high school class, such as an Advanced Placement (AP) course. You should be particularly aware of this fact because this may affect students in your class who have never programmed. Many of those students are just trying out the field, and they can immediately feel behind if they think they should already have some programming ability. I have heard many times from CS1 students that *everyone else already knows how to program!* and while it is not true, the perception can color the experience for those who are brand new to programming. Have a good plan in place before the course begins to tackle the heterogeneous nature of your class. For example, make sure that you don't over-complicate assignments, especially early on. Students who have programmed before might fly through the first few assignments, but students who are new programmers may take many hours to assimilate the introductory material. You run the risk of discouraging those students, and it is better to let the advanced students believe the course is too easy than to have the new programmers think it is much too hard.

One idea we use in the CS1 and CS2 courses at Stanford is to allow students to do as many *extensions* as they want on assignments, with the understanding that it can improve their grade, but not by a whole lot. We provide students some ideas for potential extensions, and we let them be creative with their extensions, too. Students who never do extensions can still receive a high grade in the course, and students who do the extensions don't feel that the class is too simple. You should also ensure that students who might be deciding between taking CS1 and CS2 have enough information to make a good decision. Sometimes, that is with a document that describes both courses, and sometimes that is with a forum before the course starts where students can ask questions about it. Don't be afraid to encourage students who might be on the fence to try the CS2 course if they do have enough prior programming experience.

SPECIFIC THOUGHTS ON BRAND NEW COURSES

If you are teaching a brand new course, many of the tips above won't be as relevant to you. The students don't have any preconceived notions of your course, and other faculty can't give you information about the course perception, as it is *sui generis*. Hopefully you have an idea of what you think students should already be able to do, and already know, before enrolling in your course, but this should be very clear to the students. You might want to consider holding an information session to tell students about the course (and to entice enrollment), where you can answer any questions they might have about it.

When you are planning your brand new course, make sure that you build in some ability to slow down or speed up, if necessary. You probably cannot predict exactly how the students will do on the material, and having a bit of slack in the schedule is critical to being able to make it work, especially the first time through the course. Also, plan on getting feedback regularly (see below), and be willing to act on it.

FEEDBACK

Another excellent way to understand your students is to provide a way for them to give you regular feedback on the course. Chapter 12 covers feedback in general, but it is worth mentioning here that you can learn more about your students and their perception of how the course is going by listening to them as the course progresses. This can be informal – as you meet them in office hours or before and after class, you can ask them how they think the course is going, and whether they have any feedback. It can also be more formal, with feedback through a web form or anonymously (see Chapter 12 for the trade offs on those methods).

However you get feedback, you should be willing to act on it if it is important. For example, you may think that your pacing during lectures is going well, but when you start asking students about how the class is going, you might find that students are concerned that you are going too fast. If it is possible to slow down some, then you should consider that. If it isn't possible due to course constraints, then you should at the very least address this with the students, with your rationale for pushing the class at that pace.

It cannot be overstated how important it is to be upfront with your students when it comes to course content, pacing, and difficulty level. Your honesty about the course will mean a great deal to students, especially if they are struggling in the course. Additionally, be honest with your students, especially if you make a mistake – students will forgive many mistakes (especially in your first year), and when you own up to a mistake, you gain credibility. I once taught half a lecture on a C++ topic where I inverted the terms "pointer" and "reference," and when I realized the mistake after class, I immediately knew that I was going to have to re-teach the material the next lecture, correcting the mistakes (and correcting the code I had posted in the slides). It was not easy to admit the mistake, but the students appreciated that I was honest and that I owned the mistake.

DISCUSSIONS WITH STUDENTS WHO ARE STRUGGLING

As you teach your course, you will have students who have difficulty with the material. They may be behind on assignments, or they may do poorly on assignments, exams, section participation, etc.. You can either reach out to these students when you realize they are not doing well, or you can wait for them to contact you. Either way, you may end up having a one-on-one meeting with them during the term to discuss their progress, and how they might improve.[6] Knowing the kinds of questions to ask, and the advice to give, is critical to getting students back on track. Before meeting a student, make sure you review how they are doing in the course. When they arrive for the meeting, listen to their concerns, and then pose the following questions, as applicable:

1. Have you been attending the lectures or watching them online? If you've been watching them online, do you do so at regular speed, or sped up? [Note: watching videos sped up is generally a terrible way to watch the class, and you should impress this upon your students].

2. Do you start the assignments when they are released? If not, why not?

3. When doing assignments, what is your general plan? Do you read the full assignment before starting it? Do you do any planning before writing code or attempting to answer the questions? What normally slows you down on the assignments?

4. How are you doing in your *other* classes? [Note: this is critical! Some students will only struggle in your class, and some will be doing poorly in their other classes, as well.]

5. How do you study for exams?

6. How did you do in the prerequisites for the course?

7. What extracurricular activities (if any) are keeping you from doing well in the course?

---

6 There are times, too, when it is too late for a student to improve. Some students will reach out to you at the end of the term with a plea for leniency with their grade, but when you look at their (lack of) progress during the term, they have not done enough to pass. This is why it is best to try and reach out as early as possible, and you should encourage your students to contact you as soon as they know they are behind.

Often, students have not thought about some of these questions themselves, and just asking the questions helps them out. But, you can use the answers to inform your own understanding of why the student is doing poorly, and you can suggest ways to improve. There isn't any magic bullet, unfortunately, but you can stress to them good study habits, which can help. You should also stress any help that the course provides in terms of TA help and office hours, and encourage the student to use those resources.

WHAT TO DO IF...

At the end of each chapter in Parts II and III of this book, there is a section titled, *What to do if....* These sections answer common questions that come up when teaching in general, and when teaching computer science specifically. Each chapter's *What to do if...* section has questions particular to the chapter, although there are some overlaps, as many *What if?* questions span multiple different parts of the teaching spectrum.

What if a student tells you something that concerns you?

As covered earlier, if a student tells you about a mental health issue, or tells you that they mean to harm themselves, you should contact the relevant school officials and you should already know your school's policy on such matters. If you feel that the student is in imminent danger, you should call 911 (if in the U.S.). In all cases of mental health, you should *not* try to deal with the situation yourself, and you should also avoid telling the student that they can tell you such things in confidence – it is far better to turn the matter over to personnel who are trained to help, even at the risk of making the student upset with you, then to try and handle the situation yourself without proper training. Your main goal should be to help the student, and the best help is virtually always by getting them the help instead of trying to be the help yourself.

Students may also tell you other concerning information, such as sexual harassment, abuse, or other violence, bullying, family situations, etc. Again – you should take care to know your school's requirements for you to report some of the issues, and you should also know who you can suggest the student contact.

What if a student asks you for academic advice?

Even if you are new to your school, you have been in academic environments longer than your students, and you certainly can give them advice about computer science, or even high school, college, or graduate school in general. You may not know the answers to specific questions related to your school, yet, in which case you should direct them to someone who can give them that information. You can also help the student track down the information, and you will, over time, learn the answers yourself. See Chapter 14 for more information about advising students.

What if your students want to be friends with you?

You should maintain a professional relationship with your students, at least until they graduate. This does not mean that you cannot see your students occasionally in a social setting, but if you do, limit your time with them, and remember to be professional. For students who are currently in your class, you want to make sure to avoid favoritism. That said, your students may ask you to join them for a meal (many dining halls have student-hosted faculty nights), and you should feel free to accept such invitations (though you should not feel obligated to do so, particularly if you are in a time crunch).

For past students still in school, or for past TAs, you can relax your teacher/student persona somewhat, as you don't need to grade them, and you aren't their boss. I frequently will get a coffee with former students and TAs, and it is fun to catch up with them to see how their studies are progressing.

What if a student enrolls in your class late?

You will get students enrolling late to your class, sometimes up to a couple of weeks after class starts, if you allow it. You should decide on the policies for your course, and how you will handle work from late enrolls. I normally tell the students that they must complete all the work, including everything they have missed, and I set a schedule for them to complete it. If assignment deadlines have already passed, I will give them extended deadlines, but I expect that they will concurrently work on the new material, as well, and not stay behind for long. If there is time, I will also schedule a meeting with the new students to get to know them, and to see if they have any questions about the course so far. I explicitly *won't* re-teach the material to them – I expect that they will use the resources available to catch up. Sometimes, this is as easy as having them watch the recorded videos, but if those aren't available, the students will have to do with the handouts and other material I have posted, or that is in the textbook.

What if students demand too much of your time?

Some students will try to monopolize your time, particularly if you have a so-called *open door policy*, where students are free to stop by your office when you are there. I will rarely send a student away who stops by my office outside of office hours, but I also try to limit the conversations, particularly if I am busy (and if I am super busy, I'll simply close the office door). You should be clear to students about when they can talk to you, and you are free to limit that time to office hours. I have an online calendar, and if a student wants to meet with me I will let them sign up for limited time slots.

If you do have a student or students who try to take up too much of your time, you should re-direct them to other resources, and if it comes to it, you should simply limit the ability for them to meet with you. You need time to do your work, and you can't meet with students continuously.

What if a student has a particularly bad attitude about your course?

In most college classes, students have a vested interest in doing well in their classes, and they are taking their classes because they want to. However, some courses you teach may be required for a particular major, and the students are taking them because they must. In high school, there is a greater likelihood of students being forced to take certain classes, meaning there may be a higher number of students who do not want to be there. In either case, you may have students with a bad attitude, who are trying to do the least amount of work to get through. Their attitude may also manifest itself in their classroom behavior (though this is rare in college, where they are more likely to simply skip class), or on assignments. I have had students use their programming comments to berate the class TAs and to complain about the course. Most of the time, you can simply ignore their attitude (unless the classroom behavior is the issue, in which case you should address it directly with the student or students), and they will be little more than noise. In other cases, you will have to address it – with one student who was using comments to belittle the TAs, I sent a strongly worded email to him to knock it off, and that was the last I heard of it. In all cases, continue to teach your course the best you can, focusing on the students that do want to be there and do want to learn.

What if you can't remember your students' names?

Remembering student names is hard, particularly for large classes. In most large classes, students are surprised if you *do* remember their names, and they will forgive you if you do not. I do my best to remember as many names as I can, although I will never be able to memorize the names of all of the students in a 300 person course. You will get to know some students in your course, because you will see them often in office hours, you will talk to them before or after class, or they may ask you to a student-faculty dinner. Whenever you do have meetings with students (or in office hours), do your best to remember their names at least for the duration of the interaction.

Many schools now provide picture rosters, and you can use those to help you learn student names. Again, however, unless you are very good at remembering names, your time might be better spent preparing for class than trying to cram hundreds of names into your head.

FINAL THOUGHTS

You owe it to your students to understand them as comprehensively you can when you teach a course. You have an obligation to teach the best you can, and the way to do that is to prepare material that challenges the students at a level where they can do the work with a sufficient amount of effort. By understanding that they are busy and probably overloaded with coursework and extracurricular activities, you can avoid making your course too difficult (but you can still make it challenging!). By asking the students as the class begins about their perception of the course, and about their concerns, you can address issues before you get too deep into the course. By gathering good feedback as the course progresses, you can modify the course as necessary mid-stream. If you can't change the course, then you can be straight with your students, acknowledging the feedback.

By understanding your students, you will be able to make your courses better, and your students will appreciate the attention you give to their opinions and about their own situations. You might be surprised at how much you benefit from the work that goes into knowing your audience, and you will improve your own teaching as a result.

4

KNOW YOUR SUBJECT

IN A RECENT COURSE EVALUATION for a class (CS 107e) that I co-taught with Professor Phil Levis, one of the student comments was, *Phil is like a zen master of CS107e, he seems to know it all, which I suppose comes with years of teaching it.* If your students are calling you a *zen master*, you know your subject! Knowing your subject inside and out is critical for the following reasons:

1. You understand the nuances of the material, and you know what is important, and what is tangential.

2. You can relate the sub-topics together, giving more meaning to each. For example, if you are teaching a data structures class and the topic is about trees, you can mention that some of the tree restrictions (e.g., a *root* node) will be lifted when you get to the more general case of graphs. If you didn't really know your subject (e.g., if you are staying *one day ahead* of the students), you might not make this connection until you ended up at the graph topic.

3. You can predict many of the questions students will have, and you can either build the answers to those questions into your lectures, or you can have a well thought-out answer prepared for when they do come up.

4. You will be ready for all types of questions about the topic, and you will be able to answer them without preparation.

5. Your assignments and exam questions will be easier to write, and they will be more nuanced to truly assess your students. You will have a deeper understanding of the types of problems and questions your students should be able to answer.

6. Students will appreciate your knowledge, and be confident that they are getting quality information from you.

The above list is not comprehensive, and it is fair to say that the better you understand your course material, the richer you can make the entire class.

You may notice that this chapter is shorter than many of the others – this book assumes that you already know the material you are going to teach (although there are pointers below with ideas for how to improve that knowledge, or gain new knowledge), and it is about giving you the tools to take your knowledge and skills and pass it on to your students. You are likely extremely knowledgeable in your subjects, already!

YOUR BACKGROUND

Your own educational background is going to heavily impact your own knowledge of the subjects you will teach. If you have a Master's or Ph.D. in computer science, you probably know the material well, although it may have been many years since you last thought about some of the introductory topics (in the case that you are teaching CS1 or CS2). Assuming you are going to teach a course for which you have an in-depth knowledge of the material, this is a great start. You are in a position to be that *zen master* the students will rave about.

Your background is also heavily influenced by the *way* you were taught your courses. If you had a fantastic professor for a course in college, you are likely to want to emulate that teaching style, and you also may want to borrow from the course examples, assignments, exams, etc. If you have access to those materials, by all means ask your former professor if you can use or modify some of the material for your own class. You may also want to make the class the same level of difficulty – be careful to understand your students (see Chapter 3) before making that decision.

You may also have had a professor for a course that you didn't particularly enjoy. If you have ideas of your own on how to improve the course, that is fantastic. If not, you should rely on other instructor's opinions and materials, at least as you start preparing for the course. If possible, try and see someone else teach at least some lectures for the course, whether in person or on video. See Chapter 11 for ideas about how to improve your own teaching through observing others.

HOW DO I INCREASE THE KNOWLEDGE OF MY SUBJECT?

You may be faced with teaching a course that is not in your realm of expertise, or that you have not studied in many years. If you are transitioning into computer science from another field, you may not know the material as well as you might hope. Given the desperate need for computer science teachers, you may have been convinced to take on a computer science course for which you have never even seen the material before. While this is not ideal, you do have options. It is important to immerse yourself in the material as far ahead of time as you can. This can be through a textbook, course materials from prior terms, or from a similar course taught at a different school.

There isn't a magical secret method to increase your own knowledge for a particular subject. Just like anything else you have learned, it takes time and it takes practice. At this point in your career you are probably an autodidact, and you don't need a formal course to learn the material.[1] That said, there may be online versions of the course you will teach, and if you have the time to go through them, you will certainly learn a great deal. But, sitting down with a textbook (or multiple textbooks), researching the topic online (Wikipedia has informed my knowledge of com-

---

1 Though this is a possibility, as well. If you've never taken the material for the course you are about to teach, you should consider taking a formal version at another institution, or online. The timing for that may not be feasible, of course, but if you can do it, you may have a better experience when you go to teach it.

puter science more than any other reference), and simply working on problems with the material is going to push you towards mastery of the subject. As mentioned throughout this book, you will also learn a tremendous amount by the act of teaching, but of course it is best to have a solid foundation before you start the course.

If you are going to be teaching a course that has been taught before, and you will be using some or all of the previous assignments, do the assignments yourself before the course begins. This may take a considerable amount of time, but it is worth the effort. In doing the assignments, you will be immersing yourself into the work, and although you will probably solve the problems faster than your students, you will also gain insights into the tricky parts of the assignments, and you will be prepared to answer questions about them. Furthermore, you will also have a better idea of what you need to teach the students before they begin the assignments so they will be successful.

In particular, if your assignments include programming assignments, as you write up your own solution, try and think of other ways your students might try to solve the problems. Is a problem better solved with iteration, or recursion? If the students have a choice of data structures to use, what choices would be best? Are there choices that would be poor but would be tempting for your students to make? All of these questions should inform your own teaching of the material. You should not be afraid to let your students make poor decisions when writing their programs, but you should also give them the information they need to make the better choices. For example, in a data structures course, asymptotic analysis is often used to inform choices, and preparing your students to use that tool is important.

The better you know your own assignments, the better you will be able to grade them. Chapter 9 discusses making rubrics for assignments and exams.

KNOWING YOUR MATERIAL IN THE CONTEXT OF TEACHING IT

Simply knowing the material does not automatically make you a great teacher, of course. Knowing your subject is the first step, but knowing how to deliver that material, with what motivation, in what order, at what depth, with what examples, etc., is what is going to make you a great teacher. If you have ever had an instructor who simply gave you slide after slide of material with minimal context, you know that just understanding the topics and being able to solve problems about them and answer questions about them is only part of the ability to teach. Your job is to turn that knowledge into an engaging story about the topics, and to do so such that students also learn it. Doing that is as much an art as it is a science, and there are hundreds of books written about teaching pedagogy in general. See Chapter 8 for ideas about making your lectures engaging, and Chapter 10 for a discussion about how to infuse your lectures and other class material with resources available online. You will come into your own in the classroom through practice, and Part III of this book is dedicated to improving your teaching.

No matter how well you understand the material for a course, review the course topics before you begin teaching. Having a fresh perspective of the material will make your lectures better, and will allow you to make connections between topics that you might not have otherwise done if you had not thought of it in a while. This is less critical the more times you teach the course, but if it is your first time in particular, you should absolutely re-view the material. You should also do at least a cursory literature search to see if there is anything new that relates to the topics, and do a search for online resources and recent pedagogical research, as well. There is a continuous flow of new CS teaching material online (see Chapter 10 for ideas on go-to sites), and it is always great to be able to provide your students with more resources, and a broader range of places to look to enhance their learning.

If you are in a position to teach a course multiple times, take the opportunity. The first time you teach a course, you may have all the knowledge you need about the material, but you will absolutely have ideas about how to make it better the next time. Your course will get better the more times you teach it, for many reasons. For one, after the first time teaching it, you will have written and delivered the material already, and preparing to do it a second time will be much faster. You will be able to concentrate on the smaller details that you missed the first time, while you were trying to create the work from scratch.

WHAT TO DO IF...

What if I am asked to teach a course that is outside my area of expertise?

If your department assigns you a course you aren't prepared to teach, then you can either lobby to teach a different course, or you can determinedly learn the new material, and do the best you can. You should still make the case that you need time to prepare the course, and preferably you would get paid for that time, as well. Teaching a course where you have not mastered the material isn't the ideal situation, of course, but if you have enough time to plan ahead, you can learn enough of the material to teach it effectively. The odds are good that the course has been taught before at your school, and you should be able to find a syllabus and some materials.[2] If you can find someone who has taught the course before, get as much information about the course from them.

Do your best to rise to the challenge of the new course. Take it as a chance to learn something new yourself, and you may be surprised at how much you enjoy it. If not, you can still make it

---

2 though if you happen to be in a new department, or your school is offering computer science for the first time, you may have to look elsewhere for information.

through one term, and then you can try to get a different, more familiar course.

What if I don't feel confident when teaching my course?

If you know the material and you prepare well for the course, you should have confidence that you can do a good job teaching it. But, if you can't muster that confidence, take the course one lecture at a time, and evaluate what you did well each day. Things will start to get easier the longer you teach, and you'll begin to gain that confidence as you get more experience. At the end of the course, spend some time reflecting on what went well and on what you can improve, and I guarantee that the second time through the class it will be smoother.

Often, the confidence that you feel you lack is actually performance anxiety, and one way to help with this is to practice your lectures in front of others, or on videotape. If you practice a few times before class, you will realize that you know how the lecture will proceed, and that should boost your confidence, especially after you have a couple of good lectures. See Chapter 8 for more information about overcoming a fear of speaking.

What if some of my students know the material better than I do?

If a student in your class already knows the material, they probably are in the wrong class. But, it does happen, and some students also like to show off their knowledge. While you should know your material well, there is often a student or two who know a lot about the material. Once you realize that this is the case, you can start to manage their participation, if necessary. Call on them only when you have given others a significant amount of time to also raise their hands, and do not let them grandstand. All of that said, I have had many students who have known as much or more than me about a course I was teaching, and they were generally helpful.

In some cases they led discussions with small groups of students, and in others they gave insights that were interesting to the rest of the class, including me. Before you try to clamp down on students who are already knowledgeable, give them the chance to be a productive member of the class, and often they will do just that.

What if I forget something while trying to teach it?

There are times when you get to a particular part of a class and you simply blank on how to do something. It probably won't happen often, but if it does it can be a frightening experience. More practice before lectures will limit the number of times this happens, but nevertheless you might find yourself in this position. The best way to handle it is to be honest with your students (e.g., *I seem to have done this incorrectly!* or *For some reason I am blanking on how to solve this!*). Don't linger too long, and feel free to look at notes you might have. Students will give you a break if this happens infrequently, and it provides a nice lesson for them (though frustrating for you) that your material is challenging.

What if I cannot keep up on the new advances in the topics my course covers?

If you are teaching a course where the field is changing rapidly, you may find yourself teaching somewhat outdated material. If you can't keep up with the latest and greatest information, you should be honest with your class, and tell them that things may change. You shouldn't be teaching *incorrect* concepts, and what you are teaching the students will likely still be helpful to know, even if there are more advanced or different techniques available.

If you are going to teach the course again, then you can reevaluate what you are teaching, and you can read up on the latest and greatest, with the hope that you can include it the next time around.

FINAL THOUGHTS

Knowing your material inside and out isn't going to make you a great teacher, but it is going to form the foundation of your teaching, and you can build on it. Even the best teacher cannot teach material they don't know at all, so you will want to be as proficient as you can with the topics covered in your classes. The students will appreciate it, and your teaching will be richer for it.

5

KNOW YOUR TOOLS

ONE OF THE BEST things about teaching computer science is that you get to use and (if you want) you get to create software tools for helping make your class better. Computer science does not have a lock on using computerized tools, but it is probably the field that uses them the most, simply because CS instructors love writing those tools, they are good at it, and they often make those tools available to others for free. I have written dozens of scripts, applications, and interactive websites that have made my own teaching better, and I consider it a benefit of the job that I get to spend time working on those tools.

With exploding enrollments, the judicious use of good tools, such as autograders and test grading software, has made scaling to bigger class sizes bearable – without such tools, grading would be harder, feedback would be more difficult to return to students, and the overall experience would be worse for instructors, TAs, and students.

In this chapter, I list some of the types of tools I have found that make teaching more efficient, and more fun. Your school and department may already have a set of tools that are used, and many times those tools have likely been crafted in-house by other instructors and/or students. The benefits of using in-house tools include being able to talk to the developer of the tools directly (if they are still at the school), and to be able to modify the tools as needed. The tools work with the systems and servers the department owns, and they may integrate directly into the school or department's grading and roster software.

There are, of course, downsides to using in-house tools, as well. One of the most common issues is that the person or people that created the software may be long gone from the school, and you are left with a poorly-documented, dense set of code[1] that is virtually impossible to change without a serious time commitment. This is particularly true for student-written software (often, in the case of graduate student software, called *gradware*) – students often have great ideas and can produce interesting and useful tools, but once they graduate, there is virtually no chance that they will continue to support their work.[2] Tools may break due to operating system upgrades, or changes to other software, and coaxing in-house tools back to life can be a time-consuming and thankless job.

Before starting your course, you should find out what tools are already being used in your department and school. If there are already tools in place, you should strongly consider using them if it makes sense for your class. If you already have a set of tools you would rather use, that is fine, too, but at least give the already in-use tools a chance, first. It may be possible to modify the tools to better suit your needs, but using them in their current form will make your work easier during your first term.

If there aren't any tools in use already, do not despair. The sections below discuss some options for free tools, and you can also talk to your department about the possibility of purchasing software, as well. Also, feel free to ask about tools on mailing lists and forums, such as the ACM Special Interest Group for Computer Science Education (SIGCSE). If you still cannot find a good software tool to do the job you need, you can still fall back on regular old paper, and try to solve the tools issue when you have the time. You may want to write your own tools for your classes – if you do so, just beware of the time commitment that writing tools takes, and make a decision about whether it makes sense to do so in your first term.

---

1 If you have the source code at all!

2 This is not always true, and there have been some terrific student projects that the students have built companies around. The test grading software Gradescope, started by a group of students at U.C. Berkeley, is an outstanding example.

TYPES OF SOFTWARE TOOLS

In the following subsections, I've listed a number of different types of software tools that you might consider using for your classes. You might find that some software works well for your classes, and other software does not. It does take time to get up to speed on the tooling for a course, but often it can save a great deal of time in the long run.

Assignment Submission Software

One of the first types of software tools you should consider should provide a method for allowing students to submit their code to you (and/or your TAs) for grading. The best tools allow students to submit their work before a deadline, either through a web-based form, an IDE, or via the command line. Generally, student work is placed into folders on a server and may allow for multiple submissions with each submission timestamped and available. Often, the submission software can also provide some autograding support to give immediate feedback to students. Any software with this type of support should have the ability to tailor the autograding and level of feedback, and if it is fully scriptable, that is ideal. If your school or department does not already have such a system, you should take a look at some of the open source or free alternatives, such as Submitty and OpenSubmit.

Whatever submission system you choose, you should plan on testing it thoroughly before the term begins. As mentioned above, it will take some time to learn the tools, and you do not want to be scrambling to get it working once the term has started. You should also ensure that there is a regular backup of the student submissions. Backups may be automatically handled through your department's IT group, and you should ask about this before using the software.

One thing you should consider when using submission software is the number of times you allow your students to submit.

If they will get immediate feedback, you might want to limit the how many times they can submit to a relatively small number (three or four is what I usually use), in order to subvert the "write code that passes the test" mentality. When students are allowed unlimited number of submissions with automatic feedback, students will simply write code to submit, then iterate until their code passes all the tests. This is likely not the way you want your students to code. Limiting them to a few submissions will force them to write their code well initially, and will give them a finite number of times to clean up the code that still needs work.

Autograders

If you are teaching a class that has programming assignments, being able to autograde for correctness can save a tremendous amount of time, and you can comprehensively test your students' work. Autograders can be as simple as writing a bash script to run your students' code through a battery of tests (which is easiest if you are using a command-line-based programming environment), or it can be a fully graphical solution that runs in an IDE, via the Web, or standalone. As mentioned in the previous section, you can do some (or potentially, all) of the autograding through the submission process, but you may want to also have a more robust autograder that you can run after students have submitted their work. Many instructors have written their own custom autograders, and you may want to do this, as well. Writing a robust autograder is not trivial, however, and you might be better off looking at what is already available as you begin your first term.

Be aware that most autograders require student output to be either exactly the same as the solution, or very close to it[3] You need to make it clear to your students this aspect of autograding. If the students get automatic feedback when they submit their assign-

---

3 Some software allows regular expression matching, ignoring whitespace differences, multiple correct answers, etc.

ments, you may want to allow them to submit more times than you usually would for the first assignment so they can get used to this aspect of programming. Students can become annoyed at minor output differences that penalize them even though they have solved the conceptual part of the assignment. With introductory courses, this is a good opportunity to discuss computers communicating with each other and how precise the interactions need to be.

Many instructors like to teach their students to write their own test code, and a nice feature to look for (or build into) an autograder is the ability to have students write tests that get included in the overall autograding system. If your course is in Java, for instance, some of the autograders will incorporate JUnit testing so you can have your students write tests in addition to the tests you provide.

Once again, there are many open source and/or free solutions, such as Autolab, Web-CAT, and AutoGradr.

Assignment Grading and Feedback Software

In addition to simply autograding, the software you use to assess your students should be able to provide for giving the students a grade and for giving them written feedback. Depending on the size of your class and your TA resources, you may not be able to give much written feedback, but you should have the option. Students should either be able to receive feedback through a (secure) online system, and/or they should get an email with the feedback.

For autograded work, a list of tests that passed or failed each test, with an error message, is ideal. Additionally, you should be able to write inline comments in the student code about functionality or style issues, assuming that you or a TA can take the time to look at the students' work. You should also be able to write general feedback to the student about the assignment, with suggestions for future assignments.

One nice feature for grading software used on student code is to be able to make changes to the code and to re-run the grading tests. This is helpful to check if a bug was minor or major, and you can give better feedback to the students with a comment like, *You had an off-by-one error in your loop, and if you change* i > 0 *to* i >= 0, *the test passes.*

Another necessity for assignment grading software is either integration with gradebook software, or the ability to export all grades to a format suitable for importing into a gradebook program, or into a custom grading spreadsheet.

With whatever grading software you use, you need to train your TAs with the software, and you need to instruct them on how you want the grading done. For example, you might want to direct them to provide at least an overall comment about the assignment details, and you should give them examples of good feedback for coding questions. Your goal should be to give consistent and fair grading across your TAs – this is not trivial, and Chapter 9 has more detailed information about grading effectively. You should have some oversight into the feedback your TAs are giving, and you should spot-check their work (without being overbearing) to control for consistency.

Test Grading Software

If the class or classes you teach have exams, consider using test grading software, such as Gradescope, or Crowdmark. For some software packages, you can upload scans of printed exams, and for others, you must create the exams through the software's interface. All grading is done online. If you opt for a program that allows you to scan the exams, make sure to budget in time for doing the scanning – this can be significant for large classes. Once the exams are in the system (either locally, or online), then you and/or the TAs can grade the exams in parallel, without needing to shuffle paper around. Exam scans can be kept for archival purposes, and the students receive a graded PDF via email or download link. You must create a grading rubric for each exam, and you must also ensure that your TAs are grading consistently. Again, see Chapter 9 for details on rubric creation, and exam grading strategies.

One feature of test grading software that you may or may not want to take advantage of is the ability for your students to make online regrade requests. If you do allow them to do this, be clear about how much information you want from them regarding *why* they want a regrade for their exam – without good guidelines, students are likely to submit a regrade request simply with the hope that they will get back points on a problem or problems. You should provide the students a good answer key to compare against, and the rubric you graded with (this is normally part of the grading report the students get). For coding problems, I give the students a test suite and I ask my students to try and run their code as they typed it, and then, after fixing the inevitable syntax errors, seeing how they do on the tests. Once students see that their solution does not work for the tests (some or all), they are less likely to request a regrade, and this significantly cuts back on the number of regrade requests overall. That said, there are always some errors in grading, and giving students the opportunity to claim points back on incorrectly graded questions keeps the process fair. For non-programming questions, you should insist that students provide concrete reasons why they disagree with the grade. Additionally, I tell students that I have the right to regrade the entire exam, and if they feel that they were erroneously awarded too many points on a different problem, they probably should not request a regrade for the other problems. See Chapter 9 for more information about regrade requests as they relate to exams and assignments.

Test grading software is evolving to include artificial intelligence for more efficient grading. Gradescope seems to be leading the way with this effort, and the technology is likely to continue to improve, improving the grading experience.

Test Taking Software

Most computer science exams are given on paper, even those that have a significant amount of code-writing. There are benefits to this method: from a pedagogical standpoint, students who have to hand-write code need to take their time and think through a solution before putting on paper, for example.[4] Paper exams are also relatively easy to create from a logistical standpoint – you type up the questions and print out the exams.

As mentioned in the last section, some exam grading software requires that you write the exams using the software. The exams can, in some instances, be taken on a computer, or printed out. Other software allows you to simply scan in paper exams in any format, and then designate where on each page the answers are for grading.

There are also computerized test-taking solutions that are not tied directly to grading software. A colleague of mine at Stanford, Chris Piech, and I, along with two Stanford undergraduates, Brahm Capoor and Ali Malik, have written a computerized test-taking program called *Bluebook*, which allows students to take paper-like exams on their own laptops. While it is still in *beta* testing (i.e., we are using it for some classes at Stanford), it is open source.[5] The software does not allow students to compile or test code, but because it is in digital format, it allows autograding of the work. Chris Piech has also written gradebook software that ties directly into Bluebook, as well.

There are other test taking software packages and systems, such as PrairieLearn, created at the University of Illinois, Urbana-Champaign.

---

4 This is the hope, anyway. Students are just as likely to erase or cross out solutions, leading to wasted time and more difficulty in interpreting the answer for grading.

5 See https://stanford.edu/~cgregg/BlueBook/bluebook.pdf for a write-up about the program, and contact either Chris Piech or Chris Gregg for access to the repository.

Software to Get Feedback from Students

As discussed in detail in Chapter 12, getting feedback from your students is critical to improving your teaching. There are plenty of ways to collect feedback from your students electronically. Many schools have an automated evaluation system for students to fill out anonymously at the end of the term. Some systems allow instructors to ask their own questions on the evaluations, and you should take advantage of that if you can.

There are other ways to collect feedback from your students that allow both attributed and anonymous responses. The benefits of attributed feedback are that you can address issues directly with the students who raise them (though see below for a way to do this while the student remains anonymous), and you can also limit derogatory, profane, sexist, or otherwise improper responses. The simplest way to receive attributed feedback is through email or through an online forum where you accept private comments (see below). You can also have students report feedback as part of their assignments, or after they turn in the assignments through an online form (e.g., using Google Forms).

With anonymous feedback, you are likely to get more critical responses (though it can be constructive), but students are more likely to be honest with you, which can be more helpful to improve your teaching, and your courses. My colleague Chris Piech has pioneered what he calls *Tiny Feedback*, which allows him to randomly poll a fixed percentage of students each day after lecture (he likes to poll 10% of the class). Chris sends out an email to the students chosen for that day's lecture, and it points them to a web form that asks questions about the lecture, and how the course is going. See YourFirstYearTeaching.com for a sample script you can use for your own courses, and see Chapter 12 for a longer discussion about Tiny Feedback.

There are also websites that you can use to collect anonymous feedback. They allow your students to send you feedback at any time, and some sites also allow you to respond to them while they remain anonymous. I have used a site (which is, sadly, now out of business) to have a dialog with students about sensitive topics such as gender issues in class, and harassment from other students in labs. Keep in mind that with any anonymous feedback system, you do run the risk of getting crude or unwanted comments. If you decide that you don't want to receive those kinds of comments, you may have to avoid using an anonymous system. Regardless, you should ask your students to provide you honest but constructive feedback, and if you do get nonconstructive feedback, either ignore it, or address it with the class as a whole.

Demonstrations

There are thousands of computer science demonstrations available online. Chapter 10 discusses the topic in detail. If there are online demonstrations for your topic, you should include them in your lectures, or for students to play around with. For example, Data Structure Visualizations is one of my favorite sites for demonstrating data structure concepts, such as heaps, trees, sorting, etc. In addition to web-based resources, there are standalone programs for many computer science topics (e.g., GraphTea for running graph simulations), and a targeted online search should uncover programs that you can use.

If you have written (or plan to write) your own software to demonstrate your course concepts, consider making them available online, and also consider making them open source. It goes without saying that contributing to the availability of all online tools can only help the field as a whole.

Plagiarism Detectors

Dealing with plagiarism can be one of the most frustrating parts of teaching computer science. Because it takes a great deal of effort to produce CS assignments, they tend to get used for multiple course offerings. This means that students who have friends who took the course have access to assignment solutions, and it also means that students have the ability to post their solutions online. Additionally, many course websites and assignment descriptions are available to the general public, and there may be solutions available online from people who were not ever in a particular course.

The good news is that there are tools that can be used to detect plagiarism on programming and non-programming assignments. For programming assignments, the most used tool is the Measure of Software Similarity (MOSS) web-based program, based on work by Alex Aiken and his group at Stanford. As an instructor, you can request access for submitting your students' code to an online server, and you simply run a script to run the report. The report, in HTML format, provides pairs of students and percentages that indicate the similarity of their code. MOSS also provides a direct report on pair matches, which you can look through to determine if the match was likely based on over-collaboration, or plagiarism. One caveat: as noted on the MOSS web page, MOSS should not be used as a sole determination for plagiarism, and you should look at any results thoroughly before accusing a student or students of plagiarism. In my own classes, I only begin looking at student code once it reaches the 30% threshold (and sometimes higher, based on the type of assignment), and I do my best to find *smoking guns* in the code submissions – variable names, code phrasing, or comments that are identical are extremely good indicators of plagiarized code. See Chapter 9 for a more thorough discussion about dealing with plagiarism.

For non-programming assignments, there are other software tools you can use to detect plagiarism, although the easiest to use ones are not free (e.g., Turnitin). You can see if your school or department subscribes to a plagiarism detection program, and if it does it is worth considering.

Gradebook Software / Spreadsheet solutions

At the end of the term, you will need to submit grades for your students. See Chapter 9 for thoughts on the grading process, but you will want to automate the process of collating the term's grades to determine the students' final grades, including where the grade ranges break down. There are dozens of standalone programs for grading (some are free), and many school's online Learning Management Software (LMS) solutions also have gradebooks built in. If you post the accumulated grades online as the students receive them, you can generally find mistakes when they happen.[6] Many instructors opt to use a spreadsheet to produce their gradebooks, and spreadsheet solutions can range from simple weighted averages, to finely-tuned and robust solutions with built-in statistical reports, graphs, and other pertinent information. See https://yourfirstyearteaching.com for sample grading spreadsheets.

Whatever gradebook software you choose, you should start setting it up at the beginning of the term, as this saves time at the end of the term. If you do choose an online version that students have access to, you do need to be clear about how the final grades will be calculated up front, and you should try to avoid changing things mid-term. As mentioned earlier, having the ability to easily import grades into your gradebook from other grading software you are using is critical to making the final grade calculation process efficient.

Online Forums

Your students will have many questions during the term about the lectures, assignments, exams, and other course material. In order to handle all of their questions, you can set up an online forum for the students and staff, and you should encourage your

---

6 Because the students will tell you!

students to participate fully by asking *and* answering questions (within the course collaboration guidelines). Many LMS systems have online forum capability, and there are other free solutions available, as well (e.g., Piazza, or EdStem) that students and instructors find invaluable. Piazza, in particular, seems to be the current standard for computer science forums, and its question/answer format, ability for students to post anonymously (instructors can still see names, and I suggest that you set that option), ability to send instructor notes to the entire class via email, relative simplicity make it a decent choice for many courses. Beware that some students will not utilize the online forum, although you should be able to broadcast information to students when necessary. You should post important information in multiple places (e.g., on Piazza, and on the class website, and via email) to ensure that all students receive it.

Your Course Website

Details about setting up a course website are covered in Chapter 6, but you should plan on having one. It does not need to be particularly feature-rich, but it should at least have information about the course and syllabus, meeting times and locations, assignment information, exam information, a schedule of course topics, and links to other important online information. Your course website can often be built through your school's LMS system, as well, although it may not be as customizable as a website you build yourself. Before you build your website, you should see what your school or department does already, and you may need to request a course website location before the term begins.

Your course website will probably be the first place your students (and prospective students) look to find information about your course, so it should always be up to date. You may want to designate a TA as the main person who updates the site with new information (e.g., the latest assignments, exam room locations, etc.), but you should also check it regularly to make sure it is current.

What if my school wants me to use tool X, but I want to use tool Y?

Some schools or departments ask that instructors use a particular tool or Learning Management System, and you might want to use a different one that has different features, or where you have more control. You need to find out how strict your school is, and you can always ask to see if you are allowed to use alternate tools. In some cases, you may be able to link from the school-sponsored system to another system, and no one will try to stop you. Some schools are particular about privacy (see the question below, as well), and they may have certain rules to control student privacy, which you should know about and be familiar with, as well. One thing you also want to consider is whether the non-standard tools you choose will confuse students, particularly if they are used to the same tools in all of their classes. Before making the change, be sure to consider whether certain features you want to use from alternate tools are worth it to your students. Furthermore, be sure that you know what you are getting into if you have to maintain a particular set of tools, which may take a significant amount of time.

What if school privacy rules prevent me from using tool X?

There are laws and school policies that protect student privacy, and your school may have strict rules about what kind of student information you release outside the school. Disregarding those rules could cost you your job, so find out what restrictions, if any, there are, and follow them. If it means that you cannot use certain online tools, then you need to find another way to accomplish your goals that meet school requirements. If you disagree with the rules, it may be worth your time to find out how you can work to get them changed, or to find another workaround. For example, schools will often sign contracts with software or service companies that outline how student data will be used and kept secure. You can see what you need to do to have your school enter such an agreement with the operators of the tools you want to use, and it may be easier than you think to accomplish.

What if I want to sell the tools I create?

If you write helpful software tools or services that you think others will want to use, you have every right to try and sell them, although you have to find out if the school you work for owns all or part of your tools, especially if you wrote them while working at the school. If you can sell the tools, before you do, consider whether you can still offer a free version, or a version that is ad-supported. Not all schools or instructors have the resources to purchase tools, and you almost certainly use some free tools yourself.

FINAL THOUGHTS

The software and online tools you use for your course are critical to how well your course runs, especially if you have large classes. There is a plethora of programs, scripts, websites, and other tools available to help you run a great class, and most of the tools are completely free. As you progress through your teaching career you may start to produce software tools, as well, and if you do, consider making them available to others. In the meantime, use the tools available, and know that you are probably saving a great deal of time, and making your courses better, by using the tools others have already created.

6

PLANNING YOUR COURSE

BUILDING A WELL-PLANNED COURSE is a challenging but rewarding endeavor. If you are building a new course from scratch, you need to start early and be prepared for a good deal of work. If, as is more likely, you are planning a course that has been taught at your school before, you should leverage the resources from prior offerings of the course, and focus on preparing yourself to teach the material well. Don't be afraid to make changes to the course (and you certainly want to make it the course you want it to be!), but recognize that you have limited time and choose the changes you want to make wisely.

This chapter covers all of the basic steps necessary to plan a typical, assignment- and exam-based computer science course. If your course or courses are seminars or have other special requirements, then this chapter should get you started, but you will need to adjust as necessary. All courses should have a syllabus and a schedule, at a minimum, and should probably have a website or other online area where students can get course information electronically.

WHAT DO YOU WANT YOUR STUDENTS TO BE ABLE TO DO?

When I was learning to be a high school teacher, one of my advisors, Eric Toshalis, gave me the best advice I've ever had about teaching: *Build your course around what you want your students to be able to **do**, not what you want them to **know**.* This advice works well in almost every category of teaching, and it should form the basis of your own course planning. Instead of designing a lecture with the goal, *My students should understand Dijkstra's shortest-path algorithm for graph traversal,* the goal should be, *My students should* *be able to apply Dijkstra's shortest-path algorithm in a program using the graph data structure.* When you focus on what your students should be able to do, your students gain more skills (*and* knowledge), and you make assessment easier (e.g., they can write a function that uses Dijkstra's algorithm to solve a problem).

One benefit to teaching computer science is that assignments and exams provide the practice "doing" that the students need to master the skills you want them to have. Your students will undoubtedly learn as much or more from doing the assignments than they will from listening to and participating in lectures, so your planning should focus on scheduling assignments at the appropriate time and level to maximize this learning. See Chapter 7 for an in-depth look creating assignments.

WRITING YOUR SYLLABUS

Your class syllabus is the defining document that you will use in your course, and that your students will refer to for general course information. It sets the framework for the class, which can include any or all of the following information:

- Course logistics (e.g., meeting location and times)

- Prerequisites

- Textbook and other material requirements

- Topics the course will cover, with or without the schedule

- Course assignments

- Exam dates

- Grading information

- Course policies, expectations, and guidelines

- Honor code and/or plagiarism information

You may want to break up the information above into multiple documents, which you should reference on your course website, or reference in one over-arching document. Depending on your school, you may be required to hand out a paper syllabus on the first day of class, or post your syllabus to a course registration website, or have one available for download via the course website.

You may be able to make your syllabus a *living* document that can change as the course progresses, but you should make it clear that students should refer to the latest version for their own planning purposes. You should not modify certain parts of the syllabus without good reason, such as grade percentage information (e.g., assignments are worth 60%, exams 30%, participation 10%, etc.) or lecture times, as your students should be able to plan their own time commitments around your syllabus.

There are many ways to design a syllabus, and there are hundreds of websites that will give you guidance on how to prepare your own syllabus. You should investigate some of those references as well as reading this section. However you go about designing your syllabus, you will first have to decide on the topics you want to teach. The topics will obviously be dictated by the nature of the course – if you are teaching an introductory Java course, for instance, you will have to teach for and while loops at some point. But, you need to figure out the general order of the topics, how many topics you can cover, and where in the schedule they will fit in. The amount of time you have in the term (e.g., a 10-week quarter, or a 15-week semester) and the type of students you have (see Chapter 3) will also influence how much material you cover. If you are teaching a course for the first time, build in some slack, and try to avoid scheduling too many topics. You will thank yourself when you get to a point where you need a bit more time. Alternatively, plan some topics that can be skipped, if necessary. In my CS2 class, I often leave the second-to-last lecture as a *To Be Announced* lecture, in case I get behind during the term. This also allows me to find a fun topic to teach that isn't testable, and I have taught classes on esoteric data structures, different programming languages, and computer science history in that lecture spot, and often it turns out to be a fun lecture with less pressure than a testable lecture (for both students and me!).

Figures 2, 3, and 4 show a sample syllabus based on my own CS2 course at Stanford.[1] You can find the original HTML for the syllabus at this book's website.

PLANNING YOUR SCHEDULE

Planning the schedule for your course is critically important. You are obviously bound by the beginning and end of the term, but you also have to count exactly how many lectures you have (and don't forget about holidays!), and make everything fit. As mentioned in the previous section, building slack into the schedule can be important, especially if you haven't taught the course before.

In my own planning I start with a blank calendar where I highlight the lecture days, accounting for holidays. I pick the week of the midterm exam, and then I make a rough placement for the assignment release and due dates. After that, I start placing lecture topics on individual days. Once I have the basic structure, I start looking at how the assignments and lectures line up – you should plan to get through all of the material necessary for an assignment before the assignment has been released, if possible. This will mean that you are covering material in lecture that doesn't match with the current assignment, but students need time to process the information before they jump into using it. Around midterm week, I try to go over a less-intensive topic in lecture, knowing that students are going to need time to prepare for the exam. I will also often extend an assignment a bit longer than I would give students for the same reason. Be careful to not have as-

---

1 Which in turn was based on a handout by Mehran Sahami and Chris Piech, and modified by Nick Troccoli.

CS2 Syllabus, Fall 2xxx

Logistics

Course: CS2, Data Structures
Lectures: MWF 1:00pm-1:50pm, Big Lecture Hall
Prerequisites: CS1, Introduction to Programming (or AP CS -- see below)
Piazza online forum: https://piazza.com/myclass
Lecturer: Chris Gregg, me@myschool.edu
Office Hours: Mon/Tue 3:00pm-5:00pm, or by appointment

Overview -- what is CS 2?

CS2, "Data Structures," is the follow-on course to CS1. It is taught in C++, although students are only expected to know some Java (or other object oriented language) before enrolling in the course. That said, if you are taking CS2 without taking CS1, you should probably look at the Course Placement handout from the website to see if you are in an appropriate course. Students who took AP Computer Science A (not AP Computer Science Principles) and received a 4 or a 5 on the AP exam should be well-prepared for CS2. The following course topics will be covered in class:

- C++ Functions
- Computational Complexity and "Big O" notation
- Vectors
- C++ Strings
- Stacks
- Queues
- Sets
- Maps
- Recursion (including fractals, recursive backtracking, and exhaustive search)
- Sorting
- Memoization
- C++ Structs and Classes
- Pointers
- Dynamic Allocation in C++
- Linked Lists
- Binary Heaps
- Trees (including n-ary trees and binary search trees (BSTs)
- Graphs
- Graph algorithms: Breadth First and Depth First searching, Dijkstra and A* shortest-path finding, minimum spanning trees

We may also cover some esoteric data structures such as skip lists, bloom filters, and ropes, and we may cover C++ inheritance and polymorphism if we have time.

Class Web Page

The web page for CS2 is located at https://cs2.myschool.edu

You should regularly check the class web site for handouts, announcements and other information, including the most up-to-the-date information on assignments. Please note that the class web page will have links to all class materials including electronic copies of class handouts and assignment files.

Figure 2: Page 1 of an example CS2 syllabus.

Discussion Sections

A critical part of CS2 is the 50-minute discussion section, where you will go over class problems with a section leader. Please sign up for discussion sections by **the end of the first week of class** at the following website: https://cs.myschool.edu/section_signup.html You will be able to choose times that work for your schedule, and we will match you as best we can to your choices. If you do not sign up by the time we match, you will need to sign up for a section after the fact, and we cannot guarantee that you will be able to find a section that meets your schedule.

Course Support

CS2 provides many opportunities for you to get help with the class. Section leaders are available Sunday through Thursday evenings in Computer Science Hall basement, from 7pm-11pm. Chris and the Head TA will also have separate office hours; please see the course website for times.

Texts and Handouts

CS2 has one optional textbook: Programming Abstractions in C++ by Eric Roberts. In addition to this textbook, we will also distribute additional material in the form of class handouts. Class handouts will be available electronically in PDF format on the CS2 web site. If you prefer printed handouts, you can print a copy from the web.

Programming Assignments

There will be seven (7) programming assignments, in increasing difficulty. Each assignment will be graded by your section leader, and you will have a one-on-one debriefing session with your section leader to discuss how you did on each assignment. Assignments will be rated on the following scale:

- ++ A fantastic submission that is well beyond the assignment requirements. We rarely give out ++ grades, and they are reserved for the top assignment submissions of the quarter.
- + A submission that exceeds the assignment requirements. To receive a + grade, you should extend the assignment in some interesting way.
- ✓+ A submission that meets the requirements of the assignment, and shows solid functionality as well as good style. Students that routinely receive ✓+ grades on assignments should be proud of their work.
- ✓ A submission that meets the requirements of the assignment, with a few small errors.
- ✓- A submission that has problems severe enough to not meet the assignment requirements.
- - A submission with serious flaws but does show some understanding of the solution to the assignment.
- 0 A submission that shows little work and does not meet the standard to pass the assignment.

We do not release number grades for assignments, because we do not want students worrying about single point totals. We have found that so-called "bucket-grading" is better pedagogically than grading with numbers.

Pair Programming

Most of the assignments in this course must be completed on an individual basis, but some of them allow you to optionally work in a pair with a partner. Each assignment will specify if it is to be done individually or allows working in pairs. Note that you are not required to work with a partner on assignments that allow it, but you are encouraged to do so. Working in pairs can improve student learning by giving you someone to talk to when you are stuck, or by letting you see a different way of approaching the same problem. You can also change pairings between assignments. In other words, you donâ€™t have to keep the same pairing for every assignment that allows pairs (and you can even choose to do some in pairs and others individually).

Pair programming means that **both** partners code together **at all times** for a particular assignment. You should be using one computer, and you should take turns doing the typing, with the other partner sitting alongside and contributing ideas. Both students should contribute significantly to the project, and both students will receive the same grade for the assignment.

Figure 3: Page 2 of an example CS2 syllabus.

Late Policy

Each of the assignments is due at **6PM PST** on the dates specified in the assignment. The program code for your assignments must be submitted electronically as described in a separate handout. Anything that comes in after 6pm will be considered late.

Because each of you will probably come upon some time during the quarter where so much work piles up that you need a little extra time, every student begins the quarter with two free "late days." "Late days" are class days, not actual days. For instance, if an assignment is due Thursday at 6PM, 1 late day would give you until the next class (e.g. Friday) at 6PM to submit without penalty. 2 late days would give you until the next, next class (e.g. Monday) at 6PM to submit without penalty. After the late days are exhausted, programs that come in late (up to a maximum of three class days) will be assessed a late penalty of one grade "bucket" per class day (e.g., a ! + turns into a ! , and so forth). Assignments received later than three class days following the due date will not be graded. The interactive-grading session with your section leader must be scheduled within two weeks of the due date. Note that no assignments will be accepted after the last day of classes.

You should think of these free "late days" as extensions you have been granted ahead of time, and use them when you might have otherwise tried to ask for an extension. As a result, getting an extension beyond the free "late days" will generally not be granted. In very special circumstances (primarily extended medical problems or other emergencies), extensions may be granted beyond the late days. All extension requests must be directed to Chris or to the head TA no later than 24 hours before the program is due. Only Chris and the head TA will be able to approve extensions.

Examinations

The midterm examination will be held on _____ from __PM to __PM. There will be alternate times available for legitimate excuses (e.g., symphony practice, or another class).

The final examination is scheduled for _____ from 8:30am-11:30am. For a variety of reasons (including university policy), there will be no alternate time for the final exam. Please make sure that you can attend the final exam at the specified time before enrolling in the class.

Examinations will be administered on a computer, will be closed-book, and you may use a one page back-and-front page of notes, as well as a reference sheet that will be provided. You cannot use electronic devices of any type (i.e. portable computers, phones, etc) other than the computer on which you are taking the exam, which may only be used to administer the exam (e.g. you cannot view any notes).

Grading

Final grades for the course will be determined using the following weights:

40% Programming assignments (weighted toward the later assignments)
30% Final examination
20% Midterm examination
10% Section participation

Because we cannot control for the exact difficulty of exams across multiple quarters, it is not possible to provide a "potential grade" for the course as you progress through it. Final grades will be weighted such that roughly the same proportion of students gets As, Bs, etc. as in previous quarters of the course.

Honor Code and Plagiarism

We take the honor code and plagiarism seriously. Please see the Honor Code Handout for details.

Students with Documented Disabilities

Students who may need academic accommodations should contact the Office of Accessible Education, who can prepare written accommodations that should be provided to Nick and Chris. Students should contact the OAE as soon as possible since notice is needed to prepare accommodations.

Figure 4: Page 3 of an example CS2 syllabus.

signments due on the same day as exams, as this causes students to prioritize one over the other, with the expected poor results.

If you have access to lectures and assignments from previous offerings of your class already, you should be able to create your schedule fairly quickly. Unless you plan on making drastic changes, the schedule from prior terms should work well, though beware that because of holidays the timing might need to be slightly different – again, you want to cover material before your release the associated assignments, and sometimes you will need to tweak the assignment dates or lecture contents slightly to account for differences in term scheduling.

It is rare for a schedule to remain completely unchanged for an entire term, especially the first time you teach a course. There are external factors that can affect your schedule (e.g., snow days, hurricanes, etc.), and you want to be able to change it as the term progresses. Keeping your schedule as a web page or other on-line document or calendar is a good idea, as is a disclaimer to students that the schedule may be changed due to circumstances. Obviously, if you do change the schedule during the term, you need to inform your students of this immediately.

Figure 5 and Figure 6 shows a schedule for a quarter-long (10-week) CS2 course, based on a data structures course I have taught before. I have removed the exact dates. Notice that there is a holiday, and notice that the second-to-last lecture is *To Be Announced*. The example schedule is part of the sample website available on the website for this book – see the *Website and Other Tools* section below for the link.

ASSIGNMENT PLANNING

Chapter 7 discusses creating assignments in detail, but when you are planning your schedule you need to carefully look at assignment release and due dates, and align them with your curriculum. If you are giving an assignment that have been used before, talk to someone who has used it and ask how long the students were

CS2 Fall 20xx

Week	Monday	Wednesday	Friday
1	September X **1. Welcome to CS2!** Slides Code Assignment 0 released Reading: Textbook Ch. 2	September X **2. C++ Functions** Slides Code Reading: Textbook Ch. 3	September X **3. Computational Complexity and "Big O" notation** Slides Code Reading: Textbook Ch. 8
2	September X **4. Vectors** Slides Code Assignment 0 due (6pm) Assignment 1 released Reading: Textbook Ch. 4	September X **5. C++ Strings** Slides Code Reading: Textbook Ch. 5	September X **6. Stacks and Queues** Slides Code Reading: Textbook Ch. 6
3	Date **7. Sets and Maps** Slides Code Assignment 1 due (6pm) Assignment 2 released Reading:	Date **8. Recursion 1 -- Introduction to Recursion** Slides Code Reading:	Date **9. Recursion 2 -- Fractals** Slides Code Reading:
4	Date **8. Recursion 3 -- Recursive Backtracking** Slides Code Assignment 2 due (6pm) Assignment 3 released Reading:	Date **9. Recursion 4 -- Exhaustive Search** Slides Code Reading:	Date **10. Sorting** Slides Code Reading:
5	Date **11. Memoization** Slides Code Assignment 3 due (6pm) Assignment 4 released Reading:	Date **12. C++ Structs and Classes** Slides Code Reading: **Midterm: Thursday!**	Date **13. C++ Pointers** Slides Code Reading:
6	Date **14. Dynamic Allocation in C++** Slides Code Assignment 4 due (6pm) Assignment 5 released Reading:	Date **15. Linked Lists** Slides Code Reading:	Date **16. Implementing a Vector of** `int` **s** Slides Code Reading:

Figure 5: Page 1 of an example CS2 schedule.

7	Date	Date	Date
	17. Binary Heaps	**18. Trees**	**19. Binary Search Trees (BSTs)**
	Slides	Slides	Slides
	Code	Code	Code
	Assignment 5 due (6pm)	Reading:	Reading:
	Assignment 6 released		
	Reading:		

8	Date	Date	Date
	20. Graphs 1 -- Introduction to Graphs	**21. Graphs 2 -- Minimum Spanning Trees**	**22. Breadth First and Depth First Search**
	Slides	Slides	Slides
	Code	Code	Code
	Assignment 6 due (6pm)	Reading:	Reading:
	Assignment 7 released		
	Reading:		

9	Date	Date	Date
	No Class (Holiday)	**23. Dijkstra's Algorithm and the A-star Algorithm**	**24. Hashing and Hash Tables**
		Slides	Slides
		Code	Code
		Reading:	Reading:

10	Date	Date	Date
	25. Fun Data Structures: Skip Lists and Bloom Filters	**26. TBA**	**27. Final Class -- Wrap-up**
	Slides	Slides	Slides
	Code	Code	Code
	Reading:	Reading:	Reading: Assignment 7 due (6pm)

11		Date	
		Final Exam	
		Date:	
		Time:	

Website design based on a design by Chris Piech

Icons by Piotr Kwiatkowski

Figure 6: Page 2 of an example CS2 schedule.

given to complete the assignment, and if there are any particular things to watch for (e.g., which part of the assignment is most difficult?). As mentioned before, it is a good idea to complete the assignment yourself, and to ask some or all of your TAs to complete it, as well. Don't base the amount of time for the students on your own completion, as they will be seeing the assignment and concepts for the first time, and they do need more time to complete them. Don't be afraid to give them a bit more time then you think is necessary, either, especially the first time you give an assignment – you won't receive any complaints about having too much time, but the same is not true if there is too much work for the given amount of time.

As mentioned in the previous section, try not to have assignments due on the same day as an exam. Also, be aware of how long you think it will take to grade the assignments – it is always better (but not always possible) to return the previous assignment grades before the current assignment is due. When planning assignments for the first run of course, you should err on the side of fewer assignments, and as you get more experience with the course, you can add more assignments if it makes sense to fit them into the schedule.

In the computer science field there are a tremendous number of freely available resources, and you can often find free resources in lieu of requiring your students to purchase a textbook. Today's students are used to reading everything online, so not having a paper textbook is not a burden on the students. From a pedagogical standpoint, having a paper textbook is becoming less important for many classes, and you likely will be able to avoid it by finding suitable online resources.

For any other course-related purchases your students will need to make (e.g., clickers, hardware, credits for online servers, etc.), you should try to streamline this as much as possible for the students, so they can make the purchases all at once. I have taught a couple of hardware-based computer science classes where the TAs and I put together the hardware kits for students and had them purchase them during the first week of class. If your course fits that mold, this needs to go into your planning.

Chapter 9 discusses the role of Teaching Assistants in your class, but having quality TAs can make a class exponentially better, and you should make it a priority to hire the best TAs you can. If you are in the position to hire TAs for your course, you need to plan it and do the hiring before the term begins (or right at the beginning of the term, though that is not ideal). Your department may already have the hiring logistics in place, but you need to find out what they are, and how much say you have over the hiring for your course. If you do have a say in who you hire, you should be prepared to interview candidates, or at least have them fill out a form that you can look at. You should ask them how they did in the course when (if) they took it, and why they want to be a TA for the course now. You should also ask them if they have had prior teaching or TA experience (a good thing). For some classes, you may ask them to demonstrate how they will help students, or you may ask them to give you a practice lesson (e.g., in preparation to teach a recitation section). Obviously, you may not have time to do a full set of interviews, especially if you expect to hire many TAs, but the time you spend hiring the best candidates you can will be worth it.

Ideally, a TA has taken the course you are teaching and done well, and has a genuine desire to work with students in your class to help them do well, too. You want TAs who are invested in the course, and not just doing it for tuition or a stipend. This can be hard to tease out of potential TAs, but you will generally be able to figure this out in an in-person interview, and sometimes from a form, if you ask the right questions. Although many TAs are gregarious students, this shouldn't be a requirement, and I have had some outstanding TAs who were reserved but really knew the material, and were great at explaining it. You should, to the extent possible, attempt to get a diverse set of TAs – I always attempt to make my TA cohort 50% male and 50% female, and I make it a priority to find quality TAs of color, sexual orientation, first generation students, etc. The more diverse your TA pool is, the better your TAs can model that computer science is a field that welcomes everyone.

If you have more than a handful of TAs, you may want to consider assigning a head TA, who reports to you and can manage the rest of the TAs. This should be a senior TA who has either worked for you before, or worked with the course before, and you should choose someone responsible who you think will be respected by the rest of the TAs. If there is a potential to pay the head TA more, you should make that happen, as well.

When you hire TAs, ensure that they understand their responsibilities, including how much time they should be devoting to your course. You should also make sure they know that they are responsible through the end of the term.[2]

Once you have taught a class more than once, you will start to build up the TAs that you have had in the course before (if you can hire undergraduate TAs – see below), and this can become self-propagating, which is fantastic. When you are teaching a course, keep an eye out for current students who will make good TAs, and tell them that near the end of the course. I have hired scores of outstanding TAs who had never even considered becoming a TA until I told them that they should apply. This is especially true for women and underrepresented minorities – recommending that they become TAs will not only increase the diversity of the TA pool, but it can give a needed boost the the self-esteem of a student who doesn't see many people that look like them in the computer science community.

---

2 You might be surprised how often TAs try to leave campus before finishing the grading for a course!

Graduate TAs -vs- Undergraduate TAs

Depending on where you teach, you may have the option to hire graduate students or undergraduate students. It is not possible to completely generalize the differences, but you may find that one group or the other at your school is preferable. Graduate students, while often more advanced in computer science, haven't necessarily taken the course before, while undergraduates have most likely taken the course, and probably have taken it recently. The undergraduates are therefore more familiar with the material. Undergraduates also generally think of becoming a TA as an extracurricular activity (that they happen to get paid for), rather than as a means to completely fund their studies, which is what motivates many graduate students. I have found that undergraduates have more intrinsic motivation for being TAs, though I have also had graduate student TAs who were phenomenal, and who took their TA responsibilities seriously.

MEETINGS WITH TAS

As you are doing your planning, you should set aside regular meeting times with your TAs. Weekly is best, as it keeps everyone up to date on the material you are covering in class, and you can talk to the TAs about what is expected of them for the current topics. Additionally, you can ask TAs how they feel the class is going – often, they will have more insight than you do to how the students are doing and on the students' perception of how the course is progressing. Take their advice and feedback seriously: for example, if your TAs tell you that students are struggling on a particular topic, you should build in review of that topic in your next lecture, if possible.

Your weekly TA meeting can also be a chance for you to preview exam questions, and to discuss potential troubles students might have on upcoming assignments. TAs who have worked with the class before and who have been TAs when the assignments were given before are invaluable to preparing new TAs for what to expect. Use their knowledge and experience whenever you can, and the class will be better for it.

WEBSITE AND OTHER TOOLS

Chapter 5 covers the various tools you can use for your courses, but when planning your course, you should decide what tools you will use, and then set them up and be ready to use them before the term begins. Having your course materials accessible to your students is a critical part of your course, and you will want them online. You can do this through a website that you build and host through your school, or it can be set up through your school's Learning Management System (LMS) (e.g., Canvas, Sakai, Blackboard, Moodle, etc.).

If you do decide to set up a school-hosted website, it does not have to be fancy, and you should prefer function over fanciness. The website should be easily navigable, and should have links to all of the course information. You should be able to update it and to add resources to it with minimal effort, and you should also have the ability to give a head TA access to update it, as well. You can see an example minimal website for a CS2 course at
https://yourfirstyearteaching.com/cs/example_website
You can download the website repository at
https://github.com/yourfirstyearteaching/example_cs2_website
The sample website is built with the Flask Python microframework, using a few Javascript libraries, including jQuery and Bootstrap. It is straightforward to add resources, and easy to update. It has a simple menu interface, calendar, and resource links. Although *Flask* is built to allow a dynamic website, the sample website is set up to be a static website. It is relatively easy to update the website to work with dynamic content. The sample website is available under the MIT license, and you are welcome to modify it to use for your own courses.

ADMINISTRATIVE DETAILS

When you are planning your course, there are many administrative details you will need to work out before the first day of class. Your school and department will likely have set up the room location for your lectures and labs (if your course has a lab), but you should check out the room(s) before your class begins. If this is your first time teaching in the classroom, this is critical, if only to find out how long it will take you to get to class from your office every day! If you are going to use a computer during class, bring your laptop, and/or make sure that you can log into the computer in the room. Also test the Internet access, and make sure you can log in to that, as well. If you are going to play media, test the speakers, and know where the light switches are. For the first day of class (at least), bring a hard-copy of anything you want to use from your computer, particularly slides. If a tragedy occurs and your laptop breaks, you can still conduct class without having to remember everything you wanted to talk about. Make a note of whether the classroom already has projector cables and adapters that work with your computer, and plan on bringing your own cord(s) anyway.[3]

Another benefit to visiting the classroom before the first day is to simply see what the room feels like. Are you in a large lecture hall? Are you on a stage? Will you need to use a microphone? Also, project your slides and then go to the back of the room to make sure they are readable. If they aren't increase your font sizes. For smaller classrooms, note the furniture, and if it is movable – you might want to have students in a circle, or at tables in groups.

If your class is going to be recorded, either test out the recording equipment beforehand, or if it will be recorded professionally, see if you can discuss the logistics of how lecture will be recorded and posted ahead of time, so you can add that information to

---

3 It always amazes me how often a cord or adapter that was present in one lecture is missing in the next. You should always carry around a full set of cables and adapters for your laptop.

your website or class handouts. If you plan on recording the class yourself, do a test-run to go through the recording procedures, and (as mentioned before), make sure you know any rules your school might have about posting recorded lectures.

FOR NEXT TIME...

The first time you plan and teach a course, you will find many things that you want to change for the next time you teach it. After each class, take at least five minutes to write down your immediate thoughts about the lecture. What worked and what didn't work? Were there any typos that need to be fixed on the slides? Did you get good questions that you might want to prepare for for next time? If you have the time to fix your slides, or make some changes, great, but if not you should have a file that lists the changes you will make so you can get to them the next time you teach the course. I have been in the situation where I have had mistakes on my slides that I forgot to fix, and it was no fun seeing them pop up again during class the *second* time around. Chapter 11 discusses how to reflect on your own teaching, but there is no better time than as soon after a lecture as you can muster.

You will likewise want to make changes to assignments after you give them, and keeping a *For Next Time* file for observations about assignments is a good idea, too. Maybe you need to write a clarification about part of the assignment, or you need to cover a particular topic in more detail before releasing an assignment, or maybe the assignment could be completed in a fewer number of days. Any constructive feedback you get from your students should go into the file as well, so you can re-assess the assignment before you use it again.

WHAT TO DO IF...

What if I don't have time to plan my whole course before it starts?

As this chapter has demonstrated, there is a lot to think about when planning a course, and you may not have enough time to plan it out as thoroughly as you might like. You should prioritize fleshing out the calendar, so you at least know what the course will look like. If you have to change the calendar during the term, then you do it. Your next priority should be to get the assignments prepared, at least to the state where you have written the bulk of the instructions. As you will see in Chapter 7, assignments can take a tremendous amount of time to create, and you do not want to try and create all of your assignments on-the-fly during the course. Better to have a number of assignments from a previous version of the course that you know work (ask your colleagues for assignments they have given in the past) then to try and create new assignments that are untested. After you have the assignments prepared as best you can, try to at least have your first week's worth of lectures planned out, if not completely written. The first week of the term is always hectic, and trying to plan lectures on top of it all is difficult.

What if my students aren't prepared for the course I've planned?

If you plan a course that is too difficult for your students, you will need to perform some re-planning during the term. You may not find this out until a few assignments or an exam have been graded, but if you look at the results and find that your students are not getting the material, then you should re-plan as best you can. Look ahead at your schedule, and plan on using some of the slack you built into it to allow you to slow down, or review. Re-prioritize the topics you want to teach, and then consider dropping the lowest priority topics, which can give you more time for the important topics. Consider re-assessing your students on material they didn't learn the first time – you can re-teach a topic and then give a quiz on it later, or you can re-assign a homework assignment that did not go well. In all cases, you should reevaluate what you want your students to be able to do by the end of the course, and be as effective as you can to make at least some of your original plan work. Maybe the students did not have the prerequisites you assumed they would come in with. If it makes sense, you may want to teach them some of that material before moving on. You also should consider sitting down with a handful of students to understand their perception of the course – ask them why they think they are not doing well, and ask them what you think can improve with the course. Take their feedback seriously, and make any changes you think you can that will make them more successful in the course.

FINAL THOUGHTS

Planning a class is a challenging endeavor, whether you have taught it before or not. Certainly, once you have taught a particular course a couple of times, you can minimize the amount of work that goes into the planning, but you still need to work out the schedule, choose assignments, re-purpose a website, etc. New courses can take months to prepare, and almost certainly won't be perfect the first time through the course. Courses that have been taught at your school before but are new to you are less difficult to prepare for, if you have access to the materials from previous offerings.

It may seem obvious that the better you plan your course, the easier it will be to run during the term. I guarantee that you will be surprised at how much work you will have during the term, regardless of how well prepared you are, so do your best to check as many boxes as you can before you get to the first day, so you will be able to concentrate on the aspects of teaching that you didn't expect, and the ones that are taking more time than you imagined.

Have fun planning your courses – remember, you like this stuff! When you are excited about your class, the students will see that, and they, too, will have a better experience. And maximizing student experience and learning is, of course, your ultimate goal.

7

CREATING AWESOME ASSIGNMENTS

In your own educational background, you have completed thousands of assignments, and I bet you can think back to some of your favorites, whether they were in a computer science course, or another class. Maybe it was an independent or group project, or maybe it was just a fun and interesting assignment that you enjoyed doing. I also bet you can think of your least-favorite assignments, though you may have blocked them out, or they have just faded from memory. You almost certainly have forgotten hundreds of boring assignments that you completed but aren't worth remembering.

My favorite assignment from college was a project for an integrated circuits course where we were instructed to come up with a creative use for the device we had been designing all semester, and we had free reign to make something interesting. My partners and I decided to use the device to control a twelve-foot long blimp that we purchased from a hobby store, for which we had to scavenge helium from various chemistry and physics professors around campus. The project was challenging (we had never driven a blimp before!), fascinating, and fun, and it didn't even feel like we were working on an assignment, but rather it felt like a cool project that we would be proud of. Not all assignments can be quite this fun, but you should strive to make at least some of your own assignments the ones that your students will remember fondly.

As discussed in Chapter 6, you should plan your courses around what you want your students to be able to *do*, and not what they will *know*. The most effective way for your students to learn how to do something is to (surprise, surprise) have them actually practice doing it. They get this practice from assignments, and the better your assignments are, the more your students will learn. You will prepare them to do the assignments through your lectures, examples, and recitation sections, and you need to create assignments that force them to put the skills and knowledge from lecture into practice. In many computer science courses, programming assignments make up the bulk of the work, although there are a number of theory classes (e.g., algorithms, theory of computation, etc.) that tend to have proof-based, or other written problem-solving assignments. Regardless of the type of assignments you create, you want them to be challenging but doable, gradable, and, above all, *interesting*. Computer science is blessed with an innumerable number of fascinating problems to solve, and you should endeavor to craft your assignments out of interesting problems.

Building a new assignment is challenging, and takes a substantial amount of time. Unless you are building a course completely from scratch, do not create all new assignments the first time you teach a course. Even if you think you can make better assignments, start small and create or re-write one or two assignments during your first term – you can modify the rest as you become more familiar with the course, and when you have more time. You want to create robust assignments that can be re-used in future terms (despite the possibility of cheating, which is addressed later in the chapter, and in Chapter 9), primarily because you want to be able to leverage the amount of time you will put into creating each assignment.

The best way to see how to create your own awesome assignments is to take a look at assignments that are already awesome. While this chapter can give you guidance about how to create assignments, you are going to learn exponentially more by reading and analyzing assignments that other smart people have already written. Computer science instructors have shared many assignments online, and there are repositories full of assignments you can look at, and use yourself, with proper attribution. One of the best resources for great CS1 and CS2 assignments is SIGCSE's

Nifty Assignments, curated by Nick Parlante and Julie Zelenski. Nifty Assignments are presented annually at the SIGCSE Conference, and instructors submit their best and most interesting assignments, which are put online to be used or modified for other classes. The SIGCSE mailing list is also a robust forum for questions about assignments, and if you are trying to come up with an idea for an assignment for a particular topic, consider sending an email to the list for suggestions.

Another way to find great assignments is simply to perform an Internet search for your course topics and to check out what assignments are available at other schools. You can use the assignments as examples to model your own assignments after, or you can reach out to the instructors to see if they will allow you to use the assignments for your own class in their current form.

Throughout this chapter, I will refer to an *Edge Match* assignment, which is geared towards a CS2 course and tests recursion and pruning backtracking. The full assignment is at the end of the chapter, and it is also located on the example CS2 website associated with this book.

MATCHING COURSE CONTENT TO ASSIGNMENTS

As you plan your course (discussed in Chapter 6), you are going to also plan what assignments you want to have each week, or for each topic or topics. You may have an idea of what assignments you want to have the students complete, based on the topics you will cover in class, and if so, you should schedule the assignments and then place the topics for lecture such that you've covered the requisite topic before (or as) assignments go out to the students. If you have planned out the topics and do not yet have assignments, then you will need to decide which topics you will cover on the assignments, and plan the assignments based on those topics. It is likely that you will not be able to give assignments that test each and every course concept, but you should obviously try to work out the schedule so that students practice most of the material on the assignments. That said – do not try to jam in every topic on your assignments simply to cover the material. Students will see through this, and if an assignment topic seems forced, your students will not appreciate it. If your course is problem-set based, you may have an easier time including all of the course topics in the assignments. Highlight any problems that you think are particularly important, and include more of those types of problems on the assignments.

Many courses are set up so that early assignments are easier than later assignments, possibly with a capstone assignment near the end of the term. Assignments gradually get more challenging as the students get more skills with the material. This is particularly true with programming assignments in introductory classes, where students build their programming skills throughout the course. In a CS1 course, for instance, the first couple of assignments may not have student-written functions, as you may not have covered function-writing yet. In more advanced courses where students are expected to be proficient programmers, this is less of a concern, and assignment difficulty may simply depend on the topic and not where in the term the assignment falls. If you do decide to have a capstone assignment that ties together much of the material from the term, it will likely end up being the most difficult assignment.

The length of an assignment is often tied to the material that is covered in the assignment, or the difficulty of the assignment, and you should plan your assignments with this in mind. You generally want your assignments to be compartmentalized such that they can be given independently of other assignments (though see below for linked assignments), although they often build on material covered earlier in the course. Except for a final assignment (which is often a bit longer than other assignments), you usually want to have most assignments take roughly the same amount of time.

As you match your content and assignments, you may want to build assignments off of previous assignments from the same term. If this is the case, you want to have a plan for the likeli-hood that some of your students won't complete an assignment successfully, and won't be able to use their work for follow-on assignments. You may want to provide working versions of prior assignments that they can use instead of their own work.

FINDING INTERESTING PROBLEMS AND MOTIVATING YOUR STUDENTS

Interesting assignments are the ones your students will remember. They are also assignments that your students will want to do, even to the extent that they may prioritize your assignments over other classwork. As a computer science instructor, you are lucky that there are so many cool topics and problems to choose from, and you should use this advantage to craft assignments that your students will enjoy.

When you are searching for interesting ideas for assignments, think about real-world uses for the topics you are covering in class. A popular assignment often given as the last assignment in Stan-ford's CS106B (CS2) course is an assignment where students use Dijkstra's algorithm and the A-star algorithm to create a Google Maps-type application. The students are given a graph of map locations as vertices, and they are given driving times between each node. Students use a beginning vertex and an end vertex, and their algorithm implementations create a path between the vertices, which is then graphed onto a real map. The assignment tests them on a real-world use of best-path finding algorithms, they get instant, visual feedback of their solutions, and they cre-ate an application that has become ubiquitous in their every day lives. It is a fantastic assignment because it keeps the students in-terested, and they get an insight into what is under the hood for a real tool.

Students will naturally gravitate towards assignments that have real-world applications, or solve real problems. The real problems can be historical, as well: Eric Roberts has an *Enigma Machine* assignment that he created that has students build a program to simulate an Enigma Machine from World War II. Many students appreciate problems that have social good implications, and they also enjoy assignments that have some relevance to current trends or culture. If you do decide to create an assignment that is trendy (a Twitter- or Instagram-like application, for instance), be prepared to update it as trends change, but don't shy away from creating these types of assignments.

Some students also enjoy writing games (for programming classes), but you should be careful to limit the number of games students build, because some of your students are not going to be enamored by building one game after another. Having a game or two in the mix during a term is fine; just don't overdo it. Some common game assignments are for Boggle, Scrabble, Sudoku, Adventure, Hangman, Conway's Game of Life[1], and a wide variety of older video games (e.g., PacMan, Breakout, Frogger, etc.). The *Edge Match* example assignment listed later in this chapter is an edge-matching puzzle game that uses recursive backtracking to produce puzzle solutions.

If you are teaching a course that is a lower-level systems class (e.g., networking, operating systems, compilers, etc.), consider finding assignment ideas that involve system security, as that is a hot topic with a clandestine nature that many students enjoy. You can also use the opportunity to talk about ethics in computer science, a topic that is gaining traction these days as an important addition to the computer science curriculum.

Students can find it interesting to develop tools that already exist and that they use frequently, giving them insight under the hood – re-creating some Unix tools (e.g., `cat`, `grep`, `ls`, etc.) or library functions can be interesting if motivated well.

For classes such as discrete math, probability, cryptography, algorithms, theory of computation, artificial intelligence, etc., there are many classic problems from each sub-discipline that you can

---

1 though this really isn't a *game* in the traditional sense

use in your assignments, and those types of problems can also serve as a historical computer science lesson, as well. You may want to introduce a historical topic during lecture and then have the students work on problems based on the topic for an assignment. For example, the RSA public-key encryption system can be introduced and then used as an assignment in many different classes (discrete math, algorithms, cryptography, etc.), and with different levels of complexity.[2] The ground-breaking nature of the algorithm and its importance to secure online communications on the Internet offers a wonderful historical story to tell your students, as well as giving them a challenging problem to work on in an assignment.

When you are searching for interesting ideas, you might want to scan the abstracts for current research papers in the topics that you are covering. Josh Hug, at U.C. Berkeley, developed a great programming assignment (delivered at SIGCSE 2015[3]) that is based on *Seam Carving*, which was written about in a paper in 2007 by Shai Avidan and Ariel Shamir. Solving the problem fits squarely into a CS1 or CS2 class, is tremendously interesting, visual, and useful – it is an ideal assignment.

As discussed in Chapter 3, knowing your students can go a long way towards knowing what kinds of assignments they might enjoy. Assignments that involve music, art, or language are often popular. For example, Ben Hescott (Northeastern) and Norman Ramsay (Tufts) created a Google-like *SongSearch* program to search for lyrics in a text-based song database, and the students love building the program and then using it to search for their favorite lyrics.

When you release assignments, you should motivate them to your students. Do this verbally when you introduce the assignment in class, and also provide motivation in the assignment write-up. Students want (and deserve) context for the assignments

---

2 See, for example, Kid-RSA, which is a public-key system designed for educational use.

3 http://nifty.stanford.edu/2015/hug-seam-carving/

– they want to know why an assignment is relevant, and what is interesting about it. Some assignments are easier to motivate than others – I don't have any trouble convincing my students that building Google Maps is going to be fun, but asking them to re-invent the `printf` function takes a bit more convincing. Provide some historical context for why the solution is necessary and relevant, and give them a demo of what they are about to create.

Motivation for problem sets may not seem like a worthwhile idea, but it depends on what kinds of problems you have created. Marketing your assignments will give your students more willingness to work on an assignment. If you have trouble motivating an assignment, reassess why you are giving it to your students to begin with, and look at re-framing the question, or coming up with a premise that your students will appreciate. Chris Piech, at Stanford, has re-invigorated his *Introduction to Probability for Computer Scientists* course by creating problem sets and programming assignments that use real data that often have social good implications. I have had students in my own classes that have asked me to re-write assignments with the same mentality that Chris Piech uses for his assignments, because they are so well received.

CHALLENGING BUT DOABLE ASSIGNMENTS

Students learn the most when they have to use their brains. If you give assignments that are too easy, students won't learn much, and those that want to learn the material won't be pleased. Yes, you may have some students happy that they can spend little time on your class, but you should not be proud of this. Conversely, if you give students assignments that are too hard, they will be frustrated, and they also won't learn much. Some students will also be tempted to cheat on the assignments in order to complete them, and this is certainly not something you want to encourage. It is not easy to develop assignments that are just the right level of difficulty, but you should do your best to try and find that medium.

As you develop your assignments, you should be continually thinking about the solution. In fact, you should create a solution or solutions early on when you are developing an assignment, so that you can determine how hard it will be. Keep in mind, of course, that you are able to do the assignments faster and more efficiently than your students, especially because you are the one who created it. Your students will be seeing the material for the very first time in your course, and they will not have the insight you have from years of practice, and from more advanced material. If you have TAs for your course, enlist them to write assignment solutions, ask them to keep track of how long a solution took them, and have them give you constructive feedback on the assignment. Many TAs are happy to help write assignments, too, and you should use their help if you can.

The first time you give an assignment, be prepared to provide guidance if the assignment does turn out to be too difficult. If this happens, reassure the students that you will account for this when grading, or restructure the assignment to reduce the amount of work. This is another reason to limit the number of new assignments for a course – students will forgive you if a new assignment needs to be re-worked, but their generosity will wane if *every* assignment has troubles. If an assignment turns out to be too easy, you will fight an uphill battle if you try and make it harder after it has been released. In this case, you can note that you should make it more difficult the next time you teach it. If students comment on the assignment being too easy, let them know that it was a new assignment that still needs to be tweaked, and suggest that they write their own extensions to go further with the material.

You should attempt to make your assignments challenging for the motivated students in your class who are well-prepared and are likely to do well. Because of the heterogeneous nature of most classes (see Chapter 3 for more comments on heterogeneous classes), you will likely have some students who struggle with the assignment, and others who think it is too easy (though with this second group, you should still try to make the assignments interesting). If it is challenging for the motivated and well-prepared students (not necessarily as much for the top-of-the-class students), then you can handle the other cases without changing the assignment. For the superstar students who want more work, you can encourage them to write extensions to the assignments, while giving them a nominal amount of bonus credit (if you want) for their work. In order to work on an extension, students should first complete the assignment in its original form, and then add to it. For students who struggle with the assignments, you should encourage them to come to office hours, or to get help from their TAs, for example. You want to assess their own level of motivation, preparation, and work before concluding that your assignment is too difficult, and you can base this on how their peers are doing.

SCAFFOLDING ASSIGNMENTS, AND STARTER CODE

For programming assignments, you often need to *scaffold* the assignments, meaning that you give the students a framework in which students can write their assignment, and the framework may provide tips or hints to get students started, or it may break the assignment up into small chunks that compartmentalize the full assignment. The scaffolding can be included in the project instructions (see below for how to write assignment instructions), or it can be *starter code* that the students will expand upon. You have to decide how much scaffolding and/or starter code to give students, but it is important to give them enough information and guidance for them to get started correctly.

Scaffolding can be in the form of a list of instructions on how to proceed with the assignment, with suggestions on the order to tackle the parts of the program (assuming it is a programming assignment). It is more than just the specification for the assignment – scaffolding can include best practices, or suggestions about data structures, or code layout. Assignments earlier in the term may require more scaffolding, especially if you want your students to take more responsibility later for some of the details you provided for past assignments. The *Edge Match* assignment provides scaffolding through its starter code, with detailed function comments in the starter code, and through examples in the assignment write-up.

Starter code can also be minimal or robust, and it depends on the assignment. For programs that have a graphical interface (for example), you may have to provide starter code that handles the majority of the graphical capabilities, especially if your goal is to have the students focus on the non-graphical part of the assignment. For the Google Maps-esque assignment discussed earlier, the students get virtually all of the graphical back-end to the assignment as starter code, so they can concentrate on implementing Dijkstra's algorithm and the A-star algorithm. For other assignments, you may want your students to implement some or all of the graphics code, in which case you would have that as part of the assignment and not part of the starter code. You can often tailor the length of an assignment by providing more or less starter code to your students, although you want to make sure that what you do ask the students to do is relevant to solving the underlying problem – don't make your students write a bunch of GUI code if you can't justify what they are learning by doing it.

Scaffolding assignments can also start in lecture, or in recitation section, where you can introduce a problem in a simple form, or you can have students work on practice problems that will build skills necessary for the main assignment. Introducing an algorithm in class and then having students write an assignment to implement the algorithm is a form of scaffolding, as is pointing out particular parts of an algorithm that might cause students the most trouble during implementation.

WRITING ASSIGNMENT INSTRUCTIONS

Once you have a great assignment idea, you need to draft the instructions for the students, and you need to prepare examples, starter code, testing code, etc. Don't underestimate how much time it will take to make clear instructions: you will spend more time writing and editing the instructions than any other part of the assignment-drafting process. This section will focus on non-problem-set assignments – while those assignments also take time to write, there is generally less overhead (no starter code, setup, etc.) that you need to explain, and writing instructions is a bit more straightforward.

Your assignment instructions should include, at a minimum, the following information:

1. Assignment deadline and how to submit the assignment.

2. Starter code download link, or instructions on how to setup the assignment (e.g., if it is on a server).

3. A description of the assignment, with motivation for why the assignment is interesting or important. Background information about the problem itself, with an example of what a student's solution should produce or answer, can also be an important part of the description.

4. Further examples of output, if relevant, and instructions on how students can test their solutions.

5. Detailed implementation instructions (see below for more information).

You may also want to have a *Frequently Asked Questions (FAQ)* section of your assignment handout, which you can populate with student questions on subsequent offerings of the assignments, or populate with questions you come up with based on the types of questions you expect. In addition to the example output, consider including a partial or full grading rubric for students to base their solutions on, if it makes sense for the nature of your assignment.

Your ultimate goal for assignment instructions is to clearly communicate to the students what you expect them to do for the assignment, with as little ambiguity as possible, and with enough information that they should be able to complete the assignment without any additional guidance. This is easier said than done, of course, and but extensive examples can help considerably, as can a detailed FAQ. This is not to say that you need to give students all of the information needed to *solve* the problem, but you need to *present* the problem with enough detail that a motivated and prepared student can solve it and can complete the assignment in the way you expect.

Your instructions can certainly reference the lecture or lecture notes (e.g., *use the algorithm discussed in lecture*), but the more information you can include on the actual handout (so it is in one place), the better. Your students will appreciate detailed assignment instructions that answer many of their potential questions.

Always have at least one other person (e.g., a TA, or other instructor) look over your assignment instructions before handing them out. As mentioned earlier, if you can have your TAs actually do the assignments after you draft them, that will help find unclear instructions, and will help ensure that your assignment release will go smoothly. You want your assignments to be as ready as possible when you release them, and the more eyes that look at the assignment ahead of time, the better.

WRITING ASSIGNMENTS THAT CAN BE GRADED

The primary goal of an assignment is for the students to learn how to do something. You should, however, be able to assess how successful they were at that task. Ideally, your assignment should have multiple parts that can be graded independently. You want to avoid giving an assignment that has a single solution, with little ability for students who don't get the exact solution to show what they do know. For programming assignments, you can assign multiple sub-problems, each with their own independent solution. For the *Trailblazer* assignment mentioned above, the students have to code three different (but related) algorithms: Breadth First Search, Dijkstra's Algorithm, and the A-Star algorithm. Students can complete any of the algorithms correctly and independently from the other algorithms, although it would be hard to complete the A-Star algorithm without having the others correct.

While you are writing your assignments, you should consider how you will grade each part. If you are going to grade on functionality (for programs), it will involve writing tests that will be run on each submission (and you will need to write those tests, and that test harness). You can also grade on programming *style*, which can come in many forms, including data structure choice, proper commenting, proper decomposition, etc. It is often worth grading on those elements, especially for introductory courses, where you are trying to teach students good programming habits.

As you determine how you want to grade each part of the assignment, you should start creating a *rubric* that will detail the individual points assigned for each part. If you have an autograder that will determine the correctness for part of the assignment, you should start to quantify how many points the autograder will assign per part, and what kinds of tests you need to write to gather that information. Do not underestimate how long it will take to write those tests! Write them as early as possible, preferably as you create the assignment and your own solution. Another benefit to having a TA or a set of TAs write their own solutions to the assignment is to help with autograding – testing your own solution against their submissions can validate that your own solution is correct.[4]

If you write the rubric for the assignment as you are drafting it, you will be able to quickly see where you need to make adjustments to the assignment to spread the available points out. The following example rubric could be used for the *Edge Match* assignment. Notice that the style section is generic, and could be used almost identically in many assignments.

- Functionality (note: 2 or more minor bugs equals one major bug)

---

4 and trust me, you will produce incorrect solutions at times!

- Compiler warnings (2 points):
    * 2 points: No compiler warnings
    * 1 point: 1 compiler warning
    * 0 points: multiple compiler warnings
- Tile String Constructor: (2 points)
    * 2 points: Tile string constructor correctly populates Tile sides and orientation
    * 1 point: Tile string constructor has minor issue with creating sides or orientation
    * 0 points: Has multiple issues creating sides and/or orientation
- Tile orientation Getter and Setter (3 points)
    * 3 points: All tests correct
    * 2 points: Minor bug affecting some tests (e.g., orientation is always 0)
    * 1 point: Major bug(s) affecting most tests (e.g., orientation is never correct)
    * 0 points: All tests fail
- Tile sidesstr() function: (3 points)
    * 3 points: All tests correct
    * 2 points: Minor bug affecting some tests (e.g., the string has spaces)
    * 1 point: Major bug(s) affecting most tests (e.g., the string is based on orientation)
    * 0 points: All tests fail
- Tile isMatched() function (3 points)
    * 3 points: All tests correct
    * 2 points: Minor bug affecting some tests (e.g., orientation is not used)

- * 1 point: Major bug(s) affecting most tests (e.g., matching uses incorrect location)
- * 0 points: All tests fail
- Operator « overload function (3 points)
    - * 3 points: All tests correct
    - * 2 points: Minor bug affecting some tests (e.g., does not include orientation)
    - * 1 point: Major bug(s) affecting most tests (e.g., does not include spaces, or string is incorrect)
    - * 0 points: All tests fail
- allMatch() function (3 points)
    - * 3 points: All tests correct
    - * 2 points: Minor bug affecting some tests (e.g., occasionally reports incorrect result)
    - * 1 point: Major bug(s) affecting most tests (e.g., often reports incorrect result)
    - * 0 points: All tests fail
- solvePuzzle() function (333 points)
    - * 3 points: All tests correct
    - * 2 points: Minor bug affecting some tests (e.g., does not call helper function correctly)
    - * 1 point: Major bug(s) affecting most tests (e.g., does not use recursion at all)
    - * 0 points: All tests fail
- solvePuzzle_helper() function (6 points)
    - * 6 points: All tests correct
    - * 5 points: Minor bug affecting some tests (e.g., solver misses a few correct solutions or reports a few non-solved puzzles as being solved)

* 2 points: Major bug(s) affecting most tests (e.g., only sometimes reports correct solutions)

* 0 points: All tests fail

– Extensions (extra credit):

* 0-3 points: One point for each extension (student should describe extensions in comments)

– Overall functionality score:

• Style

– Data Structure Choice and Utilization: (3 points)

* 3 points: Student chose appropriate data structures for all parts of the assignment, and utilized them efficiently

* 2 points: Student used a less-than-optimal data structure, or used it inefficiently

* 0 points: Student made multiple inappropriate data structure choices

– Code Complexity (3 points)

* 3 points: Student's code is clean and avoids redundancy

* 2 points: Student's code is more complex than necessary in one part (e.g., poor choice for loop type)

* 0 points: Student's code is more complex than necessary in multiple parts

– Code Decomposition and Redundancy (3 points)

* 3 points: Student's code decomposes the problems efficiently (e.g., small functions with a single task)

* 2 points: Student's code has redundancy that could have been removed by writing one or more functions

* 1 point: More than one function is too long (or too short), has too many (or unneeded) parameters, or over-complicates returning values (e.g., returns a single value in a vector)

* 0 points: Student's code has multiple major decomposition issues, or no decomposition was attempted (e.g., a single function for the entire program

- Commenting (3 points)

* 3 points: Student's code is well-commented where necessary

* 2 points: Student's code has useless comments, or should be commented better for complex functions, or does not have top-of-function comments

* 1 point: Student's code has multiple problems from above

* 0 points: Student did not comment code

- Variable Naming and Usage (3 points)

* 3 points: Student's code used excellent naming strategies

* 2 points: Student's code has some naming issues, e.g., using UPPERCASE for non-constants, using non-descriptive names, using strings to hold integer data, using floating point to hold integers

* 1 point: Student's code has multiple problems from above

* 0 points: Student's code is unreadable because of variable naming and usage issues

- Spacing and Indentation (2 points)

* 2 points: Student used consistent spacing and proper indentation

- * 1 point: Student's code used inconsistent spacing or has improper indentation
  - * 0 points: Student's code used inconsistent spacing and has improper indentation
  - Overall Style score:

- Overall Score (Functionality + Style):

- Grader Comments: (grader comments can also accompany code listing)

CREATING LABS

If your course has a lab associated with it, you will need to write lab assignments, which can take a variety of forms. As with homework assignments, you should focus on what you want your students to be able to *do* to complete the lab, not what they will know. Labs are excellent opportunities for students to work with a partner, and it is also a time for students to practice the class material with an expert (you or a TA) that can provide guidance immediately. One particular difficulty to creating good labs is ensuring that they fit into the lab period, especially for students who work at different rates. You can address this by creating a core lab that all students are expected to complete, and then to have extra parts of the lab for students to do as an extension (in a similar fashion to extensions on homework assignments).

As with homework assignments (and perhaps even more importantly), you must cover the material for lab before the students attend lab. While you can have a TA teach the students some of the material in lab, you want the students to spend the majority of time in lab actually working on the lab itself (and not listening to another lecture!).

When creating a lab, you must be extremely concise and straightforward with instructions – students won't have time to pour over long instructions like they will for homework assignments. Often, labs have instructions form a narrative that directs the students to do something (e.g., code a function) before moving on to more instructions. If your students are working with partners, your instructions can direct student pairs to discuss their ideas before doing a task. For example, if you are having students build a trie in lab, you can have the instructions briefly review what a trie is (which you presumably covered in class), and then you can have the partners compare data structure choices to use to build the trie (e.g., a 26-pointer array, or a dynamic vector, etc.). Then you can have them write an insert function that places a word into the trie. You can repeat this strategy with a find function – describe what find will need to do, ask the students to discuss how they will implement it, and then have them implement it. As with homework assignments, if your labs involve coding, you should provide some scaffolding in the form of starter code, particularly given the time constraint with a lab.

Labs are also a good opportunity to have students read and discuss code that has already been written. By exposing students to well-written code to discuss, you model what they should be producing with their own code. Furthermore, you can save lab time by providing them some fully-written functions to discuss (and consider having them comment the code, as well) while having them write other parts of the code themselves.

When you produce labs, you should have solutions that you or the TAs can look over before running the labs. You want the labs to be as streamlined as possible, and you don't want the TAs to have to figure out the solution on the fly. That isn't to say that student solutions need to be identical for lab results, but you should write your labs in such a way that students end up with similar enough solutions that a TA helping out can quickly give suggestions to the students during the lab.

It is important that you have someone (e.g., a TA) look at your lab and attempt to do it before the lab begins. Because timing is critical, you need to do the best you can to make the lab fit comfortably into the lab time, and you need to make sure it is clearly written so students have less of a chance to get confused. I can say from experience that it is scary to have an entire lab of students confused while the clock is ticking. If there is a point where students are confused, it is worth spending time stopping all groups for a quick overview of the problem.

One further note about timing: whoever is overseeing the lab should circle the room and gently encourage the students to make steady progress on the lab, and the instructor should have a good idea of how far students should be as the lab progresses. If students are stuck on a part of the lab, the instructor should help guide them towards the solution, so they can continue with the rest of the lab.

CREATING RECITATION SECTION HANDOUTS AND PROBLEMS

Recitation sections[5] can be run in many ways, with the instructor (often a TA) reviewing the material covered in lecture. Recitation is not the place where new material should be covered, but rather a place to solidify the concepts in a less-congested setting. With that said, a practice set of questions or problems is a good way to give students time to work on the concepts in a directed way (much like labs). Ideally, recitation section problems should model the types of problems students will see in both the assignments and on exams. The problems should be short enough so that students can (under direction of the instructor) finish a number of them during the section, although you can include more problems than will fit into the section time, as students can use them to study for the exams, or for general practice.

You should provide solutions for your recitation section problems – you may want to give the solutions to students after their section, but students should be able to see the solutions so they

---

5 In this context, a recitation section is distinct from a lab in that the students aren't working on their computers – the line between "lab" and "recitation section" can be blurry, though, and you may find that your own sections are a combination.

can check their answers, and also so they can see a well-crafted answer. Also, students may come up with different solutions, and showing them alternate solutions enhances their understanding of the material.

Your TAs should have a thorough knowledge of the recitation section problems before holding their sections. They should also have a plan for going through some or all of the problems, and they should also have your solutions. See Chapter 9 for more ideas about instructing TAs.

CREATING OPEN-ENDED PROJECT ASSIGNMENTS

In some classes you might end up teaching, you may decide to assign assignments or projects that have open-ended goals or requirements, such as a capstone project. Students are able to choose their own project, generally with some approval or oversight from you or your TAs. Often, the hardest part of the project from your perspective is going to be keeping the students scoped to projects that are reasonable for the course – neither too easy, nor too hard. The second hardest part of the assignment is going to be grading it – your rubric needs to be sufficiently robust to be able to glean how effective the students were at meeting the project requirements, which may be broad enough to allow many interpretations.

The easiest way to ensure that students know what they have to do to produce projects that meet your requirements is to give them a comprehensive rubric at the start of the project. The rubric should give them clear, concise statements about what is expected for each part of the assignment, and the students should be able to use the rubric to concretely determine if they have met the requirements. This is harder than you think to accomplish – if you do an online search for *software engineering final project rubric*, you will see many example rubrics that use less-than precise language about *demonstrating understanding, articulating requirements*, and *effectiveness of the presentation in explaining the problem*. This imprecise language confuses students, and makes grading too subjective to help either the graders or the students. A better approach is to tie the rubric to what the students *say they will do* in their own project proposal and follow-up reports.

For example, let's assume your students have to create a project proposal during the early stages of the assignment. One rubric item for their proposal could be, *Full Credit: Student / group proposal has a list of what each member of the team will do and produce for the project. The list must have concrete responsibilities, e.g., "Taylor will write the authentication for the website, to include a sign-on page, and back end authentication with secure database support. Ainsley will interface the website with an SMS service to send text messages to users." Should the nature of each student's duties change, this has been reflected in project update documents.*

One of your final rubric items could be, *Full Credit: Student presentations demonstrated all aspects of their proposal duties for each team member.* The students can then look at their proposal and their presentations, and determine how they can meet the rubric requirements. When you are grading their projects and presentations, you can check off each item in their proposal as they cover it, and you can make an objective determination of whether they accomplished what they said they would or not. You also have a ready set of questions for them, e.g., "Taylor, can you demonstrate adding a new account, and give a brief overview of the security features you implemented?"

If the student projects you are creating are long-term, make sure that part of your plan is to have the students produce relatively frequent updates to their projects. Their updates do not need to take them too long, but they should be keeping a record of where they are with the project, what their current challenges are, and how the project has changed since their last report. The more granularity, the better. Additionally, the form of their updates should be such that you or your TAs can quickly look through them, and see how they are progressing. Without frequent updates, students tend to either procrastinate, or prioritize other courses and activities, which is not what you want them doing.

Open-ended projects can be among the most interesting and fruitful assignments students do in their coursework, but it does take a good deal of planning to keep the students progressing forward in a productive manner, particularly if the projects span a large part of the term (or across multiple terms).

CREATING EXAMS

Be forewarned: much like creating a homework assignment, writing an exam will take more time than you think. I have taken twenty or more hours to create a three hour exam, and I spent the bulk of the time crafting good programming problems that were interesting, doable, and fair. The rest of the time was spent on writing the problem solutions, and making sure that the instructions for each problem were clear, concise, and unambiguous.

You will have a set of topics to draw from for each exam, but you may not be able to include all the topics on a single exam. If you focused on one particular topic for a homework assignment, then you can probably have a shorter problem on that topic, or leave it off the exam altogether. Alternatively, you can re-examine the students' understanding by having a similar problem on an exam that they solved for a homework assignment. Ideally, what you ask on the exam would have been assessed in another form already (e.g., on a homework assignment), but this isn't always the case.

While you are considering a problem for an exam, you should focus on what you want to assess about the topic. If you want to assess whether students can re-wire a linked list, make sure that the problem actually tests re-wiring, and not an ancillary linked list function, such as data retrieval (you can, of course, test both). If the students need to write a lot of code to get to the part that you want to test, then you probably need to re-think the problem.

For many types of problems, there will not be a single solution, and students may solve the problem in different ways. For programming problems, you must be clear in your problem instructions about whether you expect solutions to be efficient, and whether you will take off points for solutions that are correct but inefficient. For example, *Your solution must have a worst-case runtime of O(log n), and solutions that do not meet this requirement will lose 50% of the points for this problem.* As another example, if you want students to solve a problem recursively, you should be clear that an iterative solution will not be sufficient for credit on a problem.

Once you determine a good mix of questions you want to ask on the exam, you need to write them up. The instructions for each question need to be as unambiguous as possible, and this is another excellent reason to have someone else review the exam before you give it to the students – your own interpretation of the problem statement may seem more clear than it is to others, and in that case you should re-word it. Once you have written up a problem, you should also write the solution, and you should have your reviewers also write potential solutions. There may be many different ways to solve a particular problem, and your solutions should take into account as many as you can think of that are reasonable. If you have programming problems, actually write tests for the solutions. Additionally, once you have a solution, you should put point values on each problem, both for the students' benefit, so they know how much each problem is worth, and for your own benefit, so you can start thinking about a rubric for the problem. Try to avoid "all or nothing" problems for which students will lose a lot of points if they cannot completely solve the problem. The best problems are ones that can be decomposed into specific parts that demonstrate understanding, and that can be graded independently from the rest of the problem. For example, for recursive programming problems, you can grade separately on whether the student has correct base case(s), and if the recursion call is correct.

In-person exams are time-limited, and making sure that you haven't written an exam that will take students too long to finish is critical. Writing a too-short exam is far preferable than having a too-long exam, for you want to test your students understanding, which is impossible to do if the students do not have time to attempt a problem. Your exam reviewers can give you some guidance on whether they think the exam is a reasonable length, although because of their own expertise with the material, they may not be as accurate as you want. When you have your reviewers take an exam, you should ask them to time themselves. They should finish the exam well within the time allotted – I usually expect my TAs to take half the allotted time, and never more than three-quarters. If the exam is too long, you should remove questions, or you should scale back questions significantly. If the exam is too short (e.g., the TAs finish in a quarter of the time that the exam has allotted), then you can add more questions. Over time, you will become better at judging whether your exams are the right length.

You should start writing your exam at least a week ahead of time. That said, I know many instructors who wait until the day or two before the exam to write them, simply because of the time crunch involved in teaching in general. However, the earlier you can start writing an exam, the more time you can revise it and get feedback on it, and the better exam it will become. Don't forget, as well, that you will either have to print the exam, or you will have to format it for any online or computerized system that you are using to give the exam, and those jobs can be time-consuming, as well.

If you have trouble writing exam problems, do not despair. You should ask other instructors at your school who have taught the course before if you can see their old exams, and you can take inspiration from them (though you should avoid copying the problems directly, as students often have access to old exams and answer keys). You can also search online for exams from other similar courses, which should also give you ideas. Additionally, asking one or more TAs to help craft your exams is fine, and they often enjoy the process.

Do you need to have exams?

Exams are not always a necessary way to assess your students. Exams often provide a better grade distribution than other types of assessments (e.g., programming assignments can end up with most grades near the top of the grading range, because students have so much time to iterate on their solutions to get them correct). However, there are downsides to giving exams. Timed exams increase the pressure on students, particularly the ones who have test-anxiety[6]. Exams where students write code may not indicate students' coding proficiency, particularly if they don't have the ability to run or test their code. However, a well-crafted programming question that does allow students enough time to think out a reasonable solution should be sufficient to separate the students who do and don't know the material. But, it can be tricky to write those questions (and it is a good reason to have your TAs actually take the exam ahead of time to give you feedback).

In my CS2 class at Stanford, which I co-taught with my wonderful colleague, Julie Zelenski, twice during the COVID-19 pandemic, we experimented with a couple of different ideas to replace exams with other assessments. During the first quarter, we replaced our midterm exam with the following: we had two programming questions that we allowed students half an hour to review (and write their code) before a half-hour meeting between the student and their Section Leader (TA). The Section Leader was instructed to ask the students about both problems, and to have the student talk them through the potential solutions that they came up with, whether in real code or pseudo-code. Our goal was to mimic a coding interview to some extent, with part of the

---

6 Test anxiety could be as high as 20% of your students. See https://www.tcu360.com/2016/12/test-anxiety-pressure-on-college-students-more-common-now-than-in-past/ for more information.

rationale that many of our students would someday have coding interviews for internships or full-time jobs. The other part of the rationale was an attempt to limit the anxiety that students usually feel during an exam, knowing that they would be meeting with their Section Leader, who they saw each week in Section, and knew through other routine grading discussions. Section Leaders graded the students on their ability to describe their solutions, and on their thought process, and less on the actual code. We limited grading to a simple pass/fail metric, and over 95% of the class received a passing grade. The entire course was also pass/fail for the term, as well, which made it easy to justify the same metric for the assessment. Students who did not pass were given a second chance with different questions, and one of the core staff (Julie or I, or our incredible head TA, Nick Bowman) re-interviewed them.

In our post-mortem for the assessment, we decided that there were (as you might imagine) pluses and minuses to the assessment. On the positive side, we were confident that the students who passed indeed did have knowledge enough to pass the course (at least at the half-way point). Most of the students also said that they appreciated the format of the assessment instead of having to take an exam (though this was not universal). On the negative side, it turns out that some of the Section Leaders felt more anxious about having to do the interviews, and they felt that it was challenging to give a grade based on a short interaction. Additionally, although they generally spent about as much time interviewing students as they would have grading an exam, because the time was spread out, they felt that it was harder on their own schedules. Another negative was that we had to go to significant lengths to try and ensure that students who interviewed early were not able to provide other students with the questions, and this involved a custom scheduler that only allowed students a strict time to download their exams, and it also involved writing multiple questions that could be used over the three days that we administered the assessment. We did not repeat the assessment during the second quarter, and opted instead for a more traditional exam.

We did, however, change the final assessment during the second quarter. We copied an idea that the summer CS2 instructors, Nick Bowman (our former TA, and a TA again for our quarter), and Kylie Jue, had for their final assessment. We asked students to investigate a topic (their choice) from the term's curriculum, and come up with a question suitable for a section problem or an exam. The students wrote the question, and then two versions of a solution to the question, and then put this into a report. They then delivered a pitch to their Section Leader about the problem and their solutions. The students were graded on a more robust scale that gave us a better grade spread than for the previous term's midterm assessment, and it was, overall more successful.

GETTING FEEDBACK ON ASSIGNMENTS

As discussed throughout this chapter, your main goal when producing assignments is to give your students a task that, when completed, will mean that they know how to do something they didn't know how to do before the assignment. You also want the assignment to be interesting, gradable, and all the other topics we have covered so far. But, how can you tell whether you have met those goals? One way is to test the students on the material later in the term – if the assignment was successful, you should see that reflected in follow-on assessments. Another way to determine if the assignment met your goals is to ask the students what they thought, in the form of feedback.

I like to get informal feedback from students as they are doing the assignment – I will ask students who come to office hours what they think, and I will also ask students how the assignment is going when I walk around talking to students right before a lecture. However, I also try to get feedback in more formal, written terms, especially for new assignments, or ones that have been assigned only a couple of times. The following questions can be a starting point for feedback that you get from the students:

1. On a scale from 1 to 5 (5 being most positive), what did you think of this assignment?

2. How many hours do you think you worked on this assignment (0-5, 5-10, 10-20, more than 20)?

3. What did you learn to do from this assignment?

4. What did you like the most about this assignment?

5. What did you like the least about this assignment?

6. What suggestions do you have to improve the assignment?

7. Should this assignment be given again (possibly with revisions) in this course in the future?

You can have the students fill out the survey either anonymously (where you will probably get more honest feedback), or attributed. You should get feedback immediately after the students complete the assignment, and it is best if you have them directed to the form right after they submit the assignment, if you have an online submission system. If you have attributed feedback, and there are significant concerns from some students, address them directly with the students. If you see many of the same concerns from multiple students, you should address them to the class as a whole. If the concerns are significant enough to address the class, you should also consider being lenient on any affected part of the assignment when grading it.

Once you have feedback from the students, take any constructive criticism and re-evaluate the assignment to see if you should modify it, or to see if it needs more serious work. I have retired assignments after the first time because they just didn't work as well as I had hoped, and the feedback I received was not positive. On the other hand, I have also improved many assignments based on student feedback, and the assignments are much stronger because of it.

Chapter Chapter 12 goes into general feedback you can gather from your students in more detail.

REUSING ASSIGNMENTS

If you are going to put in dozens of hours writing an awesome assignment, you should feel free to re-use the assignment in future instantiations of your course. You may, of course, change the assignment to make it better, but you should take pride in the assignment and put it into your set of resources for the course. The question that reusing assignments brings up, not surprisingly, is, *How do I keep my students from cheating by finding completed versions of the assignment from other students, or online?* There are a number of strategies you can take. One somewhat uncommon strategy is to either count the assignments for a small portion of the course grade, or do not count them at all. If you work to convince your students that they will only learn by doing the assignments themselves, this can work, though you will have students who will gladly copy another assignment and will disregard your warning.

In my own classes, I have a frank discussion about cheating in the first week of class, and I stress to the students how dealing with cheating is one of my least favorite duties. I am also firm that I will do my best to hold them accountable, but that I also have high hopes that they will take the school's honor code seriously, and do their best without cheating. Aside from reminding them before assignments, I don't highlight cheating any more during the course.

One other idea for re-using your assignments is to modify the assignment each term in a way that makes it difficult for students to re-use past iterations of an assignment. This is sometimes difficult to do, especially if you are trying to test a particular algorithm or concept. But, if you can make a non-trivial modification easily, you can limit the usefulness of students looking at past solutions.

WHAT TO DO IF...

What if my assignment solutions get posted online?

If you are going to re-use assignments, you would rather that your students do not have easy access to the solutions. However, once your assignments have been posted, there is little you can do to stop someone from posting the solutions. You should ensure that your students are aware of your school's honor code or academic integrity policies, and you should highlight this in your course syllabus and discuss it in lecture. Although you probably don't want to take the time to police all instances, you can certainly request that whoever has published the solutions removes them. I have found that many people will remove solutions if you ask them nicely (particularly former students), though this isn't always the case. If you are in the United States, you also have a right to request that any solutions you find be taken down under the Digital Millennium Copyright Act (DMCA), and filing a DMCA Takedown request is not hard. Before you do that, however, you should discuss it with your school, and make sure you understand the ramifications of fighting that battle. [7]

Your students may ask you if they can send their solutions to prospective employers, or if they can post them online to demonstrate what they have done for your class. You should discourage them from posting publicly available solutions, and you can steer them towards private repositories that they can share directly with others. You might also want to suggest that they try and work on something that isn't directly related to a class, as some employers put little weight on school assignments when reviewing applicants.

---

7 See https://www.dmca.com/faq/What-is-a-DMCA-Takedown for information.

What if I can't finish creating an assignment before I need to release it?

There are not too many options in this case, and you will probably have to postpone handing out the assignment. You will also want to extend the deadline to give the students an appropriate amount of time, as well. Avoid handing out half-baked assignments – it is better to delay handing out an assignment to make sure it is ready to go than to hand out a partially ready assignment that you have to make changes to. The latter situation only frustrates your students. If absolutely necessary, you could hand out part of the assignment and then the rest of the assignment as soon as you can, but try to avoid this if possible.

What if the average on an exam is higher or lower than I expected?

It is difficult to write an exam that gives you the perfect spread of grades. Sometimes, it ends up being easier than you expected, and sometimes it ends up being harder. If students do very well on the exam (on average), praise them for it, and move on. If you have future assignments in the course, you can consider making them more difficult, but don't create a particularly difficult exam simply to make up for the great grades on a midterm exam. Hopefully, the other assignments you have will enable you to break out students appropriately when calculating the final grades.

If students did not do well on your exam, know that this can be discouraging for them. Plan on taking some lecture time to discuss the results of the exam, and if you expected them to do better, try to figure out what went wrong. Did they have enough practice examples? Were the test questions clear? Was there a common misconception that you did not expect? You might think about allowing students to re-do some of the questions for some credit back, as well, though you should be careful about making sure you (and/or your TAs) have the time to grade the re-dos. Regardless of what you decide to do for the poor exam, take the time to recognize what went wrong with it, and make the appropriate changes for future exams in the course.

FINAL THOUGHTS

As hard as it is to create assignments, it is just as rewarding to come up with challenging and interesting assignments and projects that help your students learn the course material. You should be proud of your assignments, and your students should know that they learned a lot by doing them. Once you create an awesome assignment, you can re-use it, share it with colleagues, and share it with SIGCSE's Nifty Assignments. Have fun writing your awesome assignments!

ASSIGNMENT X: EDGE MATCH

Due: _____, 5pm

Overview

In this assignment, you will write a program to solve an Edge-matching puzzle with nine tiles. The following images show an unsolved puzzle and a solved puzzle:

Unsolved   Solved

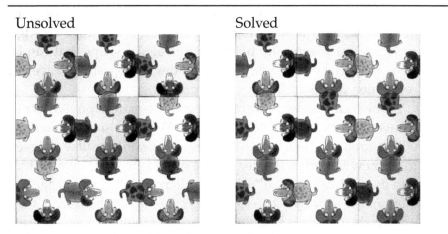

The Crazy Dog Game, Heye Concept, ©1980

Notice that each puzzle piece can be located in one of the nine grid positions, and also can be rotated into four different orientations. This is actually a challenging game to play by hand, but your algorithm will make quick work of finding the solutions!

Starter Code

Download the starter code here. You will need to have Qt Creator installed, along with the requisite C++ build environment.

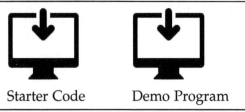

Starter Code   Demo Program

Problem Description

Edge-matching puzzles involve matching up aligned edges on polygons (typically squares, although it is possible to design an edge-matching puzzle for any polygon or irregular shape that can be *tessellated*). The puzzle you will be writing a program to solve is a set of nine tiles that fit into a 3 x 3 grid.

We provide you with starter code in edge-match.cpp that implements the user interface for the game. We have also provided you with a graphical version of the game that you can play yourself to see how it works. The goal of the game is to place all nine tiles into the grid such that all the edges align properly. Each edge can only match with one corresponding edge on another tile. For a 3 x 3 puzzle, there are four different edge combinations, with each combination having a distinct *top* and bottom or *left* and *right*. For example, the following vintage puzzle given out for advertising a brand of cola has four colors as the edges, green, red, blue, and yellow. Each cola bottle also has a top and a bottom. So, for example, a red top only matches with a red bottom, and two red bottoms do not make a match, as show in the top right corner of the image.

The following image shows one solution to the cola puzzle:

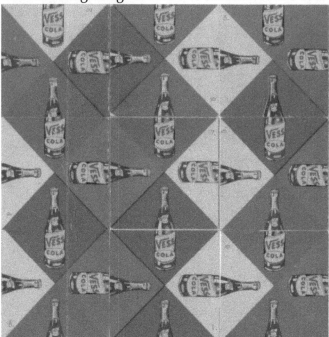

In real life, the puzzle is solved by manually matching and rotating tiles until all of the tiles line up. A brute force approach would involve trying 95,126,814,720 (over 95 billion) tile positions and rotations. This is because each tile can be in one of nine positions (9!) and each tile can be rotated in each position four different ways (49), and 9! * 49 = 95,126,814,720).

Of course, a human player won't try nine billion different combinations, because many combinations cannot produce a solution, and there is no need to permute tiles in one part of the board when other parts of the board are already incorrect. When you write your solution, you should also take this into consideration -- even though computers are fast, your solution should not continue to search in a particular way if a solution down that search path can never be found.

Matching tiles do not have to be strictly image-based. For example, the puzzle below is solved by matching up numbers in combinations that add up to 10. So, for example, a matching set of edges would have a 3 and a 7 (the puzzle below is not solved, though it does have some matching edges):

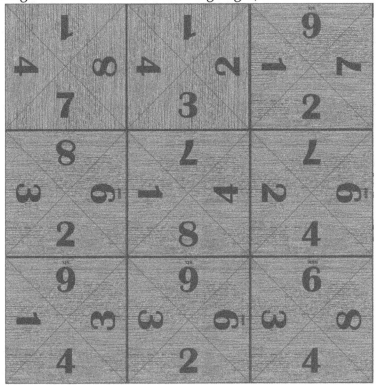

Your solution will populate a Vector<Tile> with all of the possible solutions for a particular puzzle. Note that the number of solutions for a puzzle will always be a multiple of four, as each full puzzle can simply be rotated 90°.

For your solution, you will be able to run the program in two different ways: the first is to find the solutions one at a time, and show them graphically (also populating the solutions vector). The second is to time how long it takes to find all possible solutions for a given set of tiles. You should strive to make your solution as fast (or faster!) than our solution, and we will provide you with sample times to compare against.

Implementation Details

In order to describe an edge, we must decide on a code that can be used to differentiate edges, and to describe two edges that match. We have chosen an uppercase and lowercase representation for each edge, such that a matching edge will have an uppercase letter on one tile's edge (e.g., "A") and a lowercase letter on the other tile's matching edge (e.g., "a"). As an example, the following tiles have been labeled. The letters themselves are arbitrary, but must be the same code for each tile in a particular puzzle. In this case, a yellow top is "A", yellow bottom is "a", green top is "B", green bottom is "b", etc.

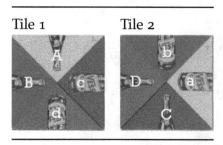

Using this code, we can describe a single tile with four edge letters. Starting with the top of the tile, and then progresing *clockwise*, tiles 1 and 2 above can be labeled as follows:

Tile 1:

A c d B

Tile 2:

b a C D

We can also add an orientation, based on how many times the tile has been rotated in a clockwise direction. Each of the above tiles has orientation 0, but we could rotate Tile 1 once (as shown below) and it would now be represented by A c d B 1:

Although the tile could also be labeled starting with B instead of adding an orientation, we will keep the original labeling and use the orientation to describe how the tile has been rotated.

You must implement the following functions to complete the puzzle solver. Some of the functions are in the Tile.cpp file (and the Tile class, and others are in the edge-match.cpp file and are not associated with a class. You do not have to modify the PlayGame class or the TileGrid class, although you will have to use functions from the TileGrid class.

Tile::Tile(string s)

- Implement the constructor for a Tile that accepts a string in *either* of the following forms:

    A b C d

or

    A b C d 2

In other words, the rotation is optional. If there is no rotation, the default rotation will be 0. We have written the default constructor for you, so you can see what is expected from the constructor you will write.

Note: the order of the letters in the string should not be modified. In other words, the string "A b C d 2" should be represented as top:A, right:b, bottom:C, and left:d, with a rotation of 2, clockwise. When shown, that tile would have C on the top, d on the right, A on the bottom, and b on the left.

```
int Tile::getOrientation()

void Tile::setOrientation(int orientation)
```

- These two helper functions simply get and set the orientation.

```
bool Tile::isMatched(Tile &other, Connection otherLocation)
```

- The isMatched function returns true if the other tile is a match in the location relative to the tile being checked. The Connection type is an enum, defined in Tile.h as follows:

```
enum Connection {
    ABOVE,
    RIGHT,
    BELOW,
    LEFT,
};
```

So, if a Tile t instance was called as follows:

```
t.isMatched(otherTile, ABOVE)
```

then the function would return true if otherTile matches t when otherTile is above t in the grid.

```
string Tile::sidesStr() const;
```

- The sideStr function should return a string in the form "AbCd". This string is used to identify a tile, and *does not* include information about the orientation of the tile.

```
ostream &operator<<(ostream &out, Tile const &tile)
```

- The overloaded << function is similar to sidesStr, but it is formatted with spaces and includes the orientation. It should output a string in the form "A b C d 2". Once you have overloaded this function, you will be able to use cout to print out a Vector<Tile> or Grid<Tile>, and this may be helpful to you as you debug your program.

```
bool allMatch(Grid &tiles);
```

- This function, located in edge-match.cpp returns true for a solved puzzle. You may want to consider what is minimally necessary to determine if a puzzle is solved, and only do as much work as is necessary.

```
Vector<Grid<Tile>> solvePuzzle(TileGrid &tg,
                               bool timeIt = false);
```

- This function, located in edge-match.cpp returns a vector of solved puzzle grids. **You will also need to write a recursive helper function that this function calls.** You are responsible for detemining the parameters of your helper function.

  If the timeIt parameter is true, your function should suppress output, drawing tiles, and asking for user input. In other words, it should solve the puzzle as quickly as it can.

  If the timeIt parameter is false, your function should draw each solved puzzle it finds (see below for the function to draw the tiles), and it should also ask the user if they want to save the solved board to a file. See below for examples of user input and output to see how you should format the user interface for your solver function.

  This is the only function that will require you to interact with the TileGrid class, which keeps track of a Grid<Tile>. There are five functions you will need from the Grid<Tile> class. This class, which we have written for you, handles the graphical interface with the tiles, and holds the Grid<Tile>.

Notice that the getGrid function below returns a **reference** to a Grid -- this is important to ensure that the TileGrid instance can draw and save the tiles:

```
Vector<Tile> TileGrid::getTileVec();
```

- This function returns a vector of all the tiles in the game.

```
Grid<Tile> & TileGrid::getGrid();
```

- This function returns a reference to the Grid of Tiles.

```
void TileGrid::drawTiles();
```

- This function draws the tiles to the screen. You should call this in your recursive solvePuzzle function every time you have a completed puzzle (but only if you are not timing your solver -- you don't want to take time drawing the grid on the screen when you are trying to see how fast your solver works).

```
bool TileGrid::saveGrid(string filename);
```

- This function saves the tile grid to a file, in the form:

```
A b C d 2
B a D c 3
...etc
```

Saved files can be loaded with the TileGrid::populate function, which is used in the loadPuzzle function, which has already been written for you.

```
bool TileGrid::toString();
```

– This function prints the tile grid to the console, in the form:

```
A b C d 2
B a D c 3
...etc
```

Example Games

Ex. 1:	Ex. 2:	Ex. 3:	Ex. 4:	Ex. 5:	Ex. 6:
cola1.txt	cola2.txt	dogs1.txt	dogs2.txt	tens.txt	penguins.txt

Style Details

You should follow the course style guide for expected coding style. You should, as necessary, decompose your solution into short functions commensurate with the problem you are solving. The following information specifically relates to the style of this assignment:

Recursion and Backtracking: You must write a recursive function to solve the puzzle. You can write as many helper functions as you need for the solution, but you must use recursion, and likely recursive backtracking to solve the problem efficiently. Your solution should be efficient and should *not* follow paths that are guaranteed to not produce solutions. You must figure out how to do this, but your grade will depend on whether you have an efficient solution. You can see the example runs of the program above to see roughly how long a decent solution should take to find all solutions to a puzzle.

Variables: This is the first main assignment where you are using classes. You are allowed to add private instance variables to the

Tile class, but you should not need to. You should *not* add any global variables, and you should use proper paramater passing strategies to move variables through your program.

Commenting: You should have a function comment at the top of each function. You should also have inline comments as necessary in your code, especially where your code may be difficult to understand without context.

Frequently Asked Questions (FAQ)

Q: When I try to run the starter code, I get an error that looks like

GImage::constructor: Cannot find an image named puzzles/dogs/.png.

Is the starter code broken?

A: You need to write some of the methods for the Tile class before you can get very far with the starter code. In particular, you need to finish the constructor, the Tile::sidesStr() function, and the orientation getter and setter. Once you write those funcitons, you should be able to play the game manually, though it won't be able to tell if you have solved the puzzle or not until you write the Tile::isMatched() function.

Q: How do I run the example program?

A: On a Mac, you can click on the "run-edge-match.sh" file, and the program should open.

Q: When I save a solved game in the program, where does it go?

A: The file is saved in the build-edge-match... folder, which is most likely one folder up from your TileMatch project folder. If you want to use your solution in future versions of the game, move it into the puzzles/puzzleType/ (e.g., for a dogs puzzle, move it into the puzzles/dogs/ folder. You can also move it into the folder in your project directory, but you will likely have to delete the edge-match.pro file and restart, re-build the edge-match program for it to automatically go into the build folder when you run the program again.

Q: My recursive strategy should work, but the program never finishes!

A: You are probably not stopping the recursion when it goes down a path that is guaranteed to not produce a solution. Look at your recursive calls and play a few versions of the game manually to convince yourself that you aren't recursing too much.

Possible Extensions

If you want to write one or more extensions for this assignment, here are some ideas:

- **Add a "hint" mode to the GUI game.** If you are playing manually, you can add a hint button to allow the user to get a tile placed automatically for them. This will involve modifying the PlayGame class. See the documentation for the GButton class to add a button to the window.
- **Change the << overload function to print a text-based version of the tiles.** If the user is playing in text mode, without graphics, it might be nice to have a function that will print the tile out in a more user-friendly way. You can also add a function to the TileGrid class to print the entire grid in text-based form.
- **Add your own tiles.** In the puzzles folder, you will find individual puzzle folders (e.g., dogs), which have images and a basic text file with the starting tile orientations. If you want, you can make your own puzzles by breaking up an image into multiple tiles. See here for many solved puzzles you can break up. You will need a graphics program, such as Gimp (free) or Photoshop ($) to break up the images. In Gimp, you can follow the instructions here to easily break an image into tiles.

- **Expand the game to include 4x4 grids, or 2x2 grids (or more).** This will take some work in the TileGrid.h header and Tile-Grid.cpp class, but it is doable. If you write your Tile class efficiently, you should not need to update it.

8

LECTURES

ALTHOUGH THIS CHAPTER is about lecturing, and preparing lectures, it is really about any form of teaching where you, the instructor, are with students, discussing the material of your course for the first time. It is distinct from recitation section, although depending on how you structure your lecture, and how big your class is, you can have the students working on problems during class.

When you lecture, you get to be an educator, a scholar, an expert, an actor, a comedian, a motivator, a symphony conductor, and a magician. Your strengths may or may not be in any of those particular areas, but you can use any of those roles to introduce your course topics to your students. When you knew you were going to become a teacher, you quite possibly thought about this part of the job first and foremost – my guess is that your first thoughts weren't about planning your syllabus, creating assignments, or grading. You likely pictured yourself in front of students, talking about some interesting topic they've never heard of, and hopefully it put a smile on your face. That said, it might also have introduced some angst, especially if you have any worries about public speaking. Regardless, here we are, and you are going to stand in front of students and you are going to teach them (and see below for tips on getting through the public speaking fear, if that is your concern).

Your lecturing role is not, as you might think, to drill all of the nuances of your topics into your students' heads. As I've mentioned a number of times in this book, lectures are *not* where your students learn the most – they learn the material by doing it themselves, not by listening to you talk about it. So, what is your role? You have a duty to *motivate* the material, to *introduce key concepts,* to provide *informative examples*, and to *teach them to think* in the context of your course material. Once you realize that your students aren't going to be able to do what you want them to do just because you told them about it, you can re-frame your lectures to focus on guiding them towards the goal of being able to do the assignments, and to really learn the material.

How you structure your lectures depends on a number of parameters. Do you have a small class, where you can know all the students, or do you have a large class where you might not even recognize all your students? Some students are more comfortable in one or the other, too. Where in the curriculum does your class fall? Lecturing to students who are taking their first CS course is different than lecturing to seniors in a capstone course. Is your class a programming course, a theory course, or something hybrid or different? Is your course 50 minutes, an hour and twenty minutes, three hours, etc.? In shorter classes, students have less time to acclimate to the material, but in longer classes students have trouble focusing for the entire duration.[1] Tailoring your lectures to your specific set of circumstances is important, and if the parameters change in future versions of your course, you may need to adjust your lectures accordingly.

PLANNING YOUR LECTURES

In the planning stages of your course (see Chapter 6), you have hopefully mapped out the schedule of topics. For each lecture, determine what topics you want to cover, and think about how much time you will spend on each one. Once you are more experienced, you will be able to more easily judge how long it will take to cover a particular topic, and in the beginning you have a high likelihood of either under or over planning, and either having too little or too much material for the day. You can recover from either case, but neither is ideal. As you start your teaching

---

1 Though there are ways to combat this, which we will discuss later in the chapter.

career, you should set aside time to practice your lectures at least once ahead of class, to gauge how the timing feels. See below for more discussion on practicing your lectures.

Your lectures should have a defined beginning. It can be a motivation for the material, or a brief review of the previous lecture's material. Many instructors actually start their lectures with administrative information, but beware that this isn't the most motivational start. Keep any administrative comments brief (less than a minute), and move on to the real material. If you need more than a minute, plan your lecture to pause somewhere in the middle to go over the administrative details – your students will welcome the break, and you will have their attention better.

Your motivational comments should frame the upcoming material in the context of the course, and in the context of the prior material (if the prior material is related). It is even better if you can motivate the material with a real-world example of where it is useful, e.g., *Facebook wouldn't be possible with the graph data structure, so today we are going to learn about the backbone of Facebook!* One my colleagues, Chris Piech, starts many of his lectures with an example that the class will be able to solve by the end of the lecture, and then as the lecture concludes, he does it.[2] Remember, you are about to teach the students about something they either haven't heard of before, or haven't used in the context you are going to describe. They want to know why they are studying it, and they want to see where it fits into the bigger picture of the course.

After the beginning of your lecture, you can get down to the details of the topics. You want to craft a narrative to inform the material, and you want to outline the details you want the students to know. Students respond to examples especially well, particularly if they demonstrate how they can learn to solve problems themselves. Remember that you are teaching them how to think, so you should compliment your examples with some of your own thought process when you came up with the solution. Remem-

---

2 And I have stolen many of his examples for my own classes.

ber, as well, that all of your students are not going to grasp the nuances of the material in class. They need time to process the information, and they need to practice using it on an assignment, in a recitation section, etc. As a topic comes to a close, summarize it, and see if there are any questions.[3]

There are many ways to check for student understanding during a lecture, and simply asking students if they have questions is not necessarily a good way to do that. First, students may have no idea if they have any questions, as they are still in the process of learning the material. They will have questions when they start to do the assignment, or when they get to recitation section, but they might not even be able to form a question in the middle of class. One strategy is to have students briefly discuss their thoughts with a neighboring student, and then ask them what questions they have. Another strategy is to ask them to bring questions for the following lecture or, even better, have them give you questions to answer before the next class so you can better prepare the answers.

Another popular way to gauge student understanding is through the use of technology, such as student-response clickers, where students have a device that allows them to answer questions from you in real-time with collated responses that you can show the class. You pose questions, often in multiple-choice form, for the students who immediately answer using their device, and then you can analyze the results during class to see if the students have understood the material. There have been many studies on how to utilize clickers and other similar technologies. Indeed, there are almost three hundred entries in Derek Bruff's Vanderbilt Center for Teaching bibliography on *Classroom Response Systems*, and eight studies specific to computer science. Using clickers is a form of *active learning* that allows students to gainfully participate in a lecture in an active manner. Active learning keeps students engaged,

---

3 A common suggestion for asking for questions is to say, *What questions do you have?* rather than *Are there any questions?* Students respond better to the former than the latter.

and it enhances their memory of the material as it is covered in class. Active learning does take time out of your class, and you must make a trade-off where you will potentially cover less material in each lecture. But, should you decide to simply cover more material, you risk students not learning as much, and not taking away as much from the class anyway.

One form of active learning that I try to fit into almost every lecture is a variation of the *think-pair-share* strategy. Think-pair-share involves having students think about a problem or question, and then pair with another student to discuss it, before finally sharing their thoughts with the class. In my modified version, after I present a topic, or as review, I will give the students a problem to solve and tell them to "talk to a neighbor" about the solution. I will pause class for anywhere from one to five minutes for the students to discuss, and I will walk around the lecture hall chatting with students about their thoughts. After I head back to the front of the hall, I will ask for volunteers to give their solution. Most students participate in the discussion, and it keeps them engaged. My jaunt around the class also gives me an idea of how students are thinking about the problem, and whether they have begun their understanding.

If you do decide to use active learning in your lectures, I suggest that you find another instructor at your school who uses active learning, and observe their class when they are engaged in an active learning session. See how the students react, and how the instructor uses the responses to inform the lecture. Then, try it out yourself. If you don't want the students to have to purchase clickers, there are similar tools that require only a smartphone or laptop (e.g., Socrative), and that can make it easier to do a trial run in your class, or to use permanently.

Concluding your lecture is an important part of the class, although don't be surprised if you often have to conclude simply because time runs out – you may have received more questions than you expected, you might have reviewed a topic after you realized students didn't understand it to your liking, or you may have simply planned too much material. If this happens, don't despair, and build in some review and a conclusion into the next lecture, or provide the students some online material that covers your concluding remarks. In other words: plan a good end to your lectures, but don't necessarily depend that you will get to it! Your conclusion should tie up the narrative of the day, and it may provide (as Chris Piech likes to do) a culminating example of how to use the lecture's material to solve a problem. You may also want to give some tips on where the students will use the material (e.g., on a homework assignment, or on the exams, or in real life).

DELIVERING YOUR LECTURE (OR, *from powerpoint to the naked lecture*)

How you deliver your lecture is critical to how your class runs, and to how your students learn. You don't have to be the world's best entertainer, but you do have to be interesting (or, at least, the material has to be interesting!), and you have to present the course topics in a way that engages the students so they pay attention and learn. You also want to present material to the students in a form that allows them to see your examples, and to get actual information aside from simply hearing it come out of your mouth. You can do this via blackboard or whiteboard (sometimes called, *teaching naked*), through handouts, or through slideshows; the latter becoming more common every year, and routinely what most students expect. Most instructors deliver their lectures using a hybrid approach, with some board-work, and some slides.

If you do decide to teach without using a slide presentation, you should probably have some notes, and use them to keep yourself on track.[4] Because it is less common these days, if you are engaging and a good presenter,[5] the students may appreciate the

---

4 But don't read your notes verbatim! I have never seen this in practice, but I do hear that some instructors do this – it is unlikely that you are good enough to make reading a lecture interesting.
5 and you have good handwriting!

break from staring at PowerPoint presentations, which they may do in all of their other classes. You may also consider posting your own notes from the class, which the students will appreciate. That said, encouraging your students to take their own comprehensive notes can be a good pedagogical stance, although your students are likely used to having published presentations from their other classes, and taking good notes is becoming a lost art. Another suggestion is to ask if any students would like to release *their* notes to the class. I generally err on the side of giving my students as much information as I can, with the realization that they may not take the best notes. I would rather they pay attention in class without having to write everything down, and lessening the burden on note-taking is one way to do that.

If you are using PowerPoint (or another slideshow program) for your lectures, you do need to be careful about boring the students, especially if your presentations have a lot of text (which you generally want to avoid). You should rarely (if ever) read the text on your slides out loud, and you should carefully think through why you have each slide. For example, if you put a definition on a slide, how are you going to elaborate to explain the definition? You may choose to have examples, or you may choose to discuss it verbally (or both), but your lecture needs to have something more than just the definition on a slide.

I find that short, key pieces of information about the topic works well on slides, but the real power of slides is being able to walk students through comprehensive examples. They can go back to the slides and see, step by step, the solution. For example, if I am talking about a sorting algorithm for an array of values, I will have a full set of slides showing one transition after another, following the algorithm. The example may be ten or fifteen slides long, but the students now have a real example that follows all of the algorithm's steps.

Some instructors put a tremendous amount of material on their slides, partially to cover everything, and partially to have a record of the course. That can be okay, as long as you and your students understand that there is probably more on the slides than you will actually discuss in detail in the class. For example, I sometimes put tables of information onto a slide, but I don't linger on those slides (I may highlight certain parts, or teach the students how to read the table), and I always verbally say that the slide is mainly for reference.

Other instructors have sparse slides with only a topic listed, or a short bulleted list that the instructor will go over in detail verbally or on the board. These types of slides act more as a place-holder and a memory jogger for the instructor, and although it works for many instructors, I am not enamored by the style. Students who are used to information-filled slides may be critical of the sparse-slide methodology, and you should consider talking to them about why you present the slides the way you do, with a discussion about good note-taking.

Regardless of whether you use slides or not, your lecturing personality is important. There are infinitely many ways to lecture, and you will find your own style. If you aren't sure about the type of lecturer you want to be, you should observe as many other instructors as you can, and take note of what you like and don't like about their styles (and see Chapter 11 for details about observing others teach). You do have a duty to present the material in an interesting manner, and you will quickly lose the attention of your students if you can't provide a forum where they can't engage with you or the material. You should work hard to make your examples relevant, and to make your description of the topics something the students will enjoy listening to. Hopefully you are teaching something that interests you, and you will be most successful if you pass on that interest to your students. If you are having trouble making your classes interesting, start by considering why *you* enjoy the topics. If you can't think of anything, then it is time for some research, or time to ask other instructors what they find redeeming about a particular topic.

ANSWERING QUESTIONS

It should come as no surprise that students will ask you questions in class. How you answer them depends on a number of factors. I have had an instructor who seemed to never answer a question with a straight answer, and although sometimes it was frustrating, he always kept us thinking, and in some ways it made the overall discussion richer. He often used a technique of answering the question with a question, phrased in such a way to make me and the other students answer the original question in our own answer. I've never been able to repeat this strategy, but it worked for my instructor. I've had other professors who would give clear, straight answers to questions, and I would say that I have patterned my own question answering after this style. I have had other professors who answered questions in a rambling, yet also interesting way, and while it tended to slow class down, I think we learned more in the detail from his answers.

You will find your own style for answering questions that you prefer, and you will get better at answering questions the longer you teach. In particular, you will get much better at answering questions when you teach a class again, simply because you will have heard many of the questions before! When you are answering questions, you may find that some of the questions are naive, or are about something you have already discussed. In these cases, *do not* criticize the student for asking, and answer as best you can. A comment such as, *Well, as we just discussed...* is not egregious, but *Were you paying attention to what I just said?* is, and you should avoid that. Remember, you want to encourage students to ask questions, so keep your answers positive, taking each question at face value. Your students are seeing the course material for the first time, and when they have questions, even simple ones, answer them genuinely.

If you are teaching in a large room or lecture hall, or your class is being recorded, *always* repeat questions for the benefit of those who didn't hear them. You can rephrase the question if necessary, but do not assume that everyone heard the question. It can take time to learn to repeat questions, but absolutely work on it. Not only does repeating the question allow everyone to hear it, but it also keeps everyone focused on your response, and it strengthens the discussion.

CLASS PERIOD LENGTH

You obviously want to tailor your lectures to the time allotted for each day. A fifty minute class feels much different than a 120 minute class, and both feel like the briefest moment compared to a three hour lecture. The overall number of minutes you have during a term is often roughly the same regardless of how long each lecture is, but preparation and delivery style can vary greatly for shorter versus longer lectures. Shorter lectures benefit from having to hold student attention for less time, and they will have less to process. Longer lectures benefit from having the ability to set the students on a problem that may take more time than you would have in a shorter class (though you still need to cover all the material, which can mean more topics per lecture, at roughly the same pace as a shorter class).

When you are preparing your lectures, try not to have more than about fifteen minutes straight on one specific topic. You should expect your students to be able to focus for that long before starting to get distracted, and if you observe other teachers teach, you will notice the phones coming out at around the fifteen minute mark if the instructor continues with a single topic. Pausing for questions, or asking a *talk to your neighbor* or clicker question provides a good break, as does providing a real-life anecdote that can give the students a mental break. Whatever you do, avoid at all costs opening your mouth during the first minute and then talking for fifty minutes straight!

Preparing for a shorter class period takes less time, in general, than preparing for a longer class. That said, you will have to prepare more lectures, so during a week you will still spend the same amount of time preparing (and you will be surprised at how quickly that next lecture approaches). During a shorter lecture, you also have less time to veer off of your planned remarks and discussion (e.g., to answer questions), and you may find yourself running out of time more often. Good preparation can account for this, and having the flexibility to pick up where you left off in the next lecture is critical. It is amazing how quickly forty-five or fifty minutes passes when you are in the midst of it, and practicing your lecture is extremely important until you get the hang of it.

There are different ways to deliver lectures in long classes. In all classes over an hour, I try to always plan a two-to-three minute break in the middle of class, for the students to clear their heads and re-focus. This is in addition to the fifteen-minutes-per-topic suggestion from above – you want to have a more definite break for the students to do whatever they want. I often get end-of-term feedback from students about how they appreciated having the break in class, and I think it is well-worth the trade-off that three more minutes of material would provide.

When planning for longer lectures, you often have more flexibility to do longer active-learning sessions, or to delve into deeper examples. You may actually find yourself covering less overall material during the term, but in greater detail, and this is okay. More involved examples can generate more questions, and you can provide more insight that can enhance student learning.

MANAGING A FEAR OF PUBLIC SPEAKING

If you are anxious about standing up in front of a class of students to deliver your lecture, you are not alone. Many instructors have some anxiety, at least on the first day of school, and it is completely normal. However, if you are dreading lecturing, or you are simply worried that you will have trouble with your nerves, or you have had public speaking difficulties in the past, there are some concrete steps you can take to combat it. First: be confident in your skills and in your preparation, and plan on practicing your lectures (see below) at least once and possibly more times before you go in front of your class. Second: go to the first class early, and introduce yourself to some of the students who also arrive early. Make sure you go early enough to set up for class, and leave five or ten minutes to walk around the class before it begins. Being well-prepared (especially on the first day of class; see more about the first day below) and introducing yourself to at least a couple of students can help calm you down a bit before class.

Almost all teachers become better at the public speaking aspect of teaching the longer they practice the craft.[6] The first day is often the worst day, and it does get better after that. Once you start the class, you automatically calm down, too, as your concentration switches from your nervousness to delivering your prepared lecture. You will find that your students are willing to give you the benefit of the doubt when it comes to delivering your lectures smoothly, and having a positive attitude, a sense of humor about it, and being honest with your students (e.g., *I guess I could have phrased that better!*) can help make the situation less intense. You may surprise yourself at how quickly you become comfortable in the classroom, and you will start to enjoy the experience more.

PRACTICING YOUR LECTURES

As a beginning teacher, you should absolutely practice your lectures after you prepare them. You will find it less necessary the longer you teach, but practice lets you time yourself, and it lets you prepare your delivery. It also lets you proof-read your material,[7] and let's you ensure that you have everything you need. If

---

6 This is not universal. If you do find that you continue to have significant difficulties, there are many possible solutions. There are organizations such as *Toastmasters International*, a club with many local chapters that fosters public speaking skills, which many teachers have found helpful. There are also therapists who focus on phobias such as public speaking, and you may benefit from that, as well.

7 I *always* find typos when I practice with new lectures.

you are going to do an example or demo, practice the demo, as well. If your example/demo requires Internet access, you should also try to practice in the room to gauge the connection reliability. If you can avoid having Internet-required parts of your lecture, even better, and there are tools to download videos (e.g., from YouTube) for offline viewing, and you can also often download Javascript demos, as well (though it can take time to get them working properly offline). If you do require Internet access for something, make sure you plan an alternative in case there is a poor connection (and see below for *What to do if...*).

It is probably untenable to ask someone else to sit in on all of your practice lectures, but if you can do so at the beginning of the term, it is worth it. A colleague who has taught the material before, or a TA who has worked with the course before would be ideal, but anyone can provide feedback. It is also a good idea to video record your practice lectures, if you have time (at least at the beginning) to review, but you won't have time to do this too often. When critiquing your own lecture, you want to look at the overall flow, and for any verbal tics or filler words you may have (e.g., saying *um* too often). Once you notice a filler word, you will naturally start avoiding it more, but if you don't, you should concentrate on turning it into a silent pause instead. Although pausing may seem awkward at first, it actually makes your speaking more crisp.

If you are practicing alone, you won't have the benefit of having someone to ask questions during the lecture. You should plan on students asking questions, and you should build that time into your lecture, with one caveat: many novice instructors talk *much* faster during an actual lecture than during their own practice, so building in time for questions will probably happen naturally. With that said, you should actively practice slowing down your speech to a reasonable speed, and be aware that you may be speaking faster than you think during lectures.

When you are practicing your lectures, make sure you carefully check any code solutions you put up for bugs. You should *always* run your code solutions exactly, and run tests on the solutions as well. You want to model what you expect from your students, and code that works is a good example. That said, if you are going to live-code in class, don't be surprised if you have bugs in your code. Some of the best teachable moments are when you as the instructor make code mistakes that you have to debug in front of students, and they appreciate it. I always keep a hard copy of the code I am going to demonstrate, and I practice writing it live a number of times before class. I am not a terrific live-coder, and having the hard copy available is a confidence-booster as well as a good crutch to use, if necessary.

THE FIRST DAY OF CLASS

The first day of class is an important one: you are making a first impression on your class, you are setting expectations, and you are giving the students a taste of the upcoming term. The students may be deciding whether or not to take the course (if they have the choice), and they want to see who you are as much as what the class is about. Every instructor has a different approach to the first day, and you should ask other instructors what their own first class looks like. Even better, go online and view the first part of many different lectures to see what others do. For the rest of this section, I will describe my own strategy.

As I said earlier in the chapter, I try go get to the first class early enough to set up and have about ten minutes or so to introduce myself to the students that have arrived early. I'll try to walk all the way around the lecture hall a couple of times saying hello, and I make my way back to the front of the class with about a minute or so before the class begins. I will normally wait another couple of minutes into the class time to actually start talking.

As I begin, I give the class a hearty welcome, and I introduce both myself and the class name. I like to give a thirty second *elevator pitch* about the course from a high level, and I also like to say how excited I am about teaching the course (and this isn't disingenuous, either – I actually am excited!). I then make a longer introduction about myself (spending up to three or four minutes on how I ended up at this school, teaching this class), and I introduce the other staff (generally the TAs and Section Leaders who might be present). I will also briefly discuss whether the course is the right one for the students, based on prerequisites, what the students are interested in, and some of the cool topics we will discuss. Then, I immediately jump into material for the course (e.g., *Our First Program*) to give the students a taste for the flavor of the course. As I discussed in the opening chapter of the book, your students may be used to boring administrative details to start out a course, and I want to give them exactly the opposite – I want them to see how exciting computer science can be. After giving them some real course content, I do make some administrative remarks. I introduce the course tools (e.g., an IDE), website address, and forum information. But, I leave bigger details about grading, office hours, etc., out of the first day – it can be covered on the website or forum, or later in the week.

I finish up the first day by finding a good example to demonstrate to the students more of the course content, and how it will be useful. For my CS2 course, I use a variation of part of a lecture I borrowed from Aaron Bloomfield, from the University of Virginia. I show the students a short program that tests four different data structures performing a large number of insertions, searches, and deletions on a data set, and I compare the results. I stress that the students may not have used some of the data structures before (e.g., a hash table), and that we will introduce them as part of the course. The comparison leads into a discussion of performance and data structure choice, which are two key concepts in the course.

I purposely do not leave much time for questions at the end of the first class, but I allow time at the beginning of the second day for questions. Many first-day questions can be answered on the course forum, and I suggest that the students use the forum for that purpose.

There are some things that you should avoid doing on the first day of class. You shouldn't be late, and you should not be fumbling to set things up after the class has already begun. Do not speak too softly (use a microphone if you think this will be a problem). Do not denigrate yourself, or give the students the impression that you are worried about the class going well, e.g., *This is my first time teaching, so please bear with me.* It doesn't matter if you are thinking those things, but don't be overt about that with your students, particularly on the first day – you want to appear confident. Although it isn't terrible to end the class somewhat early on the first day, you should avoid ending it too early, as you want to set a standard that there is work to be done in the course, and you plan on using the time allotted.

Think carefully about your own first day of class, and do your best to be welcoming and excited about your course. Students respond best to engaging instructors, and you want to give them the impression that the class is going to be as enjoyable as it will be educational.

INCLUSIVITY IN YOUR CLASSROOM

In all likelihood, you will have students from many different backgrounds in your classes. In many cases, you may have more men than women, and you may also have fewer underrepresented minority students. You should make every effort to be inclusive in both your lecturing, and in recitation sessions, office hours, and anywhere else you see your students.

A colleague of mine at Stanford, Cynthia Lee, has put together a terrific document on how to be inclusive in your classroom, and it is worth reading and studying at the beginning of each term you teach: https://bit.ly/inclusivecs. The students who are underrepresented in your classroom deserve your attention to making them feel like they belong in the class, and you have a duty to teach the class in a way that recognizes the diversity and actively combats exclusivity. The technology sector in general needs to improve their inclusiveness, and as a leader instructing students at the beginning their careers in tech, you can play a huge role in modeling inclusiveness and working to make tech better for everyone.

TO RECORD OR NOT TO RECORD

If you are in a position to record your lectures, there are some things you should consider before making the decision. If you do record the class, you should expect a drop in attendance, simply because students have an easy option not to attend. This may not be a problem in a large lecture hall (see the question about attendance above), as you will still have enough bodies to be able to do active learning if you desire. For smaller classes, however, this may become a problem, and it is noticeably harder to teach to a very small class (fifteen or less, I have found) if you are also expected to make the class worthwhile for online viewers. You will get fewer questions, and assessing student understanding is more difficult with a much smaller class.

There are some benefits to recording your lectures. Students who must miss class for legitimate reasons (sporting events, illness, etc.) will still be able to see your lectures, and they will appreciate it. Other students will also appreciate being able to time-shift their own viewing to do so when it is convenient. Videos are also helpful to students who want to re-visit the lectures, particularly if you cover a lot of material. Some of the most vulnerable students in my classes have been beneficiaries of the last reason, and it has been one of the driving reasons I often try to record my lectures even if it is not required. When I record the lectures, I can point students who don't come to class to the lecture videos, and I avoid the *I missed class, can you re-teach me the material?* question in office hours. Finally, having recordings of your lectures means that given the time, you can go back and revisit your lectures to improve your teaching. These days I don't often watch many of my lectures, but occasionally I will review the lectures if I want to recall exactly what I told students about a particular topic, or if I want to remember a particular question. I also try and keep copies of videos from previous times I taught a course, so I can go back and revisit them as a review when I teach the course again.

The biggest downside to recording your lectures is that you will likely see poorer average performance relative to when you do not record your class. Students with the best of intentions to watch the lectures often find themselves behind early in the course, and they are rarely able to catch back up. Many video services also allow students to watch the lectures at faster-than-normal speed, which helps the students watch more of the videos at the very real risk of having much lower retention to what is said. Even at regular speed, students are often more distracted and less engaged trying to watch the videos on their own than they would be sitting in class.

One option other than to fully video record you in front of your class is to do a screen capture (assuming most of your class is presented on screen). I have moved primarily to this method of recording my lectures if the course isn't being video recorded, and I think it is a nice trade-off between having no recording and having an in-person video. I have also gone to using a drawing tablet, which I use to write most of the examples, whiteboard-style, on the screen. Students are less likely to consider the screen-casts to be direct replacements of videos, so in that sense they are more likely to attend in person. Additionally, doing a screen-cast is a particularly simple task, using one program, and then uploading the video to the course website.[8] Finally, a screen-cast can avoid running afoul of any school requirements to avoid showing in-person students on camera, as all that is shown is the screen itself.

---

8 I use QuickTime Player, which comes with the MacOS operating system. There are also free screen capture applications for other operating systems, as well.

AFTER A LECTURE

Particularly as you begin your teaching career, you want to set aside some time after each lecture to give yourself feedback, and to note things that you will want to change for the next time you teach the course. You want to do this as soon after the class as is possible, preferably directly after the class. You may not be able to do it immediately after class, because you will often have students staying behind for at least a few minutes to ask clarifying questions. But, you should avoid setting your office hours or other meetings to be directly after class, and give yourself at least a half an hour window to do your review. In particular, try and answer the following questions:

1. Were there typos that need to be changed in slides or notes? (Fix these immediately)

2. Did students have trouble understanding any particular parts of the lecture?

3. Did you finish early, on time, or did you have more material to cover?

4. Were there any questions that you think you should answer organically in the lecture next time?

5. What were some of the good questions students asked?

6. Did you receive any questions after the class?

7. Specifically, would you change anything about the class (e.g., removing or adding examples, moving topics around, etc.)?

8. What is your overall impression of how the class went?

Write down the answers to these questions, and keep them in a location with your current lecture notes or slides. If you have time to work on fixing the lecture when you write the notes, do it. Likely, though, you will have more pressing issues to deal with (such as finishing preparation for the next lecture), and fixing the lecture you just finished will have to wait. In that case, you will have your notes for the next time you teach the course, and you can make the modifications when you prepare the next time.

Your students will be able to give you the best feedback on your course, and it is worthwhile to get regular feedback from your students. This is covered in more detail in Chapter 12, but you might consider polling a subset of students after each lecture to get feedback. Chris Piech pioneered the use of what he calls *Tiny Feedback*, which automatically polls a random subset of students to ask them to fill out a form online about the course. I have used a similar Tiny Feedback system, and getting immediate feedback on the lecture can be extremely helpful as you want to know the students' perceptions because they are your target audience.

WHAT TO DO IF...

Lectures do not always go as planned, and you should prepare for some common occurrences so you aren't caught off-guard when they happen. The following list is not comprehensive, but I have been in all of these situations (and I didn't handle all of them well the first time). You will get into situations that you haven't prepared for, and it is best to have a good sense of humor about it, and to roll with it the best you can. Even if you get flustered in the situation, you can rebound, and you should always use unexpected experiences to grow as an educator.

What if your computer or projector breaks?

Technology isn't perfect, and your computer can crash or the projector can break either before or during class. In both cases, you should be prepared to continue without either piece of technology, even if it does mean that your lecture will go differently than you had expected. If your computer crashes and you can't reasonably reboot it, you can ask a student to borrow a laptop, if you feel comfortable doing so. I post my lecture slides to students before class as a matter of course, but you should always have your lectures posted somewhere online (even if password protected), or on a removable device (e.g., a flash drive) so you can access them from a different device. You may also want to have hard copy slides as well, removing the necessity for trying to get a copy in the middle of class from a piece of technology.

Although it may not be your strongest method, you should also be prepared to continue the lecture on the whiteboard or chalkboard. I have done this many times when the classroom projector has broken, and the students adapt to it just fine. It may be harder to show some examples, and you may have to skip online demos that you want to show, but the situation is recoverable.

If you were relying on either your computer or the projector for the bulk of your lecture, you can always change tactics and ask the students what questions they have about already covered material, or you can use the time to review other material. This does take a certain amount of on-the-spot thinking, which can be difficult, but you should do your best to pivot or adapt to the current situation.

In certain circumstances, it makes sense to simply cancel the rest of the lecture (e.g., if the power goes out and doesn't come on in a reasonable amount of time), but if you can avoid this by being prepared to use less technology, then this is the better option.

What if a student dominates asking or answering questions?

Sometimes there are one or two students who seem to ask all of the questions, or provide all of the answers to your questions. In both cases, you should try to limit this behavior to the extent that it interferes with other students participating in class. If your class expects to raise their hand to be called on, one of the key ways to combat the over-eager behavior is to simply wait longer before calling on anyone. Wait time is critical when asking for questions or answers, because students need time to process them. As mentioned earlier in the chapter, you can also have students talk to their neighbors about what questions they have, and this will extend the time students have to think about questions or answers, meaning that you will likely have more than one group to call on.

If you find that it is always the same students asking or answering, with no other hands going up, you can create a rule that you will not call on a student more than once before letting others ask or answer, and again, you should provide plenty of time to think before you call on anyone.

In rare cases, you may have to talk to a student individually outside of class, to ask them to let others participate more. Try to phrase it in a positive way, e.g., *You have a lot of great questions and you are a fast thinker, but I would like more people in the class to participate. If you could hold some of your questions until after you see others ask theirs, then this will be easier.*

What if students don't ask questions?

As covered above, you should always wait for enough time to let students formulate their questions. If you aren't getting any questions, then there are a couple of possibilities. First, you may not have a topic that leads to many questions – in that case, you could be lecturing very well, but be wary of this happening all the time. Students who are engaged will almost always have some question about all but the most trivial material. If students never have questions, you also might be on the other end of the spectrum and you have covered the material too fast and none of them are able to formulate questions. In both cases, you can use the strategy outlined earlier to ask student pairs to discuss their understanding of the material, and to formulate questions using a think-pair-share method.

Another option, sometimes useful nearer the beginning of the course, is to come up with your own questions that you think the students might have. You can say, *You might have the following question...*, and if you have a few of these ready it may encourage the students to follow-up, or to give them ideas about what types of questions are reasonable.

What if you have low attendance?

At some schools, low attendance can be a problem, particularly when the course is recorded and available to watch online. You should encourage your students to attend lectures, because it is harder for many students to motivate themselves to watch a video for every class than to simply attend. See the section above, *To Record or Not to Record*, for a discussion on whether you should even record the lectures.

In a high school environment, attendance is likely required, but in college it is often not required, particularly for larger classes where taking attendance becomes difficult. If you do want to enforce attendance in larger lectures, technology can help – you can get ID card scanners, and you can also take attendance via clicker. You can also hand out a paper-based ID system, although this would require manual labor to collate and be untenable in a very large lecture. However, I would suggest that rather than simply requiring attendance, you create an incentive scheme for students to attend – this could be a bonus for attending class, or a release from other work (e.g., letting the students drop an assignment if they attend a certain percentage of the lectures). You could also limit the maximum grade the students can obtain if they miss a certain percentage of lectures (e.g., *If you miss more than 10% of the lectures, you can not get a grade higher than B+*). Positive incentives work better than negative incentives, and talking to your TAs about how they think students will react to a certain policy is a wise idea.

If you do end up with low attendance, do the best you can for the students who do attend. My general feeling is that as long as there is a quorum of students in attendance who are eager and engaged, I don't worry too much about the non-present students, and as college students I expect that they will take responsibility for their learning (when I taught high school, where attendance was required, this was not my attitude, and I expected all students in class). In a large lecture hall it can be discouraging to see a sparse set of students, and you can also request that they move closer to the front, or to the center of the room. But, teach the class as you would with a packed hall, and focus on the students that do attend.

What if you can't answer a question?

You will get questions in class that you don't know how to answer. You should honestly say that you don't know the answer to the question. Often it is nice to say that you will try to find out the answer after class though this isn't strictly necessary – you can also suggest to the student to try researching the answer, and to see you during office hours to discuss it in detail if they can't figure it out. You can also open the question to the rest of the class in case someone else knows the answer, and you should not be ashamed if someone does when you do not. You should absolutely avoid making up an answer, though postulating one with the caveat that you aren't sure is okay.

What if a student answers a question incorrectly?

Whenever a student attempts to answer a question in a lecture, you should understand that they are putting themselves in a vulnerable situation, in public. If a student does attempt to answer a question and gives an incorrect answer, you should be kind and complimentary, while acknowledging that the answer was incorrect. You want to instill a sense of safety for answering questions, and the last thing you want to do is reply with a curt, *no* to a student who has volunteered an answer. Rather, you can reply with something like, *Well, that is an interesting idea, but not correct. How about thinking about this....* You don't have to give the student another chance, but if you can coax a better answer out of them, all the better. If you can't, moving on to another student is fine, and as long as students know that they are free to make mistakes when answering, they will be more likely to volunteer in the future.

What if you answer a question incorrectly?

If a student asks a question, and *you* answer it incorrectly, the best strategy is to correct your error as soon as possible. You might only realize you made a mistake after the class. In that case, posting a correction on your course forum, and also re-addressing the question in the next class is reasonable. If you happen to know the student who asked the question, you can also follow up with them.

Always own up to mistakes you make in class – students are happy to re-adjust their understanding if you made a mistake, but they will not appreciate if you attempt to stick to an answer that is incorrect. If a student disagrees with your answer, the best strategy is to ask the student to stop by after class to discuss it – getting into an argument with a student during class is a no-win situation; at best it wastes time in class, and at worst it just makes everyone uncomfortable. By postponing the discussing to after class, you can also take more time to think through your answer and you can reason with the student in a non-public situation.

What if you provide inaccurate information during lecture?

While similar to the previous question, in this case you have actually prepared your lecture and had incorrect or misleading information in the lecture. I have done this before (specifically, I
had an incorrect understanding myself of C++ pointers and references, and told the students about *pointers to references*, which is
illegal in C++, instead of *references to pointers*, which is legal), and
I only realized it after class. Your response should be the same as
when you realize you made a mistake answering a question: you
should own up to the mistake and you should correct it as soon
as you can. In the case I just mentioned, I sent out a correction on
the class forum, and I re-taught the incorrect part of the lecture
the next day, apologizing for my mistake. The students appreciated my honesty in correcting the mistake, and they may even
have learned the material a bit better after my explanation of the
mistake and the correction.[9]

What if you can't find a bug in your live-code?

As mentioned in *Practicing Your Lectures* above, live coding can be
a great pedagogical tool, allowing you to demonstrate coding in
real-time to your students. However, you might introduce a subtle
bug into your code that is difficult to find, especially when a class
full of students is staring at you. If this happens, don't panic. I
always have a hard copy of what I prepared to code, and if you
have that, you can compare what you have with what you typed.
If you don't have a copy, or if you can't find the code (and the
students don't know, either), you may just have to either start over,
or back up to a point where you know things were working. In
the worst case, you may have to move on from the example and
come back to in in the next class, after you have debugged the

---

9 Note that I do not encourage *purposely* misleading your students only to correct
yourself later!

code. I have been in this situation before, where I swapped two integer parameters when calling a function, and both the class and I missed it. I had to end class with a comment that I would debug after class. I ended up finding the bug a few minutes after class, and I posted a fix online, and showed the corrected demo again the next day in class.

What if you have an unanticipated day off (e.g., a snow day)?

If you have finely crafted your course schedule to perfectly utilize every minute of every lecture, you can still be caught off guard by an unanticipated cancellation of class. There could be a snow day, or a water main break, or a power outage. Alternatively, you could be sick, and have to cancel a lecture. In the latter case, if you can get a replacement lecturer (a colleague, or a TA), that may work out best, but canceling class due to illness is reasonable.[10]

If class gets canceled, re-evaluate your lecture schedule, and adjust it as necessary. This may require leaving out some topics that you would have liked to cover, or it may involve providing information in another form to the students. I have video recorded missed lectures due to snow days before, which I have posted to students. This isn't ideal (this misses out on active learning, and student questions), but it was sufficient given the circumstances.

You may have to reschedule an exam or extend an assignment for a missed class day, and you should be as flexible as you can be. This is another reason to build in some flexibility into your term schedule, so that you can more easily adjust if necessary.

What if you run out of time in a lecture?

This is not as rare an occurrence as you might think, especially if you have a class of students that ask a lot of questions. Much

---

10 Please don't go to class if you are contagious, or too sick to be effective. Virtually all other options provide a better choice.

like the answer for the previous question, you have to adjust your schedule to either fit in the missed material into a subsequent lecture, or you should provide it to the students in another form (e.g., as online material). If you find yourself not finishing your lectures too often, then you should build in less material to future lectures, and plan the rest of your schedule accordingly. If you are required to cover all the material and you routinely find yourself running out of time, then you need to determine if there are inefficiencies that you can remove from lectures, or you should determine why you have too much material for the course. In the latter case, talk to other instructors who have taught the course before, and find out their strategies. If you are responsible for the course content, then you should consider removing course topics if you can't cover them in class to your liking.

What if you finish early in a lecture?

Finishing lectures early on occasion is not bad. Information design expert Edward Tufte is fond of saying that no one has ever complained about a presenter finishing early. You should strive to fill your lecture time appropriately, but if you finish up a few minutes early, your students will not be upset. You can use the extra few minutes to discuss further questions, but beware that once students recognize that you are done presenting the material for the day, they will start to get anxious in their seats. You might secure one or two questions, but drawing it out too long will be counterproductive.

If you are finding yourself finishing much too early regularly, then you have a good opportunity to add more active learning into your class, or to go deeper on certain topics. As important, you also can give students more time to process the information by assessing their understanding more often as you finish individual topics. You can also assess whether you are finishing early because you are talking to fast, and you can work on modifying your speed to talk slower and be more deliberate.

What if you are interrupted during class?

In class interruptions are rare, but they do happen. Once when I was teaching a CS2 class on Valentine's Day, a bare-chested male student waltzed straight into class with a bouquet of flowers, asked if a particular female student was in the room, and then (to her palpable embarrassment) delivered the flowers to her. I later found out that it was an athletic team's fund-raising event. My reaction to the interruption was to simply realize that this was happening and I wasn't going to help matters by intervening. It was obvious that it would be quick, and as far as student pranks / interruptions goes, it was relatively benign, so I just kept my mouth shut and waited for the student to leave. I made a quick joke about it after the student made his delivery, and then I resumed teaching.

Your best strategy for interruptions is to deal with it maturely and quickly, and then to get back to your regularly scheduled lecture. You don't need to linger on the interruption, nor do you need to make a big deal about it. Your students will recover quickly, and one or two minutes missed from class is should not ruin your lecture. Once again, having a good sense of humor about it helps, as well.

What if a student has an emergency during a lecture?

One interruption that you do need to deal with in a serious way is in the very rare case of a student emergency, such as a seizure or other critical medical event. Your students will also react to the situation (some better than others), but you should do your best to keep the situation under control, and to call the necessary emergency personnel (in the U.S., call 911, for example). You can also delegate to a student to make the emergency call, but you should be assured that it is happening. A situation like this can be traumatic to students other than the one directly involved in the emergency, so this is another situation where canceling class after such an event may be warranted. If you can, following up with the student after they are stable is a nice gesture, although you should not make a big deal of it, especially because the student might feel ashamed of causing the interruption.

What if your students don't seem to understand the topic?

If you find that once you have taught a topic in lecture and you are assessing student understanding, that many of the students haven't picked up the material, you have a couple of options. If you feel comfortable going into more detail on the spot, that is appropriate. If you can formulate another example, or you can review the material or talk about it from a different perspective, that is terrific. If you don't think that is a viable strategy, then you should tell the students that you will work to come up with another strategy for them to understand, and you should cover this in a subsequent lecture, or online. Sometimes, students don't grasp enough of the material during class, but they do once they go to recitation section, or they start the problem set, or they work on the assignment. If you think this may be the case, make this clear to the students, e.g., *This topic is difficult to wrap your head around immediately, but when you go to recitation section you will see many more examples that should help you understand it.* If this does happen, you should also go back and re-evaluate how you taught the material, modifying it for the next time you teach it.

What if you are being observed?

In many schools, instructors get observed and evaluated by another faculty member, department chair, principal, etc., during the school year. Sometimes the visits are scheduled, and sometimes they are unannounced. Regardless of the situation, *don't change anything about your lecture.* If you have planned a good lecture, you should be proud to have anyone watch the lecture, regardless of whether it is a student, faculty member or administrator. Although it may not be easy, try to perform as you would for any other lecture, and try not to get nervous about the visit. If possible, you should ask for a follow-up meeting to go over the observer's feedback (and sometimes this will be a normal part of the observation). You should always welcome constructive feedback to improve your teaching.

If you want to improve your own teaching, getting feedback from other faculty members is a terrific idea, although it is often difficult to find a time where a colleague is willing to watch your whole lecture. But, it does not hurt to ask someone you respect to come to class and give you feedback. Many schools also offer directed feedback through teaching centers on campus, where someone from the center will observe you and give you constructive feedback.

What if students complain you are going too slow or too fast?

Once again, welcome all constructive feedback from your students (and see Chapter 12 for a longer discussion about feedback in general). However, this is a difficult piece of feedback, because you likely have a heterogeneous class that has students who are having difficulties to students who are acing the material. If a student gives you this feedback directly, you should talk to the student about why they perceive the course to be going too slow or too fast. It can be difficult to determine if the pace of the class is wrong based on a single student's feedback, which is a good reason to try and get feedback from a wider swath of students. If, after talking with the student (and potentially, other students), you decide that you think the pace is reasonable, then you can suggest to the student ways to make their experience better by either working on building their skills (if they think the class is too fast), or to direct them to more advanced material (if they think the class is too slow). If, on the other hand, you do think the student has a reasonable criticism, then you have to go back and

re-look at your pacing, and adjust as necessary. You will probably
find that more than a handful of students will reach out to you if
they think the pace is too fast, particularly.

What if you have visitors (prospective students, non-affiliated, etc.)?

I love having visitors in my class, and I welcome them. Sometimes
visitors are prospective students with or without their families,
and other times visitors are other faculty, or other people from the
general public. Unless your school has requirements against visitors, you should feel free to welcome visitors into your classroom,
assuming they are not causing any disruption. If I recognize that
there are visitors in the class (sometimes difficult in a large lecture hall), I will introduce myself and tell them that I hope they
enjoy their visit. I will also approach them after class if I see them
to thank them for coming. Often, if they are perspective students,
they will have questions, and it is a good opportunity to represent
your school positively by being cordial and supportive of their application to the school. I also don't mind having them contact me,
and I have also put prospective students in touch with current students to find out more information about computer science, and
the school in general.

FINAL THOUGHTS

Lecturing can be the most interesting and most rewarding part
of your teaching experience, but it can also be a tremendously
time-consuming endeavor, from the planning, practicing, and delivering of your lectures to gathering feedback and revising of
your lectures the next time you teach the course. The more effort
you put into creating lectures the first time you teach a course, the
less time you will have to spend on future versions, but don't expect your lectures to be perfect the first time you plan them, and
expect to make some revisions. Additionally, I can't state enough

how important it is to give yourself enough time to plan your lectures, as it will take longer than you think.

Have fun with your lectures, and enjoy the teaching – it is an intellectual endeavor that can be hugely gratifying and is a bedrock of our educational system.

Why are we doing this?

In my first term as a full-time tenure-track faculty member (after a year as a lecturer), I was teaching a discrete math class. About two-thirds of the way through the semester, during a lecture on the pigeonhole principle, one of the women in class, sitting in the back of the room, raised her hand. I called on her, and she asked:

"Why are we doing this? We don't do anything like this at my job."

I stumbled through an answer about the importance of discrete math as foundation for other courses in the CS curriculum. I don't know if she bought it, but she didn't follow-up on the question, and class resumed.

After class, I retreated to my office, feeling the shame of another poorly-executed class. And then it occurred to me. While the question wasn't offered in the most polite manner, it was an important question, and was worthy of a good answer.

The question changed the way that I think about delivering content in courses. I always try to make sure that I connect each course to other courses in the curriculum, and to the wider world of CS. I don't get that question anymore; I think it's because I answer it before it gets asked.

— Dr. Jim Huggins, Associate Professor of Computer Science, Kettering University

My First Whirlwind Lecture

I spent about forty hours preparing my first lecture for a graduate networking course (it felt like it took forever!). I then delivered the whole lecture to the students in about thirty minutes, and found myself with about forty-five minutes still remaining in the class. When I looked up, I noticed the students were shell shocked, and I had gone through the material *way* too quickly! I spent the next forty-five minutes going back over the material.

— Dr. Tracy Camp, Professor of Computer Science, Colorado School of Mines

9

GRADING (AND THE ROLE OF TEACHING ASSISTANTS)

LET'S FACE IT: GRADING IS probably not the part of teaching you are most looking forward to doing. Assessing your students is, however, an essential part of your job, and is as important for the students themselves as it is for your own determination of how your course is going. Grading can be an overwhelming task, particularly if you have too many students per person doing the grading. You may be the only person grading your students, or you may have an army of teaching assistants to help you. Or, you may have a few (or no) TAs and many students, which is, unfortunately, becoming more frequent as computer science enrollments are exploding. Your TA allotment (if any) will be dependent on how many students you have, and the resources available where you teach. If you are able to hire undergraduate TAs, this can help the situation considerably, and lobbying for a good group of undergraduate TAs is worth your time.

Hopefully you are in a position where you will be able to assess students effectively without having to spend a burdensome amount of time doing it, but if you do think you will have difficulties getting the grading done, there are strategies that can help. If you have TAs, you will have to instruct them on how to grade effectively and to your standards, and you will have to manage them in general. After reading this chapter, you will have a number of grading and TA management strategies to use to make your grading efficient and to utilize your TAs grading skills effectively.

One important point to understand related to grading is this: your students understanding of the material–and being able to do something based on their understanding–is more important than grading them on their work. You want to be fair and thorough when you grade, but you also want to focus less on your students grades and more on their understanding. Students sometimes have a hard time separating the two ideas, as well, although with fair and honest grading, most students will correlate their grades with their understanding. You should do your best to align your grading with their understanding.

WHAT KINDS OF ASSESSMENTS SHOULD YOU HAVE?

As discussed in Chapter 8, you should be informally assessing your students' understanding often during lectures. This can be in the form of questions you ask the students in class as a whole (with, for example, think-pair-share questions), and/or more individual assessments through technology such as clickers or online response systems. Some of the more formal and obvious ways to assess students is through homework assignments or projects (individual, pairs, or larger groups) and quizzes or exams. In computer science, it is rare to have students write papers as they would in a humanities course, but some CS courses lend themselves to longer-form writing based assessments.

You should strive to provide a good balance of assessment types to your students, in order to get a wide view of their performance and understanding. Furthermore, students can perform differently on different types of assessments. Some students have more difficulty with exams than with assignments, for example, and giving them multiple ways to demonstrate their understanding makes a fairer overall assessment.

If you are teaching a small class, or if you have recitation sections, you may want to give your students short, low stakes problem-solving quizzes to test their understanding. With clickers or online response systems, you can also have students in larger classes take short quizzes, although it is difficult to have problem-solving quizzes (though well-crafted problems can have multiple choice answers). These types of assignments should be quick to grade and should give students good feedback on whether they understand the current material.

Some courses have an end-of-term project that is worth a large portion of the course grade, and it can in many cases replace a final exam. For group projects, it is often difficult to separate individual student work to grade it. See Chapter 7 for ways to craft a rubric that helps with this. If possible, try to have at least some assessments in the course be individual, to further help differentiate students. If that is difficult (e.g., in a course that is completely team-project based), one useful tool is to have teammates rate each other's work on their project. Students will be surprisingly honest with their peer assessment, although you should not overly weigh this for course grades.

Although time constraints sometimes limit the amount of feedback you can give students for their graded work, you should attempt to give concise feedback on what was incorrect (and positive feedback on what was correct!) so that students can understand where they made their mistakes. Only some students will actively try and fix their mistakes (e.g., on a programming assignment), but that can be a tremendous learning experience, and you want to provide them as much information as you can to allow them to find and fix their errors.

TEACHING ASSISTANTS AND GRADING

In courses with teaching assistants (TAs[1]), those students will often perform the brunt of the grading. This means that you need to train them how to grade effectively, and you need to be clear about how you want the grading done. It also means that you have to trust them to do the grading to these standards, and they need to take the job seriously. Teaching assistants can be a tremendously important part of your class (and not simply because of

---

1 The term *Teaching Assistant* is meant to be generic. Your school may call them teaching assistants, course assistants, teaching fellows, section leaders, or another unique term.

the grading), and the more you foster a good relationship with your TAs, the better your class will be.

TAs that have actually taken the same course you are teaching will have the most knowledge about the course, and should be able to provide excellent support. This is not to presume that TAs who haven't taken the course won't be excellent, but they may need more instruction about how the course runs before being as knowledgeable about it. The flip side is that TAs who have taken the course before may expect the course to be the same as it was when they took it, and if you make significant changes to the schedule and assignments, they may push back. If you are going to make changes to the course, be upfront with your TAs about this decision, and also be clear that you want them on board with the changes. You should take TA feedback and constructive criticism seriously, too, especially if they have been involved with the specific course long than you have. Ultimately, however, the course is yours to change (barring any department-specific requirements), and your TAs should support those changes the best they can.

If your TAs are going to be grading assignments, you want to have a clear rubric (see Chapter 7 for an example assignment rubric, and see below for an example exam question rubric), and you want to give the TAs training on what you expect. This training can be accomplished in a number of ways. Some schools have TA training courses that are specific to particular classes (e.g., CS1 and/or CS2), and either they are taught by veteran TAs or by faculty members. Sometimes the courses give students credit, and other times they are paid. This kind of training can be outstanding, particularly because it gives veteran TAs a leadership role among their peers, and it also provides continuity from senior TAs to new TAs. If such a course exists at your school and is meant for your class, you should plan on integrating yourself into the TA training to the extent that you can see how grading happens, and make changes if it is warranted for your own grading expectations. This is especially true if you are going to teach the course for the first time, as you will gain valuable information about how the course has been run in the past.

If you don't have a course that will train the TAs on how to grade, you should have a meeting after the first assignment is due where you discuss your expectations for grading, and you should have the TAs practice grading in a setting where you can give suggestions and can correct any misconceptions about what you are looking for. These so-called *grading parties* can be a productive time for TAs to at least begin on the grading, and to do so in a supportive environment. It also provides you and veteran TAs the ability to help less experienced TAs with any questions they have about the grading process, or with specific examples.

You can also hold grading parties for exams,[2] and if you schedule enough time, you can grade the entire exam within a single meeting (which may be many hours long, depending on the exam and your student to grader ratio). With exams, try to assign veteran TAs to lead a particular question for grading. See below for more information about grading exams in general.

You should feel comfortable trusting that your TAs are grading assignments and exams correctly, but for novice TAs, you should occasionally spot-check their work to ensure that they are on track. If a TA isn't grading appropriately, discuss the issue with them and try to correct it. Students in your class may also ask you to review grades from the TAs, and you should investigate in that case, and if necessary, fix the problem. You should always use these types of situations to give your TAs feedback and to help them become better – unless you feel there is negligence on their part (which is rare), it is a teachable moment for them.

---

2 And feed your TAs! TAs will be happier and will have more stamina if you offer them food during a grading party.

As discussed in Chapter 7, you want to create assignments that are gradable, and you don't want students to be surprised at how they performed on an assignment. Assuming you have written a decent assignment that meets these goals, grading it should be a matter of following the rubric and applying it. There are a multitude of different types of assignments, and I've broken them down into a couple of different types you may assign below.

Programming Assignments

Programming assignments can be graded in a number of ways, depending on the feedback you want to give the students, and what you want to stress. Functionality, based on tests (hopefully automated), is generally a key component of a grade, as is style, to include good decision making (e.g., choosing the right data structures, decomposing the problem properly, etc.), formatting, commenting, and so forth. You can also ask students to write tests for their own code, which you can grade, as well. You can grade student-written tests on code-coverage, independence from other tests, or integration between code sections. If you have emphasized code testing in your course, you will have presumably demonstrated good testing practices with your students, and then you can grade them on the effectiveness of their own tests.

Think carefully about the feedback that you want your automatic tests to provide to your students. You may not want to disclose the actual tests you run (or only disclose some of them), but you should be able to provide feedback that gives students enough information to write their own equivalent tests. For example, you may write a test that checks for memory management on input strings, and your test provides an abnormally long string. If a student's program fails the test, the feedback could be:

```
Failed test for long input string (over 1024 characters).
Error: segmentation fault.
```

Be as specific as you can – if you are using a programming language that has stack traces available, provide them to the students in the failed-test message. Ideally, a student will see the failed test, and then go back to their code to figure out why the test failed. The easier you make it for the student to find the location of the bug, the better. The grading report should not try and hide that information from the student, and at this point in the process you want to give them as much information as you can.

For introductory programming courses, you should give students at least some feedback on their programming style. All decent IDEs will do a competent job formatting code for your students, and if you use an IDE for class, you should teach your students how to auto-format. They won't catch all the formatting issues (e.g., such as having two end curly braces on one line), nor will they fix many whitespace issues. You can provide feedback (and a style grade) on redundancy in code, proper commenting, decomposition, variable naming, scope, proper types (e.g., double -vs- int), proper constants, use of global variables, and good design choices. You cannot just assume students will know about all these issues, of course, and you should model them in class and on any code you give the students. You should also have a style document that lists the style elements you expect from the students so they have a document to reference.

If you have a grading system that allows you to provide feedback inline with student code, you (and your TAs) should utilize this feature. Students can see exactly where you note a problem (either functionality, or style), and this provides a better context than a list of errors on its own.

How much time you and your TAs spend grading is relative to the number of students per grader you have. If possible, each student should get at least ten or fifteen minutes of a grader's time, which allows the grader to comment on functionality and style. Even better is for you or the TA to also have a one-on-one meeting with each student after grading to discuss their assignment, but this is, understandably, rarely possible. If it is possible, you will probably have to have a student-to-grader ratio of less than fifteen-to-one so that the graders have enough time during the week to hold one-on-one meetings. One-on-one meetings can be instrumental for students early on in their computer science training (e.g., CS1 and CS2), and I strongly recommend them if you can find the resources.[3]

Problem Set Assignments

Depending on the type of problem sets you assign, grading may involve simply marking answers correct or incorrect, or (more likely) spending time looking at how students attempted to solve the problems. For proofs, you and/or your TAs will have to make a judgment as to whether the student solved the problem correctly, and whether the proof meets your expectations for rigor. Training your TAs to do this efficiently and fairly is not trivial – you will need to spend a significant amount of time ensuring that they can grade to your standards. If they cannot, you will have many frustrated students who do not understand why their answers were marked incorrect. Your burden is two-fold: you need to give the students a clear expectation of how they need to solve the problems, and you also have to ensure that the TAs are precise in their grading.

Because of the difficulty of grading proofs and other intricate problems, you may want to consider giving your students an assignment or two that are worth less than later assignments. This gives the students time to see what they are graded on and to cal-

---

3 This is important enough to lobby for extra resources from your department or school, and is especially important for underrepresented students who may feel out of place in the course. Having a person individually sit down to discuss assignments and progress can be influential to students to make them feel included.

ibrate their responses to be consistent with what you are looking for. Alternately, you could consider letting students re-do problems they got wrong, although this requires further grading time, which may not be available.

When you provide feedback on problem set assignments, you should be clear about what the students did incorrectly, and you should (as best you can) direct them towards a better solution. Having problem-set keys is also reasonable, though this may limit your ability to re-assign the same problems in the future (this is less of an issue for problems that have multiple solutions, where the answer key solution is one of many choices, where it would be easier to determine if a student used the answer key to inform their own work).

Projects (Individual or Group)

As discussed in Chapter 7, when assigning projects, you would be wise to have a public rubric for your students to base their work off of, and the rubric should be precise enough to grade student work as objectively as possible. If the project is long-term (i.e., the better part of a term, or longer), then you should have multiple assessments as the students work on the project. An assessment a week is worthwhile, as it keeps students focused on the assignment. Without a weekly check-in and assessment, students can be lulled into procrastinating, which makes for worse projects and higher student stress near the end of the projects when they are scrambling to finish them. One strategy that works well is to have a calendar of checkpoints that students must meet, with an assessment of some sort at each checkpoint. The checkpoints could include a project proposal, a demonstration, a short oral presentation, or a stand-up group report to you or a TA. Each of these can be graded, and will help keep students on track.

Final projects can involve a combination of written work (a paper, poster, website, etc.) and an oral presentation, and each of the parts should be graded as separately as possible. The earlier you can grade a portion of the assignment the better – leaving the entire project to grade at the end of the term is likely to involve long hours grading that you could have spread out more during the term.

If the project involves student presentations, be sure to allot enough time for each presentation, and have someone time the presentations and keep to the schedule. Fifteen minute presentations by ten groups is two and a half hours of time, without any inevitable slack between presentations. With five minutes extra per group (which ends up being shorter than you might think), that two and a half hours turns into three hours and twenty minutes, and that is a lot of time to spend watching presentations.

If you decide to have full-class feedback on presentations with a form the students fill out, make sure you have a way to collate the responses – if there are nine groups of four students grading each of the ten presentations, you will have to collate three hundred and sixty responses, and doing that on paper is rather time consuming. Often, you will want to provide the feedback to the student groups, as well, and this adds another level of administrative work. If possible, set up an online form for each group for the student audience to fill out (e.g., use Google Forms documents). The time you spend up front to automate the feedback process will be well worth it when you go to collate the responses.

Grading individual work on group projects can be quite difficult. Try and produce rubrics that force students to discuss what each individual group member has accomplished, and consider having groups provide self-assessments where each member grades the others on their participation and delivery (as discussed in Chapter 7). Too many times I have received feedback from group members that they felt like a particular member did not put in a comparable effort, and you want to be able to reward students who do put in the work. In the interest of fairness, you should do what you can to differentiate among group members.

ASSESSING QUIZZES AND EXAMS

If you decide to give frequent quizzes, make them as easy to grade as possible, while still providing reasonable problems for students to work on. Multiple-choice problems that force students to actually work to get the answer are terrific (e.g., *What is the output of the following program?*), as are other questions or problems that have an answer that is easily scanned for correctness. If you ask your TAs to give quizzes in recitation section, a good strategy is to give the quiz (which should be no more than 5-10 minutes) and then have the TA put the students to work on another problem while they quickly grade the quizzes. The TA should be able to grade the quiz, record the scores, and hand the quizzes back to the students by the time they finish the other work, and this should be less than ten minutes, as well (as I said, the quizzes need to be easy and quick to grade).

As discussed earlier in the chapter, exams can take a significant amount of time to grade. But with enough grading help and through the use of grading parties (*with food*), you and your graders should be able to get through the exam grading in one sitting. If that isn't possible, you should still have a meeting with the graders to ensure that everyone is on the same page as far as understanding how the problems they are assigned to should be graded.

The more you can automate the exam grading process, the better. If you have paper exams, consider scanning them into a grading program such as Gradescope, which will enable you to grade them online, and to return the graded exams via the Internet. If you don't want to use technology to help with the process, I would even more strongly suggest a grading party so that the inevitable paper-shuffle is limited to one room.[4]

---

4 When I was in graduate school, I was a TA for a course where each of the four TAs would get a box of exams and would have a few days to grade their problems. We shuffled exams between each other, and it took us the better part of two weeks to grade each exam. The logistical nightmare, combined with the

When you go to grade an exam, you will obviously need an answer key. You should put together the answer key as you create the exam, and you should make sure to test any coding problem solutions. If possible, you should also have someone else, such as a TA or TAs, review the exam, and also provide potential solutions. Keep in mind that for many CS exams, the answer key represents *one* way to solve each problem, and there may be many solutions. If you expect significantly different solutions to a particular problem, then you should consider putting more than one solution for that problem on the key.

Once you have an answer key, you will need to put together rubrics for each question. If you put the point values for each question on the exam itself (which I recommend), then you will know how many points the problem is worth, and you can start assigning points to parts of the solution that you are looking for. This requires decomposing each problem into sub-parts that students can get points for, and it is not a trivial process (in other words – don't wait until the last minute before grading to try and write up the rubrics). See below for more information about creating rubrics.

THE ART OF CREATING RUBRICS

The rubric is the document that provides a scoring guide for your assignments, and it is a key part to grading any assignment. The rubric for an assignment should help the graders be consistent with their awarding (or deducting) points, and it is often a good policy to show your students the rubric after you hand back an assignment (or, in the case of project-based assignments, showing them the rubric ahead of time can give the students a good guide as they complete the project). Sometimes, you may *not* want to hand back the exact rubric, particularly if you want students

---

all-too frequent paper cuts led me to embrace technology for exam grading as quickly as I could.

to get a grade that is not points-based (e.g., a check-plus, check, or check-minus) – in this case you should provide them enough feedback that they can understand what they did correctly or incorrectly, but without the fine details of the number of points they received. This is to avoid students trying to win back individual points when it is better for them to concentrate on their overall performance.

Learning how to create good rubrics can take time, and you will start to get a good idea of what makes a decent rubric as you grade more assignments. You want the rubric to be as clear as possible on what a student needs to do to receive credit. If there are multiple solutions to a problem, than this can get difficult – again, it helps if the problem statement on the assignment was unambiguous as to what the student needs to accomplish. Your rubric must be general enough to cover all the cases that students might come up with, and it can be difficult to create a perfect rubric before you have seen all of the student responses. If this is the case, you can change the rubric while grading, as long as the change won't affect other students who have already been graded (or, you can modify those scores after the original grading was completed).

As an example, the problem on the following page was a question I asked on a final exam for a CS2 course. You can see the problem and the solution that I wrote, as well as the rubric that the TAs and I created. The rubric didn't originally start with all of the point deductions, and we added some during the grading party, as we looked at new student solutions. For example, we added the *Does not properly track lemons rotten during a single iteration* deduction after we found that students were not correctly tracking the graph nodes in each iteration of their loop.

You can notice for the rubric that there are more point deductions than the total number of points in the problem (15). This is because of the different ways students attempted to solve the problem, and we had to be flexible based on the various answers we received. For example, students who did not have a reasonable algorithm, but did attempt the problem (e.g., if they tried to use a depth first search) with a decent solution, they might only lose seven points. We were lenient on syntax errors (e.g., missing semicolons), but we did take points off for major syntax errors (e.g., trying to get the index value of an element in the queue).

When you first start grading with your TAs, it is a good idea to all work a few of the same student answers together, to see how each TA grades based on the rubric. The TAs should eventually gravitate to scores that are roughly the same. It is also a good idea to have the same TAs grading one particular problem, so that they can be consistent. I always assign one TA as the head grader for a particular problem, and the head grader is the only one who can update the rubric, when necessary.

For a rubric, you can either grade *down* or grade *up* for a particular problem. The rotting lemons problem is graded down from fifteen points. In other words, the student starts with fifteen points and loses points as rubric items are matched. The other option is to start students with zero points and have rubric items count up, so a rubric item might be, *+1 checks all neighbors of BROWN lemons when they have been dequeued*. It depends on the type of problem you have whether it makes sense to grade up or down. If you have different problems on the exam with different grading schemes, tell the students about this, as they are likely to be confused when reviewing their exams if you don't tell them about the differences.

Problem 3: Graphs -- Time to Rot All Lemons

(15 Points)

Consider a graph of nodes for which every node represents a lemon (the fruit). The `color` of each node (an `int`) is either YELLOW or BROWN, where YELLOW represents a fresh lemon, and BROWN represents a rotted lemon. As each day passes, a rotted lemon causes all of its neighbors that are fresh to become rotted.

Write a function, `daysToRotAllLemons`, that determines how many days it will take to rot all the lemons in the graph:

```
int daysToRotAllLemons(BasicGraph g);
```

Notes:

1. If it is impossible to rot all lemons, return -1.

2. Return -1 for an empty graph.

3. You may declare helper functions as necessary, and you may construct auxiliary collections as needed to solve the problem.

4. You can assume that both YELLOW and BROWN are `int`.constants that have been defined already.

5. You can assume that when you receive the graph the `visited` state is set to `false` for all nodes, and the color for each node is set to either YELLOW (fresh) or BROWN (rotted).

Answer:

```
int daysToRotAllLemons(BasicGraph g) {
```

Problem 3:

```
int daysToRotAllLemons(BasicGraph g) {
    // basic algorithm: bfs that enqueues all rotted lemons,
    // then dequeues each one step at a time,
    // keeping track of the time step through the queue
    struct TimeRotted {
        Vertex *v;
        int time;
    };

    int rotTime = 0;
    Set<Vertex *> totalRotted;

    Queue<TimeRotted>q;
    Set<Vertex *>lemons = g.getVertexSet();
    for (Vertex *v : lemons) {
        if (v->getColor() == BROWN) {
            q.enqueue({v,rotTime});
            totalRotted += v;
        }
    }
    while (!q.isEmpty()) {
        TimeRotted tr = q.dequeue();
        if (tr.time > rotTime) {
            rotTime++;
        }
        // rot all neighbors
        Set<Vertex *>neighbors = g.getNeighbors(tr.v);
        for (Vertex *v : neighbors) {
            if (v->getColor() == YELLOW) {
                v->setColor(BROWN);
                totalRotted += v;
                q.enqueue({v,tr.time+1});
            }
        }
    }
    if (g.size() != totalRotted.size() || g.size() == 0) {
        return -1;
    }
    return rotTime;
}
```

Table 4: Rubric for *Time to Rot All Lemons* Problem

0	Correct
-15	Incorrect
-1	Does not return -1 for empty graph
-1	Does not return -1 for disconnected graph where at least one YELLOW lemon cannot be reached
-7	Does not select a reasonable algorithm for this problem
-1	Does not properly keep track of days for each step (i.e., dequeueing cannot track when a new level has been reached)
-1	BFS: Does not enqueue / check all BROWN lemons first
-1	Does not check all neighbors of BROWN lemons when they have been dequeued
-1	Re-enqueues already-rotted lemons
-1	Does not set YELLOW lemons to BROWN when they have been rotted
-1	Does not enqueue each newly rotted lemon
-1	Does not finish if all lemons are YELLOW to begin with (and does not return -1 days)
-1	Does not properly handle case where all lemons are BROWN to begin with (does not return 0 days)
-3	Does not properly track lemons rotten during a single iteration
-3	Completely wrong approach to count days
-1	One major syntax error
-2	Two major syntax errors
-3	Three major syntax errors

MANAGING THE GRADING WORKLOAD

If you aren't careful, grading can take up more time than you have. Obviously, it doesn't help if you have too many students and too few resources (you or your TAs) to help with the grading, and if this is the case, you have to start being creative with the time you have. For programming problems, you can rely more heavily on automated tests than you would if you were able to devote more resources to grading. Some CS instructors with extremely large classes (over 1000 students in some cases) either have only automated tests, or they do not grade programming assignments at all. In the latter case, student grades are completely dependent on exams, which is less than ideal. If you are forced into this position, you should have more quizzes or exams then you might otherwise, so that you can at least give students more individual assessments.

If you find that you must make exams that are auto-gradable, you should invest some time looking at methods for writing good multiple choice exam questions. It is possible to make challenging multiple choice problems, but it takes time and creativity. You want to ensure that the students don't have any shortcut to the correct answer, which means that you have good distractor answers, and answers that can only be dismissed when the actual solution has been found. If you search the Internet for *creating good multiple choice problems*, you will find a multitude of good advice to peruse.

KEEPING TRACK OF GRADES

As discussed in Chapter 5, you should have a computerized gradebook in some form or another. This can be as simple as a spreadsheet with your student names and grades, or it can be a standalone gradebook software package or part of your school's learning management system (LMS). If you have online grading software, it should be able to export to CSV format for easy import into your gradebook software.

The students should have access to their grades as the term progresses, and if you can keep your gradebook in a form that is online so students can check their scores and report any errors or concerns to you, that will save some time at the end of the term. Try not to wait until the very end of the term to start collating the grades, as you will want to spend some time making sure that you've calculated them correctly. In my first semester teaching college CS, I miscalculated all the student grades for one course, and I had to re-submit them on paper (which was painful) after I realized my mistake. Had I triple-checked the grades before I submitted, or had I started preparing the grades earlier, I possibly would have caught my mistake and saved a good deal of time.

Your syllabus should have listed the grade breakdown for the assignments in your course, and if so it should be straightforward to put the calculations into your gradebook software. You may still need to do some finer-grain calculations depending on your assignment breakdown (e.g., if you say that 50% of the grade will be assignments, you still need to put in the individual calculations for each assignment). If possible, have someone else (e.g., a TA) check your calculations to ensure that you haven't missed anything, and also spot check a few of the scores to ensure that you haven't made any mistakes.

SUBMITTING GRADES AT THE END OF THE TERM

If your school has a traditional, U.S. grading system, you will have to provide letter grades for your students, which will involve turning numbers into letters. You also need to decide where the grade differentiation points are (e.g., the number grade that differentiates the A grades from the A-minus grades, and so forth). Depending on where you teach, there may be a standard grade distribution, and you should ask your colleagues what they do. You have some choice in setting grades – you can either give students fixed grades depending on a set standard, or you can fix the grade distribution based on what you want the grade distribution to be. An example of the former case would be if everyone who got above a certain percentile average got a particular grade, no matter how many students achieved it. If everyone got above a 93% (for instance), then they would get an A, and you could have the entire class get As if that is what happened. In the latter case, you look at the grade percentages, and choose the division points for each particular letter (A, A-, B+, etc.). If you only want roughly fifteen percent of the class to get As, then you fix the division at around the 85th percentile, no matter what the average is. If your school publishes the grade breakdowns for classes, you may want to strongly consider matching the average breakdown, at least the first time you teach the course. Otherwise, you may find that students complain, and that is not a particularly fun conversation. However, as long as you can justify your grading scheme, you are within your rights to assign the grades as you see fit.

Both methods to determine the grade divisions have their proponents. Some instructors have a standard, and anyone who achieves the standard can get the highest grade. The instructors consider this a fair way to judge student performance. Other instructors always want similar percentages for each particular grade. They argue that because assignments vary in difficulty from term to term, this more fairly assesses one class relative to another class. You will have to decide which method you prefer, and you should tell your students how you will calculate the grades, either in the syllabus, or near the end of the term.

You do not, however, have to be completely transparent with the grade calculation, although this is certainly your decision. One of the reasons to keep that calculation somewhat hidden is simply to avoid students who try to argue that they should get a point back here or there on various assignments, simply to break through to the next higher grade. That is not a conversation you want to have with students – you should be clear that you are fair and have done the calculations properly, and they have to trust you. One response that I use when a student thinks that they deserve a higher grade for the course is to send them their rank in the course relative to the other students. A student who sees that they are in the 50th percentile for the class is not likely to continue to demand an *A* for the course.

How you submit the grades to your school is dependent on the system they use. Ideally, you should be able to upload a file with the names (or IDs) and the grades, although even these days you may have to manually enter the grades. If you can submit them via a list, spot check at least a dozen or so grades to ensure that everything is correct. If you have to manually enter the grades, you should double-check them before pressing the *submit* button. Even better is to have someone help you enter the grades so you can both double-check them. If for some reason the grades aren't correct, you will likely hear from the student or students involved, and all schools have the ability to change grades if necessary.

Make sure you get your grades in on-time. That said, I have never been at a school where there was a penalty for being a bit late. But, it is better for everyone if you submit the grades on time. If you have seniors who are going to graduate, you may have an earlier deadline for their grades, and you should ask your department about this before the end of the term. If you have students who you suspect have cheated in your class, you may want to either hold back their grades, or give them an incomplete, depending on your school's policy. Again, ask your department and colleagues how you should handle these cases. See below for more information about how to handle cheating cases.

WHAT TO DO IF...

What if a student asks about or complains about a grade, or asks for a regrade?

Students are justifiably concerned about their grades, and in your career you will get many students who are disappointed in their grade, and/or who think they deserve a better grade. You should clearly lay out your policy on asking for regrades for each assignment. For exams, I often give students a week to look over their test and ask for a regrade, but I am clear that their grade could go up *or* down, depending on the regrade. Most students who ask for a regrade have a legitimate reason for asking, though they don't always get what they want. A few students try to get regraded on many assignments, in the *hope* that they can get more points, and these students are the ones that you need a policy for. I always tell my students that both the TAs and I make grading mistakes, and if they genuinely feel that they were graded incorrectly, they can ask for a regrade. Some grading software allows students to automatically request regrades, but you should be careful with that because it can make it easy for students who don't have a legitimate concern to simply press a button to start the process. I force my students to write out exactly what they want the regrade for, and I also make them run a test suite (for coding problems) before they make the request. I use a computer-based exam (called *Bluebook*, that Chris Piech wrote, and that we have written about at SIGCSE), and it allows students to get their code in digital form so that running the tests is straightforward. With these policies in effect, it is rare for students who don't have a good reason to ask for a regrade to actually request one.

If a student has a realistic question about a regrade (and they aren't simply trying to win back points for the sake of it), then you should listen to them and make an honest assessment about their grade. If you have many students, you can delegate this to a TA or a set of TAs, and students should only raise the issue to your level if they feel that the TA has not been fair.

Again, setting a good policy about regrades and asking about grades is the key to minimizing the number of illegitimate requests.

What if you make a mistake when grading?

Grading mistakes happen frequently (though hopefully not *too* frequently), and you should fix the mistakes when students bring them to your attention. If the mistake affects many students, fix it as soon as possible and let them know that you have fixed it. Students appreciate honesty in this regard, and they won't hold grading mistakes against you if you fix them. As discussed in the previous question, you can let students ask for regrades, or ask about their grade, and you will find the mistakes quickly enough.

What if your TAs don't grade by the deadline you set, or do not grade effectively?

Managing TAs can be quite challenging, and they don't always meet your grading deadlines. If it happens infrequently, you can ask them to do better next time, but unless it is critical (e.g., at the end of the term), giving them a break once in a while isn't terrible. If it becomes frequent, you do need to have a talk with the TA, and if necessary, take steps to relive them of their duties if they can't work to your standard. Before you do this, talk with your department chair or a colleague about the procedures, and make sure you follow any human resources guidelines. TAs are busy, and most want to do the best they can. Some do not want to put in the necessary effort, and you may need to fire TAs in that situation.

If a TA isn't grading effectively or correctly, this is more serious. You should try and re-train them, and you should ensure that either they or someone else re-grades the work in question. Again, if it becomes serious, you should take steps to remove them from the position, and you want to do it with the backing of your department with the proper human resources procedures.

What if all of your students do poorly on an assignment?

You will, at some point, give an assignment that many or most of your students won't do well on. If the motivated, well-prepared students don't do well on the assignment, then you should think about either removing the assignment from everyone's grades, and/or you should give them a replacement assignment. Your responsibility is to the students who study hard and are motivated, and it is primarily your fault if that contingent doesn't do well on your assignments.[5] Either the assignment was too difficult, or the students were under prepared, and this is not their fault if they are putting in the work required. You owe it to them to do better, and therefore you should make it right by them. Be honest with them, and make a good decision on how to proceed based on making the situation right.

What if all of your students do perfectly on an assignment?

There is usually nothing wrong with this situation, except that you may not have made the assignment challenging enough. When you re-teach the course, you can evaluate the assignment again and make it more challenging. If the assignment grades are going to adversely affect your grade distribution, you can consider making future assignments a bit more difficult, but be careful, as it is not easy to re-calibrate on the fly. Often, if I find that my midterm exam for a class is too easy or too difficult, I will try to adjust the final exam to compensate, although again, this is not an exact science. It is better for your students to consistently do better on the assignments then worse on them, but if you know your students well (see Chapter 3), you will be able to tell if your assignments are too easy or too hard based on the students who demonstrate that they are hardworking and prepared.

---

5 If this happens, don't be too hard on yourself, especially in your first year! I have given out assignments that were too difficult more than once, and you will be hard pressed to find an instructor who has never done this.

What if a student cheats on an assignment?

Cheating, (called, at some schools, *violating the honor code*), is a serious issue. As discussed briefly in Chapter 5, there are tools that can help determine whether or not a student has cheated on programming or other assignments. You may also find out about cheating from TAs, or from other students. In all cases, you should investigate the accusations to the best of your ability, even though it can be a time-consuming and tedious endeavor.

Before you accuse any student of cheating, be absolutely sure that you understand your school and your department's policies on cheating, and do your best to follow any procedures to the letter. Some students will do everything in their power to fight the accusation, even if they are completely guilty. They may claim that they had family problems, or mental problems, and they may try to justify their behavior in other similar ways. They may, even in the face of certain evidence, deny the accusations to the end, and they may even accuse you of trying to ruin their lives. In all of this you should remain professional and you should avoid getting into any kind of heated discussion with them about the accusation. If you feel pressured by the student, or unfairly accused yourself, talk to your department chair and address your own concerns.

You want to do your absolute best to avoid accusing innocent students of cheating. If you are unsure and decide to investigate, be very clear with the students that you will do a thorough investigation and you won't make an accusation unless you have no doubt about the case. Students who are unfairly accused of cheating endure a stressful time, and if they are indeed innocent, it can feel like a terrible slight to even be accused. I have been accused of cheating before when I was innocent, and I can tell you that it is a difficult time.[6] I have let many cases go after I have investigated

---

6 This was in my first semester of graduate school, when I was asked to practice writing a Ph.D. proposal for an "Introduction to graduate school" course everyone had to take. I had already been working with my advisor on a big project, and when I wrote it up, the instructor for the course said that he didn't

them because there was still some doubt in my mind, and I could not prove the case. I have also had cases where I knew the student in question was guilty but I didn't follow the proper procedures, and the student got away with it. However, I have also had (too) many cases where I was able to prove that the student violated the honor code, and the student either admitted it and took the punishment, or they went to a judicial hearing where they were found guilty by a committee.

When you first decide to pursue a cheating case, you should let the student or students involved know about your concern. You don't have to do this immediately, but if you need to withhold a grade (i.e., at the end of the term), you should tell the students what is going on. I usually send an email to my students that describes the situation, with as much information as I can tell them. The following is an example of an email I have sent in the past:

> Dear <redacted>,
>
> As I discussed in class during the first week of the quarter, we routinely run tests on student submissions to determine if the school Honor Code is being up-held. There was an anomaly with one or more of your assignments, and I have forwarded the results of our tests to the Office of Community Standards (OCS) for their review. You should be hearing from that office in the near future, but in the meantime, we must with-hold your final grade for the course until that gets straightened out.
>
> Unfortunately, I cannot comment on the tests or as-signments, and I would suggest emailing or calling

---

believe I had written the document (and he also accused a number of others of the same offense, some of whom he was correct about). I had to clear things up through my advisor, and the matter was dropped. When it was still ongoing, I was nervous and concerned, and it was not a fun time.

the OCS if you have questions pertaining to the situation. I can assure you that OCS does a thorough investigation, and you will have full access to the evidence presented against you. Should you be found innocent of the charges, your grade will be unaffected and I will consider the matter closed.

Once you officially accuse a student of cheating, you should avoid discussing the situation with them until you are finished with your investigation, or whatever school body you have turned the case over to has completed their duties. In most cases, students will want to talk to you, and often they will send an email admitting their guilt. I generally respond to those emails with a brief response that thanks them for reaching out, but it is out of my hands until the school office (in our case, OCS) makes a decision. I also reiterate that I will not discuss it further with them.

If you are expected to handle cheating cases on your own at your school, talk to your colleagues or department chair about how they have handled similar situations. You do not want to tackle the situation completely alone if you can help it, and the more support you have, the better.

Once a decision has been made on a cheating case, you should accept it, whether you agree with it or not (of course, if you are making the decision, you will probably agree with it). If the student was found guilty, you should follow any policy your school might have to penalize the student – this could be a grade deduction (I frequently give students a zero on the assignment, and then re-calculate the grade, giving no higher than one letter grade below their original grade with the assignment intact), or it could be failing the course. There could also be school penalties, such as suspension, that you do not impose directly. If your school does not have a particular policy, or if you are able to decide on the penalty, you should talk with others in your department about how they penalize students.

If you do accuse a student of cheating and they are found guilty, you should not be surprised if they are cold towards you in the future. However, I have had a number of students repent for their mistakes, and we have been on cordial terms since. Sometimes students who are caught cheating turn over a new leaf, and it is nice to see this when it happens.

FINAL THOUGHTS

I would be surprised if grading is *any* teacher's favorite part of the job, but it is necessary, and it is worthwhile. Grading can be frustrating at times, and it can be time consuming, but with good planning and enough resources, you can make it bearable and you can make the most of it. As with most other parts of teaching, talking to others about their best practices can help inform your own grading strategies. Even though grading may seem like a chore now, rest assured that you will improve your grading efficiency and make your grading better as you progress through your teaching career.

10

ONLINE RESOURCES

IT SHOULD COME AS NO SURPRISE that there are an almost limitless number of resources on the Internet that can inform your teaching and your course material. Computer Science instructors are a creative group, and are also, by the nature of their career and skills, well suited to creating online resources, demonstrations, and other teaching tools. Many instructors (and other developers in general) publish their work freely, making it available to everyone. If you teach CS1 or CS2, you will find a tremendous number of informative explanations, tutorials, visualizations, and demonstrations to augment your curriculum. If you teach more advanced material, it may be more difficult to find resources that are specific to your course, but you also might be surprised at what you can find, and doing a search may turn up something useful. Of course, if you do create material yourself, consider posting it online for others to use and to benefit from, as well.

This chapter is potentially going to become stale somewhat quickly – new resources appear regularly, and older resources sometimes disappear. Some disappearances are simply because the author decided to stop hosting the resources, or because there are other, better resources available. Furthermore, some web browsers stop supporting the technology underlying the resources; Java Applets and Flash are two examples of technologies that once flourished but have now been deprecated. Authors who wrote tools using those technologies are not always going to rewrite them in newer technologies, and therefore they will disappear.

The best and most obvious resource for finding online CS resources is to perform a good search using your search engine of choice. For example, performing a Google search for "algorithm

animations" produces a substantial number of links for outstanding animations:

https://www.google.com/search?q=algorithm+animations

When you are searching for online materials, make sure you
understand the nuances of the search engine you are using. For
example, many search engines allow you to include or exclude
certain search terms, and all have comprehensive operators that
you can use to refine your search. Here is a link to Google's page
on how to refine your search:

https://support.google.com/websearch/answer/2466433

Some of the resources will be interactive, some will be static,
and some will be videos. You will also find slideshows, lecture
notes, exams, study tips, etc. You will also find resources that only
work on a particular platform or operating system (e.g., Microsoft
Windows only, or iPhone/Android). When you do find resources
that you want to share directly with your students, the best way
to share them is via the link you find. If you decide to copy and
share the resources, make sure that you cite the author and put a
link, as well.

As with all online usage during lecture – make sure that you
test the resource out, and have a backup plan if for some reason
the resource does not work in real time. If you can download the
resource for offline use, that is ideal, though this is not always
possible.

The rest of this chapter is a list of resources, with some comments regarding each resource. As mentioned above, the list is
fragile in that the resources are external links and may not be
up to date. It is also certainly not a comprehensive list – treat
the following as an example of *some* of the resources you can
find online, and you will certainly find more as you do your
own searching. This list will be kept as up to date as possible
at https://yourfirstyearteaching.com/cs.

COMPUTER SCIENCE TEACHING RESOURCES

csteachingtips

Colleen Lewis, formerly at Harvey Mudd College and now at the University of Illinois, Urbana Champaign, runs *csteachingtips*, a comprehensive, curated repository of CS teaching resources, sponsored by the National Science Foundation. The site has tip sheets for a number of topics, and it hosts hundreds of teaching tips that cover general teaching practices, specific programming language suggestions, suggestions for reducing bias, lab rules, assessment, and a multitude of other useful tips for anyone teaching computer science.

cseducators.stackexchange.com

cseducators.stackexchange.com is a relatively new site for CS educators that is part of the StackExchange network. As with the other StackExchange sites, it is a question/answer forum that has a focus on teaching computer science.

https://sigcse.org/sigcse/membership/mailing-lists.html
Archive

The *Special Interest Group on Computer Science Education* (SIGCSE) hosts a vibrant mailing list for SIGCSE members, and it is well worth becoming an *Association for Computing Machinery* (ACM) member in order to be able to receive list emails and to post to the list. Topics include pedagogical discussions, job openings, conference announcements, and other important information that you will want to keep abreast of in your CS teaching career.

GENERAL PROGRAMMING AND COMPUTER SCIENCE RESOURCES

There are an uncountable number of general programming and computer science resources online. As mentioned above, a general search for any particular topic is bound to bring up links that may prove useful to your teaching. My favorites are listed below.

Wikipedia

It is hard to overemphasize how important Wikipedia is to the world today, and within the scope of Computer Science, it is a phenomenal resource. It is outstanding for technical details, and it is also a great place to find historical context for your course material. As it is sourced by collaboration, and anyone can contribute, you do have to be slightly careful when using Wikipedia as a source. I have found (and fixed) a number of Wikipedia articles that had incorrect information (e.g., I have fixed programming mistakes and inconsistencies, and algorithm errors), but the technical details are almost always correct, and they are surprisingly thorough. I have used Wikipedia to prepare for lectures in CS1, CS2, systems, architecture, discrete math, and computer history classes, and I invariably come away from reading a Wikipedia article with more knowledge than before I started.

StackOverflow

StackOverflow is a gold mine for programming help, and a good search on the site will often reveal interesting discussions about topics such as algorithmic efficiency, programming language nuances, and good programming practices. Your students will invariably stumble upon StackOverflow at some point when they are looking for programming answers, and it is a good idea to discuss the best way for them to learn from the site. StackOverflow is not necessarily geared towards novice programmers, and you should make sure that your students know that if they do end up finding answers on the site, they may either be too advanced or the answer may not quite fit for their question. Also, you should caution them against looking for code snippets to use, as you likely want them to write their own solutions for their coding problems. As an instructor, I use StackOverflow more often when writing the various tools for my classroom, than I do for actually teaching. However, I often post links to excellent StackOverflow answers to more advanced questions from students on our course forum.

YouTube

YouTube and other video aggregation sites provide a wealth of computer science information. There are numerous videos demonstrating programming and theoretical concepts, and they can be useful in your lectures as well as extra resources you can provide to your students. There are also many humorous videos that are also instructive, and I have used many as a fun post-instruction few minutes (e.g., search on YouTube for *dance sorting algorithms* and you will find dozens of cute sorts that are illustrated with dance. Another of my favorite search-related videos is 15 Sorting Algorithms in 6 minutes, which provides a unique audio and visual representation of common sorting algorithms). Additionally, there are hundreds of computer science courses that have entire quarters or semesters worth of lectures available. If you are planning a concept and want to see how someone else teaches it, you can often find a video example, especially for CS1 or CS2 material.

YouTube is also a wonderful place to find videos about computer science history. YouTube channels such as Computerphile are full of interesting historical (and current) information that you and your students might enjoy.

Quora Computer Science

Quora is a less technical computer science question and answer community than StackOverflow, and answers are often opinions about various computer science topics rather than specific information. However, it is sometimes a better place to get information that would not be appropriate for StackOverflow, such as *What are the main differences between artificial intelligence and machine learning?* As with Wikipedia and StackOverflow, anyone can contribute to answers on Quora, but answers are voted on by readers, so there is a modicum of accountability.

CODE PLAYGROUNDS AND ONLINE COMPILERS

There are a multitude of online code playgrounds which can be useful to demonstrate programming in an easily shareable way. Code playgrounds allow both you and your students to modify code and see the results immediately. The downsides to code play-grounds are that they may not include some of the libraries you want to demonstrate, and they generally do not support graphics easily. You are also limited to a relatively short amount of code, in general. There is a collated list that is kept up to date on Wikipedia:

https://en.wikipedia.org/wiki/Comparison_of_online
_source_code_playgrounds

CS1 AND CS2 RESOURCES

The most resources by far that are available online are for CS1 and CS2 courses. As the main introductory material for computer science curricula, CS1 and CS2 are taken by the most students worldwide, and there are more teachers for these classes than for any particular sub-discipline in computer science. The following list is just a taste of the type of resources available online, but I have used each of the following websites many times in teaching both CS1 and CS2 courses over the years.

https://www.toptal.com/developers/sorting-algorithms

This sorting animation is one of my favorites, as it allows you to visually compare a number of common sorting algorithms with different types of data (random, nearly sorted, reversed, and few unique). My only quibble is that I would like to be able to slow down the animations to be able to more easily concentrate on what is happening in each sort.

https://visualgo.net/en

This is a robust set of data structure visualizations with a number of tree, graph, and hash table visualizations I have not seen elsewhere. The examples include code, descriptions, and excellent instructions, and the animations can be run one step at a time, or in a range of speeds.

https://www.cs.usfca.edu/~galles/visualization/ This site includes dozens of data structure visualizations, and it was the website where I first learned about fantastic online resources for

CS2. If this site disappeared, my lectures on heaps and AVL trees would be worse-off.

http://pythontutor.com

If you are teaching a course using Python, this is a site you must bookmark. It combines live-coding with an interactive debugger and presents data connections graphically. The debugger allows both forwards and backwards step-by-step code execution, which can significantly help students understand what the code is doing. It is a terrific tool to use in lecture, and it is also great for one-on-one help and for students to use in lab or individually. The website also has versions that support C, C++, Java, Javascript, and Ruby.

https://codestepbystep.com

https://codingbat.com/java

CodeStepByStep (Java) and CodingBat (Java and Python) are two sites that allow students to practice code problems, with feedback. Students are presented with a coding exercise and then multiple tests are run on their code solutions. The students get a report on what tests failed. Both sites are terrific for students to practice for both exams and for coding interviews.

https://www.hackerearth.com/practice/algorithms

This site provides both tutorials and code for a number of CS2 topics, and it also includes a nice section on dynamic programming.

http://rosettacode.org/wiki/Rosetta_Code

RosettaCode is a site with close to a thousand code solutions to different tasks, written in many languages (sometimes more than one hundred different languages). It is worth looking at if you want to see different solutions to particular problems (e.g., the *knapsack* problem), and how they can be coded in different languages.

https://llimllib.github.io/bloomfilter-tutorial/

https://people.ok.ubc.ca/ylucet/DS/SkipList.html

I included these two websites to show that there are also more advanced data structure visualizations online – you may be surprised at how often a search turns up a cool visualization that you want to show students.

SYSTEMS (CS3) RESOURCES

Often the course in CS curricula after the introductory sequence is a systems course that delves deeper under the hood than in prior courses, and often includes low-level C and assembly language programming. This is sometimes the first introduction students have to a Unix or Linux terminal, and they are often faced with needing to use a text-based debugger. There are many resources available online that can help. There are also resources built into the terminal (e.g., *man pages*).

Listed below are a few resources.

https://godbolt.org (Compiler Explorer)

If your class has assembly language (x86, ARM, MIPS, among others), this is a phenomenal resource that shows how a number of languages (including C, C++, D, Go, Haskell, Rust, and others) will be compiled into assembly language for a given compiler. You can choose from dozens of compilers with various versions, and you can set all compiler options (e.g., -Og for debugger-friendly output). It also includes many libraries (e.g., Boost).

https://www.h-schmidt.net/FloatConverter/IEEE754.html

https://babbage.cs.qc.cuny.edu/IEEE-754.old/Decimal.html

http://stanford.edu/~cgregg/107-Reader/float/convert.html

If you cover IEEE floating point, there are a number of converters that perform the conversion. I have also included a link to a simple binary-to-decimal and decimal-to-binary converter I wrote that helps students with the process of manually performing the IEEE conversion.

https://www.onlinegdb.com

This resource provides a web-based gdb instance, which is helpful for showing during class. It incorporates a visual representation of where in the code the program is during debugging, as well, which is often easier than relying on gdb's list function or the (sometimes buggy) tui functionality in gdb.

TECHNICAL INTERVIEW RESOURCES

Your students will invariably ask you for advice on how to do well on technical interviews. See Chapter 14 for ideas about having this conversation. In terms of online resources, a simple search will bring up a multitude of web pages, some helpful, some less helpful. For example, the following GitHub page is often cited as a top-notch resource:

https://github.com/yangshun/tech-interview-handbook

Unless you want curate your own list of excellent resources, you should suggest to your students to focus on the sites that are most likely to provide them with the types of questions they will get in their interviews. This means that it is wise for them to ask their contact where they are applying about what kinds of questions they should prepare for, and *then* do a search for resources.

PUBLISHING YOUR OWN RESOURCES

As mentioned a number of times, when you create resources that you use for your classes, consider posting them online for others to benefit from using. Not only will you be helping other instructors and students, but you may also end up helping people who are learning the material on their own, and this is particularly important for students in developing countries that do not necessarily have brick-and-mortar schools to attend, and who get all of their resources online.

When you publish your cool new resource, you should try and make it easy to use, and you should include as much documentation as you think is necessary for someone to start using the resource. Some resources don't need any documentation, but just make sure that it is clear what the purpose of the resource is, and how it works. You may also want to put contact information in case a user finds a bug, or has a question about the resource. It should have an informative title so search engines that find the page will have a decent chance of funneling people to it.

Where you publish your online resource is not particularly important, as long as it is in a location that will be scraped by search engines. If you put the resource on your school-based website, beware that you will need to move it if you change schools.

When you publish your resources online, be prepared to do some upkeep, if people send you bug reports. You may or may not want to take suggestions on improving the resource, and that is up to you and how much time you have. If your resource does become popular, support could take a considerable amount of time.

Also consider open-sourcing your resources as well as posting them. This is as easy as having a GitHub repository for the source, available on the web page of your source (near your contact information, for instance). Again, you will have to decide if you are going to respond to suggestions, or pull requests, and this is up to you, bearing in mind that you only have so much time to work on the resource. You should also consider attaching a license to your work, so you can control how the work can be re-used or re-purposed.

There are some online resources that are supported by advertisements, and you may consider doing this for yours. If you do, then be sure that you own the resource (you may not own it if you created it while working at a school, and the school may own it), and be sure that you are allowed to host ads on your website (you may not be allowed to do so for a school website).

WHAT TO DO IF...

What if I can't find an online resource for a particular topic I am teaching?

Well, there may not be such a resource. Make sure you are performing a good search on the engine, and feel free to ask others (e.g., on cseducators.stackexchange.com or through the SIGCSE mailing list) if they know of any resources that fit your needs. Eventually, you may decide that you want to create the resource yourself, or you can also encourage an enterprising student to create the resource. Students are often looking for interesting projects to work on for classes or on their own, and they may appreciate your suggestion of a cool tool to work on that you will use in your course.

What if the resource I have been using disappears from the Internet?

This does happen, and sometimes it is disappointing. If have a resource that you love and want to continue using in case it does disappear, you can try to download the source for it, whether it is a web site or on a repository. Keep in mind that you won't be able to access any backend server scripts, in general. Otherwise, you can fall back on asking whether others know of similar resources, as mentioned above.

What if someone re-publishes a resource I put online?

If you have open sourced your work, and the license allows others to use the material as they see fit, then you should be happy that your resource is getting more traction. If you do have an issue with where it is being hosted, or how it is being hosted, then you should contact the person hosting it, if possible, and start a dialog about your concerns.

What if I find a great resource that isn't listed here?

Please let me know! You can submit resources to https://yourfirstyearteaching.com/cs, and there will be a curated list on the site.

FINAL THOUGHTS

Online resources can be an outstanding way to supplement your teaching, and resources that have a strong visual component can help many students understand the material easier than seeing code, or listening to you explain it in words. There are thousands of websites dedicated to helping teach and understand computer science, and you should consider looking into the resources as your plan your courses.

Part III

IMPROVING YOUR CRAFT

11

OBSERVING OTHERS TEACH, AND REFLECTING ON YOUR OWN TEACHING

YOU SHOULD CONTINUOUSLY STRIVE to improve your teaching. Teaching well is not something that you simply learn once and then apply unchanged for the rest of your career. You want to grow in as many ways as you can, to improve both your delivery during lectures, your support of students in office hours, your assignment and exam writing, and all of the other things that Part II of this book has covered. No one is the same teacher in the beginning of their career as they are in the end of their career, and with an open mind about what you want to improve, you will steadily become a better teacher the more you practice it. This part of the book covers strategies for improving your craft, and learning how to inspect your own teaching to become better at it. You will make teaching mistakes that you won't want to repeat again, and you should recognize when this happens, and you should take steps to change. You will also grow in your own teaching by observing how other instructors teach (that is the focus of this chapter), and by accepting constructive feedback from others–most importantly, from your students (covered in Chapter 12). You will want to keep abreast of research related to teaching, and in particular, teaching computer science (covered in Chapter 13). You may also want to perform education research yourself, and contribute to conferences and journals (also in Chapter 13). Hopefully, you will have an outstanding first year of teaching, but you can absolutely improve, and being conscientious about how to do that is the key to being a better teacher next year than you are this year.

OBSERVING OTHERS TEACH

In the United States, teaching a course is predominately performed by a single teacher who is responsible for all aspects of the class. Co-teaching does happen (and I strongly encourage you to co-teach if you have the opportunity!), but most often you will be the sole teacher for your course. In this sense, teaching can sometimes be lonely – only your students are watching you and (hopefully) providing feedback, and you don't regularly see others teach, nor do you regularly have other instructors watch you teach. However, you presumably work at a school where others *do* teach, and you should prioritize observing your colleagues as often as you can. By observing others teach, and by concentrating on the teaching itself (and not the curriculum), you will start to get ideas about what works in a classroom or lecture, and also what may not work. Indeed, don't simply observe teachers that you know to be amazing – you can learn plenty from observing teachers that may need to improve their own teaching.[1] Do not limit your observations to just those teaching computer science. You may be in a school where you are the only CS instructor, or one of only a few, and seeing how other classes and instructors operate can be just as worthwhile as watching a CS course. You will often learn the most from observing a course that is similar to your own course (both in the topic and in the size of the class), but it isn't necessary.

Your job when observing another class is to concentrate on the teaching, not the content. That is not to say that you shouldn't pay attention to a nice way to teach a topic that you might also teach at some point, but that is a secondary concern. In addition to focusing on the instructor, you should also observe what students are doing – are they paying attention? Are they taking notes? Are they distracted by an electronic device, or a neighbor? If you get

---

1 But don't go observe a teacher simply because you may hear that they struggle, of course. If you happen to observe a teacher that has a less-than perfect class, then take what you can from it. Also, if the instructor asks you for feedback, be honest but gentle and constructive.

the chance either before or after the class to introduce yourself to some students, you can ask them what they think of the course and get their general impressions.

Before you observe a class, ask the instructor if they would mind if you observe, and ask if they have a particular class they would like you to see. Some instructors are happy for you to visit their class whenever you'd like, and others do not like observers – if you get the impression that the instructor does not want you there, then find someone else to observe.

When you observe a class, arrive early, and find a spot near the back of the class (or, if it is a small class, ask the instructor where they would like you to sit). You want to be able to observe the students as well as the instructor. Avoid anything more than a quick hello to the instructor, as the few minutes before class are often not the time for chit-chat, especially with you. Observe anything that the instructor does before class – are they setting up? Are they talking with students? It is helpful to have either a computer or a pad and paper to write down your observational notes.

One way to organize your notes is to keep a running tab of what is happening during class. When I was getting my Master's degree in education, my advisor, Eric Toshalis, observed me student-teaching a number of times, and he introduced me to a note-taking strategy that works great, and is shown in Table 5. As the class progresses, jot down the time on the left, and then your observations and any notes you might have. Keeping these kinds of notes can help you recall what you thought was important in the class, and any questions you might have for the instructor.

During your observation, write down anything that you think is unique, or that you think is interesting about the way the instructor teaches. For example, in Table 5, note the comment on the amount of time given to the students to think through the problem. Highlight anything that you would like to include in your own teaching, and also highlight the things that didn't work

Table 5: Example Note Sheet for Observations

Time	Observation (e.g., what is happening in class?)	Notes
10:30am	Class begins, instructor welcomes students and introduces topic.	Room looks about half full. Students are still trickling in. PowerPoint slideshow on screen.
10:31am	Instructor reminds students about the homework assignment. Student has a question about the due date, which has been changed.	Ask instructor why the due date was changed.
10:33am	Instructor briefly reviews last week's material (binary search trees), and stresses the importance of the topic for the midterm.	No questions from students, and they are paying attention. Some still arriving.
10:37am	New material starts (hash tables). Instructor relates it to the previous material with an example of how today's material is going to be a more efficient solution.	Comment from student that the slides don't seem to be online. Instructor pauses to ask the the TA to post them.
10:40am	Instructor describes the purpose of a hash, and shows a simple example. The instructor then polls the class using an online response system what the hash value would be for a particular string.	
10:43am	Instructor lets students think of the answer and discuss with their neighbors for a few minutes. Then she posts the results of the poll.	Virtually all students got the correct answer, and it looks like almost everyone participated in the poll. I originally thought she gave too much time, but it looks like it worked well.
...	...	...
11:15am	Instructor starts live-coding example of creating a hash table. She uses onlinegdb.com for the demo.	Some students seem distracted, though many are following along. (Go look up onlinegdb).
11:20am	Class ends; instructor doesn't quite get to finish the example, but says that she will post it on the course forum and that they will start with the example in the next class.	
11:21am	About five students approach the front to ask questions, and the TA also is getting questions.	

that well (e.g., the fact that students are distracted near the end of class is something to consider).

After the class is over, you should thank the instructor, and you should consider asking the instructor if you could go over your notes some time with them.[2] You can ask any questions you have (e.g., *Why did the assignment due date get changed?*), and you can discuss what you liked about the lecture. You should not focus on feedback (unless the instructor asks), but rather you should discuss some of the things you thought were excellent in the class (e.g., *How do you determine how much time to give the students for clicker questions?*), with the intent of possibly using some of the methods yourself.

Right as the class ends, you can also ask any students nearby what they thought of the lecture, particularly if you introduced yourself to them earlier. Getting the students' perspective can be helpful to compare against you own observations.

Once you have observed the class and after you have debriefed with the instructor, you should take some time to reflect on where in your own classes you might want to use some of the techniques you observed. You should also reflect on anything that you didn't think went well, and think about whether you can limit those elements from your own teaching.

In your first year of teaching, you will not have too much time to observe others teach, but do try to observe at least a few teachers over the course of the term. I have been at schools that have given new teachers reduced duties (e.g., committee assignments) to give them more time to observe, and you should ask your department chair if that may be a possibility for you. The more teachers you observe, the more techniques you will see in action, and you will invariably gain useful insights that will improve your own instruction.

---

2 Inviting them for a coffee (on you) is always a nice gesture.

REFLECTING ON YOUR OWN TEACHING

Improving your own teaching is a personal endeavor, and can be both challenging and rewarding. In many ways improvement is like training to become a better athlete: it takes dedication, time, and it can be tiring, but you will see rewards along the way. You should try to reflect on your teaching as often as you can, with the understanding that you only have a certain amount of time to dedicate to improvement, especially during your first year.

Before each class

Before you teach each class, think of one key thing (or possibly two) you want to do well. Maybe you want to facilitate a detailed class demonstration of a certain sorting technique, or maybe you want to introduce a proof by asking students key ideas that will lead them towards the solution. Jot down a couple of outcomes that will indicate a success (e.g., *lots of students participated, and we ended up with the correct proof*), and an outcome that indicates that you still to work on the technique (e.g., *students were confused about what I was asking and I had to give answers a number of times*). As you prepare for that part of the lesson, consider what you will do in the case that things veer off-track, and how you might recover. While you want to plan out these sorts of contingencies in general, make sure that you have thought thoroughly through the one topic you have decided to focus on, in particular.

If you have taught the class before, you may have notes that you took after the class, and you should review those notes and make any necessary changes or additions. If you have a recording of the previous time, watch any parts that you recall may have been a bit less than perfect.

After each class

For the topic or topics that you wanted to focus on, go back and look at the potential outcomes you wrote down, and see how you did. If you achieved the successful outcome, congratulations! If you ended up with the unsuccessful outcome (or somewhere in between), write down a few words about what else you think may have been going on at the time – were the students ill-prepared for the topic? Did you get to the topic late in class when students may have had less attention? Were your recovery techniques successful? What do you think the students learned, and is it worth repeating during the next class, or via another means? Should you instruct your TAs to discuss the topic in recitation section? You should write down anything that you can think of with regard to the main issue you were focusing on, and do a deep dive into how it turned out.

You should also take some quick notes on anything else you thought worked or didn't work during the lecture. If there were any typos in your materials, fix them immediately, and if you realize that you misspoke, correct this as soon as possible with your students. You don't have to have elaborate notes, but you should have something that indicates what worked and didn't work. Keep that list of items with your materials so you will find them when you teach the course again, and you can see what you have to focus on to improve.

You should consider asking some of the students in your class about their impressions of the class (see Chapter 12, which discusses getting feedback from your students). If you had any other visitors to the class, elicit feedback from them, as well.

Do your own post-class reflections as soon after the class as is possible, preferably directly after class, when your memory is fresh. Taking even five or ten minutes of time will be worth the effort long-term.

After each assessment

Once you have finished an assessment, whether it is an assignment, exam, project, etc., you should reflect on how the assignment went. Again, getting feedback from your students is a good idea, as is getting feedback from your TAs. Think about how you could improve the assessment the next time, including whether you need to re-tool the assignment, or if you need to spend more time crafting questions (e.g., for an exam). For exams specifically, jot down some notes on how well each problem worked – did the students struggle with anything in particular? Could the problem have been stated better? Should you focus more on a particular idea if you want to ask a similar question in the future? If a problem was great, highlight that, and try to include similar problems in future exams.

For assignments you may use in the future, keep a document with your notes on what worked and didn't work with the assignment, so you can adjust it in the future. As with your lectures, fix anything simple (typos, etc.) immediately. Otherwise, make sure your document has enough information to give you a good head start on making changes when you use the assignment again.

At the end of the term

When you finish a term, the first thing you should do is congratulate yourself on getting through it, especially during your first term. Teaching a class or multiple classes for a whole term is a challenge that is worth celebrating. The next thing you should do is reflect on the term holistically: how do you feel after teaching the course? Did you meet your goals for the course? Are your students able to do what you wanted them to be able to do, based on their final exam, project, etc.? Are there any big issues related to your teaching that you think need improvement? Write down your answers to these questions, and keep them with your course materials so that the next time you teach the course, you can see what you thought directly after teaching it before.

Most schools give students the option of providing course evaluations after they take a class, and you should read the evaluations carefully. Chapter 12 goes into detail about course evaluations, and they are an important post-course resource for reflecting on how the course turned out. They can also be a source of much consternation for an instructor, particularly if course evaluations are used for continued employment or promotions. For the purposes of reflecting on your teaching, take any constructive feedback that you have in your end of course evaluations and consider steps you might take to address the comments. If you see many of the same comment, e.g., *I would have liked more example problems to solve before exams*, then give those comments more weight in your reflection.

Before you teach a class for the second time

Teaching a class the term after you have taught it for the first time is a tremendous way to improve the course. At this point you have a great deal of information you can use to inform how to teach the course again, and it will certainly go smoother and you will be more efficient. You have already done the brunt of the work to prepare the materials, and you can concentrate on improving what you already have created.

If you have notes from the previous time you taught the class about what you think you should improve, review those notes and work on making the improvements. Try to do this with enough time before the term begins. If you try to make the improvements the night before you release an assignment, for instance, you may find that you don't have time to test the changes, and you don't have time to enlist review from your TAs, or otherwise.

When you teach a course the second time, your pre-lecture thoughts on what you should focus on will probably be different. Eventually, you will have a rock-solid lecture that you can rely on without much thought (though you should still review each lecture to see if it needs any updating), but the first few times through the course you should be able to find something each lecture that you want to focus on to improve.

Recording your lectures for reflection

If your lectures are not already recorded, you should consider recording some lectures during the term for your own review. Not only will you get to see your entire lesson, but you will be able to take your time and think about what worked and what potentially didn't work during the class. You won't have time to do this for every class, but every so often it is a good idea to see your own classes from the perspective of your students. When you watch a class recording, you can use the same note-taking strategy outlined for observing others teach, or you can simply jot down some notes as you watch. Pay attention to any verbal tics (e.g., saying *um* too often), and work on removing them. As discussed in Chapter 8, once you realize you have a verbal tic, it will be relatively easy to work on removing them.

If you have recordings of your lectures, you should also think about asking a colleague to sit down with you to review your lecture. You may be too focused on watching yourself teach (and it can be hard to sit through sometimes!) to observe your teaching enough so that you can determine what went right or what needs improvement. Many schools have teaching centers with staff members who would be willing to watch a recording to discuss how your teaching is going. They are also trained on what to look for in a lecture, and will give you very good feedback.

WHAT TO DO IF. . .

What if I am observing a class and there is a group activity? Should I participate?

Participating in a class you are observing is up to you, though remember that you are observing the teaching and don't need to be paying close attention to the material. I encourage all visitors to my own classes to participate as much as they would like. When I am observing other classes, I usually ask the instructor if they want me to participate in those types of activities. If the instructor has students talk to a neighbor, I will generally look around and if I see a student nearby who isn't talking to anyone, I will engage them. I would avoid otherwise disrupting the course, though—don't ask or answer questions as if you are a student, and primarily play the role of an observer and not a participant.

What if the instructor I am observing says something that is wrong?

As an observer, you should let the class play out as if you were not there. It may be difficult to watch an instructor make a mistake, but avoid correcting or challenging them in their class. Remember that instructors make mistakes all the time, and recovering from a mistake after the fact (e.g., in the next class) is perfectly fine. If you want to bring up the matter with the instructor after class, go ahead, but as with any other feedback, be gentle and constructive.

What if I can't find anyone to observe?

It would surprise me if you can't find *anyone* to let you observe their class, but if you do find yourself in that position, there are thousands of hours of videos on YouTube and other video streaming websites that you can watch. You may not be able to see the students, but you will still be able to observe the teaching. Make sure you are watching videos that are taped in front of a real class, and not videos that are made strictly for online viewing.

If you are not sure who would be a good instructor to observe, the easiest way to find out is to ask your students who *they* think the best teachers in the school or department are. They see teachers all the time, and they talk to each other, as well, and you can be guaranteed that the students know who the great teachers are.

What if I don't have time to reflect after each class?

The reality of the time crunch, especially in your first year of teaching, may mean that you won't have time to do much reflecting on your teaching. I would urge you to try and take five or ten minutes (surely you can spare that?) and at least put some notes in a file with your thoughts about each class. You will be glad you made the effort. If you don't end up reflecting on your teaching, you will still be able to do so at the end of the term or year, and that will still be impactful and important.

FINAL THOUGHTS

When you explicitly think about teaching, you will start to see areas where you can improve. By observing others teach, you will be expanding the number of teaching techniques that you know about, and you may start using some yourself. Spending time reflecting on your own teaching whenever you can will also spurn your own growth as a teacher, and it will make your classes better. Although it may not be the highest priority task to spend your time on, it is an important part of the path to becoming a great teacher.

12

HANDLING FEEDBACK

YOU SHOULD ENCOURAGE AND WELCOME feedback on your teaching from as many people as possible. If you are uncomfortable receiving feedback, that is common, but keep in mind that external feedback is an important part of growing as a teacher. You will get feedback in some forms whether your like it or not, whether it is from end of term evaluations (most likely in anonymous form), from your department chair or other observer who is evaluating you, or from your students directly through email or in person. Accept all constructive feedback for what it is, and if you agree with it, then you have something to work on or change with your teaching.

INVITING OTHERS TO OBSERVE YOU TEACH

You are seldom the best judge of your own teaching. When you teach, you are concentrating on delivering the material, asking your students questions, and making sure the flow of the class works out. An outside observer can concentrate on the teaching, and can give you better feedback than you might be able to generate yourself.

When you ask someone to observe your class, you can either ask them to view the class holistically, and to let you know what they thought about the class in general, and how individual parts of your lesson went. Alternatively, you can give them more concrete guidance, e.g., *I will be teaching Dijkstra's algorithm, and I'd like you to judge whether I explained the topic well enough, and whether you think the students understood it. I will also have them working on an exercise to go along with it, and I'd like feedback on how you think that went.* If you only want them to give you feedback on a particular part of the lesson, you should ask them to arrive roughly when you think you'll get to that part of the class.

If you are being formally reviewed by someone as part of your job, that person may or may not ask if you want them to concentrate on anything in particular, as they are likely going to review the full class. If they do ask, then you should give them a concrete part of your lesson to focus on, as above. After the observation, you should ask for feedback, whether this is the normal procedure, or not. If your observer says yes, then you will get another piece of good feedback to inform your teaching.

One thing you want to avoid if you are being formally observed is to change your lesson from what you were originally planning. If you know that you are going to be observed, there is no harm in doing an extra practice run-through before the observation, but you should do your best to teach as you normally would. If you prepare well for your lessons regularly, then you should be confident that you'll shine during a formal observation.[1]

Your school may have a teaching center with the sole purpose to help instructors improve their teaching. Often, these teaching centers will offer to have someone observe your class and then sit down with you to give you feedback. If this is available, take up the offer, as you will get excellent feedback from professionals who know what to look for and know what to concentrate on for their feedback. Teaching centers also host teaching workshops, or have longer classes dedicated to helping instructors become better teachers, and you should strongly consider utilizing these resources.

---

1 I have seen a teacher actively try and subvert the observation process by having a well-prepared lecture ready to go strictly for observations. The reviewer for this particular teacher came into the classroom unannounced half-way through a lecture, and the teacher put down the materials they were currently using, took out the observation lecture, and attempted to start it half-way through. The students were utterly confused by the mid-lecture topic swap, and a number of them told the observer explicitly what happened. That teacher was fired within two weeks after this fiasco.

GETTING FEEDBACK FROM YOUR STUDENTS

Believe it or not, your students will be able to give you excellent feedback on your teaching. Students see teachers every day, and in addition to commenting on your teaching, they will also be able to give you suggestions about what other teachers do that they like. As an example, the reason I started giving a short break in the middle of long classes was because a student told me that she really liked it in another class she was taking. Students will also tell you honestly what they think, and they will be frank if they found a particular lesson boring, incomprehensible, or irrelevant. You do have to be prepared to hear this kind of feedback, and having a thick skin for it is also a character trait you want to build if you don't have one already. But, by and large you will get constructive, on-point feedback from your students, and you should ask them frequently to give you their assessment of your teaching.

Frequent feedback (daily or weekly)

You should try to get some feedback from your students as often as daily, before or after a lecture. I arrive early to class and informally ask students how they think the class is going, and if they have any concerns or suggestions. The students will tell me about whether they understood a topic, or they will let me know how an assignment is going. I also ask students in office hours the same types of questions, as well. Don't worry too much about sampling bias (e.g., the students who arrive early may be better than average), and as long as you do your best to ask a number of students, you will get good feedback.

My colleague Chris Piech turned me on to an idea he calls *Tiny Feedback*, which I have referred to earlier in the book. In the Tiny Feedback model, the instructor sends an email to a certain percentage of the class (e.g., 10%) after *each* lesson, with a link to an online form that has simple questions about the lecture. Figure 7 shows an example form that I have used in my class (thanks to Chris Piech for the inspiration). The following is an example of the email I send to the students:

```
Dear _____,

Hello! You have been randomly selected to provide feedback
for CS 106B!

Please go to https://forms.gle/ddVZFSNetwkfj3aeA and fill
out the form located there.

I always appreciate constructive feedback about the course,
as I am constantly trying to improve it to make it the best
course possible. Thank you for participating!

-Chris

Chris Gregg, Ph.D.
Lecturer, Computer Science
Stanford University
```

As you can see from Figure 7, the form is short and simple, and it only takes students a minute to contribute feedback. The students are prompted for their positive thoughts about the lecture, and also for criticism, and they are asked to give a score for the lecture. They are also able to put a random note to the course staff, and in that field I often get both amusing notes and other pertinent feedback about the course itself. I look at the feedback a couple of days after each lecture, and if I send out a request to 10% of the class, usually about half of those students respond. Over an entire term, I try to ask each student submit feedback for two lectures. Incidentally, the feedback form I use is anonymous, and if you would rather have attributed feedback, you can ask for the students' names, as well. With attributed feedback, you

Tiny Feedback

Tiny Feedback for CS 106B Spring 2017

* Required

Lecture date *

MM   DD   YYYY

/   / 2018

What did you like about the lecture?

Your answer

What would you improve about the lecture?

Your answer

Overall quality of instruction today *

	1	2	3	4	5	
Poor	○	○	○	○	○	Excellent

Random message for Chris and or the TAs?

Your answer

How did you watch lecture *

○ In Person

○ Online

SUBMIT

Never submit passwords through Google Forms.

Figure 7: Example of a Tiny Feedback form.

may not get quite as much honesty (i.e., students may fear retribution in some form for poor reviews), but you will also forestall unconstructive feedback which you may want to avoid.

The feedback you will get from the Tiny Feedback form is well worth the effort (which, with the script, is minimal). You will get students' opinion on the lecture in question, and you will immediately find out whether they are confused about the lecture. Some will also report whether you went too fast or too slow (in their opinion), and you can use this information to refine future lectures.

You can find the Python script I use for Tiny Feedback at https://yourfirstyearteaching.com/cs.

End of term feedback

Most schools ask students to fill out end of term course evaluations. The evaluations are generally anonymous, and they ask about the course and the instructor. There are free form questions as well as numerical ratings, and the ratings can be averaged into a score for the class and instructor. In some cases, these scores are used as a contributing factor for instructor retention, which can be stressful for instructors, particularly if they feel that the students base their scores on aspects that are unfair, such as the difficulty of the course instead of whether the course met its goals.[2] Because of the anonymous nature of the feedback, as well, students will not necessarily be nice, and almost all instructors have their share of unconstructive feedback that they would rather not have seen (see below for further discussion on the topic of unconstructive feedback).

End of term feedback can be an excellent way to provide you with information with which to reflect on your course. Students

---

2 Or, more ominously, based on the instructor's gender, age, etc.. Unfortunately, this does happen, and some school administrators are just starting to realize that there is this kind of bias in student reviews. But, there is still much work to be done to fairly evaluate instructors.

will report on what they liked about your course, and what they liked about your teaching style in particular. They will also provide critical feedback, which you can use to improve your teaching in the future. You should feel justifiably proud of the positive feedback you get – for students to take the time to praise your teaching on their evaluations is a tribute to your hard work. For the critical feedback, you do need to have a thick skin, but if the feedback is constructive, use the information wisely to reflect on how you can improve in the future.

In the beginning of your teaching career, do not be too hard on yourself if you receive end of term feedback that is more critical than you might like. You are learning, and there are many ways you can improve. Make it your goal to improve on specific parts of your teaching that students are critical about, and try to turn those opinions around in future courses. Also beware of comparing your scores with other instructors. Some instructors are simply phenomenal, and rather than comparing yourself to them (especially early in your career!), go observe their classes, and see what they are doing to garner those high marks.

GETTING UNWANTED OR UNCONSTRUCTIVE FEEDBACK

Unfortunately, there may be times when you receive feedback that is not constructive, and it is not useful to you. The feedback can be rude or insensitive, and it can include ad hominem attacks that are just intended to make you feel bad. Students sometimes give this type of feedback when they are frustrated with their performance in a class, and they think the instructor was unfair with the grading, or didn't teach the course well. Instead of admitting their own responsibility for their grade in the course, they want to blame someone, and often that someone is the instructor. If you do receive this kind of feedback, be confident that you did the best you could with the course, and you can safely ignore these comments and concentrate on the constructive feedback you receive.

Sometimes, however, the feedback crosses a line and is sexist, racist, homophobic, or otherwise completely uncalled for and offensive. If the feedback is anonymous, there is likely nothing you can concretely do about it, but you may want to consider bringing it up with someone on the faculty you trust, such as a colleague or your department chair. There may be a school policy for reporting those kinds of comments, as well.

BENEFITS OF ANONYMOUS FEEDBACK

The message from the section above notwithstanding, there are times when anonymous feedback can be useful, and not only to garner honest feedback from students. For a number of years I have used an online anonymous feedback website that allows students to write feedback for me with the added ability for me to reply to the students (if they provide their email to the website) without knowing who they are. I have had a number of discussions with students that were sensitive enough that the student was only comfortable talking to me while remaining anonymous. One student had constructive criticism about an example I used in class that referred to male and female names – the student commented that, as a transgender student, they felt uncomfortable at the assumption that a name had to be gendered. I wrote the student back and apologized for making them feel uncomfortable, and we had a fruitful back-and-forth discussion about how I could improve on the example in future courses. The student did not need to provide their identity, and we were able to discuss the issue through the system without any trouble. In another case, a student wrote me that she was upset at a sexist comment made by a TA during a lab for the course, and I was able to reply to her that the matter was serious and I wanted to address it. In that case, the student did decide to identify herself to me to make the investigation easier, but I did not require her to do so. Regardless, the student's initial contact with me was fully anonymous, and I doubt she would have come forward without the ability to do so.

If you are worried that allowing anonymous feedback for your courses may lead to comments that you are not comfortable with, there are ways to buffer yourself. One way is to agree with a colleague to preview all anonymous feedback for each other, and simply delete unconstructive or offensive comments before the intended recipient has a chance to see them.

No one is going to criticize you for not having anonymous feedback for your classes, but you might want to consider that there are benefits to encouraging it that you might not realize.

WHAT TO DO IF...

What if I get feedback about my TAs?

If you get positive feedback about your TAs, share it with them! TAs, like any other teacher, appreciate positive comments about their performance, and you should not keep that to yourself. You can also encourage the student giving the feedback to you to also explicitly give the feedback directly to the TA, which makes it even more personal and rewarding for the TA.

If, on the other hand, you get negative feedback on the TA, you have to consider whether it makes sense to tell the TA, or to handle it differently. You want to be honest with your TAs, but at the same time you want to buffer any feedback to turn it into constructive feedback so the TA does not feel discouraged by it. For example, a student might tell you that a particular TA gets frustrated in office hours and is mean to the students. This is not something you want to relate directly to the TA. Instead, set up a meeting with the TA, and ask them how office hours are going. They may tell you that they get frustrated with the students, and this is an opportunity to talk to them about being kind and having patience. Even if they don't admit their frustration, you can say that you have received feedback that the students perceive some frustration (you can leave out the *and is mean* part), and then you can discuss remedying it, as before. You do want to address this kind of feedback directly with your TAs, but be as kind and provide constructive remedies, if possible.

Some feedback about TAs may be more serious (such as the sexist comment mentioned above), and in that case you want to investigate the matter. Before you launch an investigation, talk to your department chair or another trusted faculty member about how best to proceed, and as always, make sure that you are doing things in accordance with any human resources guidelines at your school.

What if I disagree with feedback I get?

You will disagree with plenty of feedback you get as you go through your teaching career, but you should always consider the feedback and spend some time thinking about it. Your students might not like your late assignment policy, for instance, and they might give you feedback that you should change it. But, if you have the policy for a reason, and you think it is a worthwhile reason, then keep the policy and if the feedback is attributed, thank the student and give them your reasoning about why you won't change it. They still might not be happy about it, but by acknowledging the feedback you have addressed it sufficiently.

You may find that after thinking about feedback that you thought was misdirected, you do want to make changes based on the suggestion. This kind of introspection will only make your teaching better, and giving all constructive feedback sufficient time and thought is absolutely worthwhile.

What if the thought of reading my end of term evaluations distresses me?

You would not be alone among teachers! Some teachers hate reading their course evaluations, and some never read them at all. As discussed earlier, you sometimes do need a thick skin to read criticism about your teaching, but you should do your best to overcome your fears and read them, for you will get constructive feedback that can improve your teaching.

Although for some people this may seem even more stressful, it can help to ask a colleague to read your evaluations and discuss them with you. They can filter out any potential unconstructive feedback, and they can help you process any critical feedback you get, with the intent on helping you improve your teaching.

As I have said many times in this book: if you prepare well for your course, and you give it your best effort, you should be confident that you are doing a good job. Yes, you may (will!) get critical feedback, but processing it is an important step towards becoming a better teacher, and even if it is difficult, your teaching will improve because of it.

What if my end of term feedback response rate is low?

At many schools you can find out the number of students who respond to the end of term evaluations, and sometimes it is a low percentage. This can skew results (and more often than not skew them negatively), and in the interest of getting a true picture of what your students thought, you should do what you can to get a better response rate. Some schools delay sending out final grades to students until after they submit their evaluations (up to a certain date), which tends to increase participation, though some students do the least work possible to successfully submit their online evaluation.

During the last lecture in my classes, I encourage my students to submit their evaluations, and I tell them (in much the same way as in the letter I send for Tiny Feedback) that I welcome constructive feedback that will help me make my teaching, and the course, better. I also send a reminder out to them after the last lecture with the same sentiment. With enough reminders, the students often rise to the occasion and submit their feedback, and the response rates in my classes are usually sufficient.

FINAL THOUGHTS

Getting feedback from your students and from colleagues is a tremendous way to inform and improve your teaching, and your courses. It isn't always easy to receive feedback (especially anonymously), but when you filter for constructive feedback only, then you have more information to use when deciding how to change your classroom, your interaction with students, your policies, and anything else you get feedback on.

13

STAYING CURRENT ON, AND CONTRIBUTING TO CS EDUCATION RESEARCH

TEACHING IS A DYNAMIC field, and computer science education in particular has a vibrant community of scholars dedicated to ensuring that the discipline continually improves with new and interesting teaching methods and resources. Should you desire to see the latest and greatest pedagogical methods to potentially use in your own teaching, you can do so in a number of ways. If you are a member of the Association of Computing Machinery (ACM), you can look at all current Special Interest Group on Computer Science Education (SIGCSE) papers accepted to the SIGCSE conferences, including the main conference and its many sub-conferences (the three main conferences besides the SIGCSE conference itself are CompEd, ITiCSE, and ICER). You can also attend and/or participate in any of the conferences, as well. No matter what level of computer science you teach at, you can also create resources and perform research that can further the field, and if you do that you should consider publishing the work via the SIGCSE or other conferences.

This chapter discusses how to keep up to date on computer science pedagogy, and how you can contribute to that body of knowledge, as well. This is not something you may get the chance to do during your first year of teaching – you will have a tremendous amount of work – but as you progress through your teaching career you should try to avoid stagnation in your teaching, and one way to do that is by keeping up with the current state of the art for computer science education.

COMPUTER SCIENCE EDUCATION RESOURCES, CONFERENCES, AND JOURNALS

SIGCSE, mentioned above, is the most prominent organization that has a focus on computer science, and you should strongly consider joining the ACM in order to have access to SIGCSE publications and resources. As described in Chapter 10, the SIGCSE mailing list is an excellent resource where you can see what CS educators are currently discussing. The topics span the spectrum of CS education, and there are always vibrant discussions happening on pedagogy, resources, student advising, etc. You can browse the list archive without being a member, but in order to ask questions or participate in the discussion you must be a member of ACM and affiliated with SIGCSE.

SIGCSE maintains a list of places to publish work, and although it can be overwhelming, you will be able to find virtually all CS education related publications by looking through the following list:

https://sigcse.org/sigcse/resources/publish.html

Most often, if you are looking for specific CS research, you can find it through an online search, either through the ACM, through your library, or through a Google Scholar search. Your school's library may have access to many of the conference and journal proceedings, and with library access you will not need an ACM membership to see the papers.

There are four main SIGCSE conferences, around the world. If you can get funding–and have the time–to attend one or more of the conferences, they are a tremendous shared experience, and attendees often return from a SIGCSE conference invigorated about computer science education.

SIGCSE conference

The SIGCSE conference, held yearly in the United States, is the largest of the SIGCSE-affiliated conferences, and is often just referred to as "SIGCSE", despite the potential confusion between the SIGCSE *organization* and the SIGCSE *conference* itself.[1] SIGCSE hosts a number of prominent CS Education keynote addresses, and it accepts research papers, tools papers, and experience reports reflecting the current state of education research and pedagogy. Additionally, there are numerous teaching-related workshops and panels at SIGCSE, and many so-called "Birds of a Feather" discussions, which are group chats about particular facets of CS education (e.g., I have been involved with discussions about teaching students to debug, about being in a teaching faculty position, and about advising CS students). Birds of a Feather discussions are informal and I always come away with new information from attending them. Additionally, because SIGCSE is so well attended, you will see familiar faces and will start to get to know the prominent educators. SIGCSE holds something for all CS educators, from K-12 teachers to undergraduate and graduate instruction, to education researchers.

In addition to other faculty members, you will see many students at SIGCSE. Some are graduate students presenting a paper in conjunction with a faculty member, and others are there to present posters for their research. There are grants available to help send students to the conference, as well.

As mentioned in Chapter 7, SIGCSE also hosts the *Nifty Assignments* presentations, which are a great way to see new and exciting assignments. There are also frequently sessions on diversity, inclusion, mentorship, and there are round table discussions on current hot topics in CS Education. If you attend SIGCSE, you will be inundated with a tremendous amount of computer science education research, discussion, and camaraderie, and you will be glad you were able to go to the conference.

---

1 As in, *I'm looking forward to seeing you at SIGCSE this year!*

Consortium for Computing Sciences in Colleges (CCSC) Regional Conferences

The CCSC is a geographically based set of ten U.S. regions made up of universities and colleges. The CCSC has a focus on computer science education, and the organization holds ten regional conferences each year. Because the conferences are regional, you may be able to find it easier to attend your local conference, and you also will be able to see what schools in your area of the country are doing with regard to CS Education.

ITiCSE

The Innovation and Technology in Computer Science Education (ITiCSE) conference is held worldwide (most often in Europe), and is similar to the SIGCSE conference in scope. It is a great choice for a conference if you live in a country nearby where the conference is held, and it is also a relatively small and intimate conference.

ICER

The International Computing Education Research (ICER) conference is focused most specifically on CS research, and it is considered by some as the more technical and *wonky* conference of the main SIGCSE conferences. It is held yearly, with alternating locations in North America and abroad (including Australia). Like ITiCSE, it is also small, with single-track sessions so attendees can go to all sessions.

CompEd

CompEd, formally known as the ACM Global Computing Education Conference, is the newest of the ACM's education focused conferences. It is held every other year, and generally outside of North America and Europe. It will have similar papers, presentations, panels, and sessions as SIGCSE, and will be focused on issues affecting the global CS student population.

Grace Hopper Celebration (GHC)

The annual Grace Hopper Celebration is the world's largest event focused on women in technology and computing. With over 18,000 attendees, it is vibrant and thrilling for attendees, particularly if it is your first time going. While not specifically targeted towards CS education, it is the premiere conference to go to if you have an interest in women in computing, and it is a great opportunity for your female students to attend, as well.[2] There are also opportunities for faculty members, specifically with a mentoring program that pairs junior and senior CS faculty together.

Tapia

The ACM Richard Tapia Celebration of Diversity in Computing (Tapia) conference is a yearly gathering focused on celebrating diversity in computing. There are sessions, research papers, posters, Birds of a Feather discussions, panels, and workshops, and it is a terrific event to participate in discussions about all aspects of the computing field (including educational and professional) with regard to diversity, inclusion, and participation.

AP Computer Science Workshops

If you are teaching AP computer science (either AP Principles or AP Computer Science A), you should do what you can to go to an

---

2 Grace Hopper has an enormous job fair, and many of my female students have returned from the conference with internship offers and full time job interviews scheduled.

AP Workshop, sponsored by the College Board.[3] The workshops, normally held during the summer, are either one day or one week offerings, and they are a tremendous opportunity to learn pedagogy and teaching tips specifically targeted towards the AP exam. I have attended week-long AP workshops for both AP Physics and AP Computer Science A, and they have been among the best professional development I have had in my teaching career.

PERFORMING RESEARCH IN COMPUTER SCIENCE EDUCATION

As mentioned many times in this book: if you have a great idea about teaching, share it with others. This goes for awesome assignments, online demonstrations or resources, tips, etc. One way to share your work is to publish it in one of the conferences discussed in the previous section. SIGCSE, for instance, accepts papers and posters that are based on both research and experience, so you can publish your work even if it isn't strictly a research project. For example, if you have instituted a novel assessment for a course that you think others may benefit from using as well, you can write it up as an experience report and submit it for peer review. It is best if you do have some ability to assess whether your idea made a difference, which means that you should attempt to have either a control group, or data from a prior course that you can use to compare against. That said, I have published experience reports in SIGCSE for new courses, and for test-taking software, and neither had a control group comparison.

Not everything novel you do in your classroom is going to merit submitting to a conference or journal, but you should still consider sharing your ideas and successes with colleagues, even if that is only at your own school, via the SIGCSE mailing list, or on your own web page.

---

3 It is important enough to lobby your school and/or department chair to fund you to go. There are also competitive grants you can apply for as well, particularly if your school serves predominantly underrepresented students.

Funding Your CS Education Research

Many CS education research projects are performed without specific funding, and many CS educators perform research strictly as a non-required, and non-explicitly paid part of their employment. However, as with any research, it is possible to get funding for resources (student researchers, equipment, etc.) through channels (in the U.S.) such as the National Science Foundation, the Department of Education, and many companies (Google, Facebook, Microsoft, etc.). The process normally involves submitting your research idea with your goals and potential outcomes to the organization providing the funding, and in most cases the process is competitive. You can also search for grants in your state, which often have funding for STEM[4] ideas. Grants can be large or small, depending on the scope of the project, and you should investigate past grants to see what kinds of projects have been funded to see if yours will be competitive.

Depending on your own school's or department finances, you may be able to request funding locally. Your first step is to talk to your department chair about the types of projects that have been internally funded previously, and present a pitch for your idea. Some schools provide teaching staff with a small budget of discretionary funds that can be used for small research projects as well.

IRBs

If your research is going to be investigating actual students in your classes, you will likely need to go through the *Institutional Review Board* (IRB)[5] process at your school. Your school's IRB oversees all research on human subjects, and you must have permission from the IRB to conduct research on your students. You may

---

4 *Science, Technology, Engineering, and Mathematics*
5 Sometimes this is called an *Independent Ethics Committee* (ERB) or a Research Ethics Board (REB)

also be required to go through human subject research training, and to provide your students with research consent forms to get permission from them. In some cases, you may be able to get an IRB waiver, for example for studies that involve non-attributed data about how students performed on an assessment. Regardless, before you begin any research on your students you must check on the IRB requirements at your school.

Once you have gone through the necessary IRB protocols for your school and if you are doing a project which requires consent from your students, plan on spending a bit of class time to discuss your research with them, and to hand out the consent forms. Be prepared to answer questions about the work, and about their role. Most students will likely consent, however if you do have students who do not want to consent, you must keep any data you collect from them separate, and not include them in the research. You may also have students who are not able to consent on their own – for example, you may have high school students taking your course, and you may have to either exclude them from the research, or figure out how to get their guardians to consent. Again, make sure you have all of the information you need about IRB requirements before starting the work.

What research should I do?

You may already have research ideas you want to pursue, but if you don't, one way to generate ideas is to start browsing SIGCSE conference papers for examples of what has been done in the past. Papers often include *future work* sections that can be instructive for producing new work that branches off past ideas, or furthers them in meaningful ways.

Another good way to generate ideas for research is to keep track of specific things that your students have difficulties with in your classes. Not only will this give you something specific to concentrate on when you teach the concepts in the future, but when you are brainstorming ways to improve your teaching, you may come up with testable ideas that merit research on the topic.

Collaboration with other colleagues is another way to start participating in CS education research. It is easiest to work with colleagues at your own school, but many research projects happen between faculty members at different schools. You should also consider talking with your students about ideas, as well – many students want to do research and they can add considerably to the planning, execution, and writing about it.

Writing up your work

Again, it is very likely that you have written technical papers before, but in case you have not, here are a few suggestions on preparing your work.

When you decide to write up your work, start early! Deadlines approach much quicker than you imagine, especially if you are trying to write your paper while in the middle of a school term when you have a myriad of other responsibilities. Ideally, you want to be done with a draft of the paper early enough to allow someone else to read it and provide feedback for a second draft. If you have collaborators, set early deadlines and do your best to keep everyone on schedule.

Use the correct format for your paper, based on the *Call for Participation* notice for the conference or journal you are submitting to. Conferences generally provide LATEX and Microsoft Word templates for you to use, and you should produce your PDF for submission from one of those templates.

Create a compelling title for your paper. The title is the first thing anyone will read about your paper, and the title should entice the reader to actually read the paper (or at least the abstract). Your abstract is also vitally important, and a reader should be able to understand what your research accomplished through the abstract. Do not hide results from your reader in the abstract. For example, instead of, *We will show the difference in student perfor-*

mance when using our new method, you should prefer to say, *We show that students performed 28% better on assignments when using our new method*.

Make sure any diagrams in your paper are clear and have descriptive captions. A reader should be able to understand your figures without having to dig into the text for an explanation. Obviously, you should elaborate in the paper text, but don't be afraid to include one or two full sentences in your captions to describe the figure.

If you are having trouble figuring out how to structure your paper, read through other, related papers. You don't have to structure yours exactly like any specific paper, but you will see certain standard sections that you should include.

Provide a robust *References* section for your paper. Take time as you are considering the research, and as you perform it to find related work to cite. If you choose to write a *Related Work* section (and this is a good idea), you should clearly distinguish why your work is different, follows, or adds to other prior research.

You should also include a *Future Work* section to discuss how your work can be improved, or what direction you might take future research. Even if you don't end up doing any of the future work you suggest, others may use the ideas for their work.

Submitting your work

The conference you submit to will have explicit directions on how to submit your paper, which will usually be in PDF form. Make sure you know exactly when the deadlines are and submit early. Many conferences will not accept any late submissions without valid reason, and "my internet went down" is not one of them. You will always have the ability to update a submission up until the deadline, so submitting a draft early is a good idea in case you do end up missing the actual deadline.

Once you submit your paper, you have to wait to receive feedback, which generally comes in the form of a set of reviews with comments and scores, which are often 1-5, with a corresponding description associated with each number. Based on the reviews, the paper will either be accepted or rejected in the conference. In some cases, there will be a second round of reviews once authors make suggested changes. If your paper is accepted, congratulations! You can then prepare to present the work at the conference. If it is not accepted, look thoroughly though the reviews, and take any constructive feedback seriously. If you think that the paper could be improved by either re-writing, or adding more research, you can consider re-working it and submitting it to another conference, or to the same conference the following year.

Presenting your work

Once you have a paper (or poster) accepted into a conference, you need to prepare to present it. Paper presentations generally allow a short (15-20 minute) fixed time for you to present, and papers are often grouped with others that discuss a similar topic. Your presentation should be concise and you should highlight your paper – you probably won't be able to go into too much detail in the short time for the presentation, so make sure you choose the main points to discuss. If you have collaborators, you should generally only have one person present, as the time is likely too short to allow a smooth transition. This isn't a hard rule, though, but if you want to present with a collaborator, make sure you practice together and have a good transition in place.

WHAT TO DO IF. . .

What if I don't want to do education research?

This is okay! Being an outstanding teacher is a triumph on its own, and doing your own research is certainly not required to achieve it. Unless you are in a faculty position where education research is expected, you can spend your time focusing on and improving your teaching in myriad ways without doing your own research.

What if my papers keep getting rejected from conferences?

It can be discouraging to work hard on research and a paper only to get it rejected from a conference. Many conferences have competitive acceptance rates (e.g., SIGCSE only accepts about a third of the papers that are submitted every year), so you should not be too dispirited with a rejection. You are welcome to modify and resubmit the paper if you desire. You can also submit the paper to a different conference, as well, but you should still modify it if it was rejected from one conference, unless it just simply fits better in a different conference. If the rejection came with reviews, read them thoroughly and take suggestions about improving the paper seriously. If the reviews suggested a different research approach, or to gather more data, this is something you can consider, too. It is up to you whether you want to continuing working on a rejected paper, and if you decide not to continue with it, you should at least think about what *you* learned from the research and how it may inform your own teaching.

What if I teach in a high school? Can I still perform research?

A number of high school computer science teachers conduct education research in their classrooms. The process for getting consent to do research on high school students will involve their parents or guardians, and you should also ensure that your district's administration (specifically, your principal or headmaster) allows research. You may also need to get approval from the administration to conduct it in your classroom. At the very least discuss it with someone knowledgeable in the school or administration before beginning any research. The SIGCSE conference gladly accepts research from primary and secondary school teachers, and you do not need an advanced degree to conduct research.

FINAL THOUGHTS

Teaching is not a static field, and many researchers present novel teaching ideas, tools, and pedagogy every year. Once you have time to start thinking about improving your own teaching, you should consider attending conferences where you can see the latest research and you can mingle with like-minded colleagues about teaching computer science. As you continue to progress through your career, you should also think about sharing your ideas with the community by doing your own education research, and submitting the work for publication.

Part IV

INFLUENCING STUDENTS (AND OTHERS)

14

INTERACTING WITH STUDENTS: HOLDING OFFICE HOURS, MEETING INDIVIDUALLY WITH STUDENTS, ADVISING COMPUTER SCIENCE MAJORS, AND WRITING RECOMMENDATION LETTERS

ALTHOUGH IT ISN'T ALWAYS the first thing that people consider when they think about teaching, you will spend more time interacting with students outside your lectures than you will speaking to them in front of class. You will hold office hours that could attract many students at once, and you will also have individual meetings with students to discuss their progress in class, to discuss special circumstances, to discuss computer science in general, or to talk about a myriad of other topics. You may also serve as the academic advisor to students who are majoring in computer science or other majors. You will also inevitably be asked for many recommendation letters for students who wish to pursue graduate school (or college, if you teach high school), who are applying for fellowships and other scholarships, or who need a reference for employment.

In some of the scenarios above, you will be dedicating your time to students for the purpose of doing better in your class (office hours, individual meetings about performance, etc.), but in other cases you will be acting in a capacity that doesn't directly affect the courses you teach. You will be advising students on their collegiate career and their future career, and you will be communicating to others about your students' performance in class, or their potential to do well in college, graduate school or in a job. In these latter cases, you will need to be judicious in what you say and how you say it, and you will need to compare the students asking for recommendations with other students you have had in the same or similar classes.

If you teach a collegiate-level course, you are generally going to want to hold office hours to give your students the opportunity to discuss the course with you directly. Your TAs will likely also have similar office hours. Your school or department may dictate how many hours worth of office hours you should hold each week, but if it isn't prescribed, you can choose however many you want. I normally have about four hours worth of office hours per class per week, although if I am teaching multiple different classes I may combine some of the office hours together.

When you hold office hours, you need to be clear with your students about how much help you are going to give them, particularly if they are asking about specific homework assignments. If you want to have a policy where you will not look at their code, for example, then you should be clear with them about it. Do your best to have a welcoming attitude in office hours, as well – you want your students to feel like they can come to your office hours for constructive help, and you should be as helpful and as encouraging as possible.

You will see some of your students in office hours, and you will never see others. In fact, you will probably see the same core group of students week after week, and this gives you a great opportunity to get to know them better than in lecture. Different types of students show up at office hours – you will often get struggling students, and you will also get students who are doing well but want the extra benefit of talking to you directly. You should encourage your students to come to your office hours, with the recognition that your office hours may end up becoming very busy, especially if you have a very large class. Some instructors ask a TA to hold office hours at the same time in the same vicinity so that you can manage the student load better.

Often, you will have to modify how you hold office hours depending on where you are in the term. You will get more students at your office hours as assignment deadlines or exams approach, and you should be ready to handle the increase when it happens.

There are many different strategies for holding office hours, and you may already have your own ideas about how you will have them, and in what capacity you will help your students. For example, some instructors will not look at any student code and limit themselves to helping with conceptual issues. Some instructors hold office hours one student at a time, and others hold group office hours. The following sections describe each type in detail.

Individual Student Office Hours

Meeting with students individually during office hours is beneficial to students because they get your undivided attention. If you have more than a few students showing up, you should have a sign-up sheet so you can talk to them in the order in which they arrive. If necessary, you should also cut off the list before your office hours end, or you are likely to have students you need to talk to past the end of your office hours.[1] Another downside to holding individual meetings is that sometimes you end up answering the same common conceptual question multiple times. However, if a student has a question that is personal in nature or about a specific issue that affects only that student, you can discuss it directly without asking other students to leave.

One note about meeting with students in your office – you should use good judgment about if and when to close your door for privacy with a student. If a student wants to discuss something privately, you may or may not feel comfortable closing the door, for many reasons. Keeping the door at least somewhat cracked usually works for all but the most sensitive conversations (if a stu-

---

1 Or, you can simply extend your office hours. But, just plan ahead if this is your strategy and don't schedule meetings directly after your planned hours.

dent breaks down into tears, for example[2]), and is generally good practice.

You may find that having individual student discussions during office hours breaks down if you have too many students in attendance. If this is the case, your options include moving to a group strategy, holding office hours more often, asking a TA to help during your office hours, or scheduling individual meetings outside of your regular office hours time allocations.

If you do have a full schedule of students waiting to talk to you during office hours, make sure you limit the amount of time you talk to each student. This can be difficult to do, as you can't predict what the students want to talk to you about, or how long the discussion will take. But, to be fair, you should enforce a time limit to the extent that you can talk to as many students as is possible.

Group Office Hours

My preferred method for holding office hours is a group method, where I reserve a room big enough to hold the students I expect to attend (not my own office, usually), and I walk around to talk to each student individually for a few minutes at a time. This works particularly well when students have questions about homework assignments, and they are all working independently on their own assignments. If you employ this method, you should try to group students together who have similar questions or are working on similar parts of an assignment. This method scales relatively well to a moderate amount of students (roughly twenty is about the maximum I like to have at once), and the constant rotation means that you can quickly discuss an issue with a student,

---

2 Do not be surprised if this happens. Students can be fragile, and there are many reasons for students to be very upset: grades, family emergencies, significant-other issues, being away from home, etc. If you feel uncomfortable talking with a student about a particular issue, you should rely on your list of contacts to put them in touch with who can handle it better.

and set them off on figuring it out while you move to the next student. You should try to get to all the students in roughly the order they arrived, and then check back with students regularly.

The group method allows students to get help relatively quickly, and it gives them the ability to ask follow-up questions after they have thought about their problems for a while after first talking to you. Students are less worried about getting all of their questions answered immediately, and those that do have more involved questions can get a longer session with you.

Group office hours can also get unwieldy with too many students, and your options for mitigating this are similar to those for individual office hours. I will often extend my office hours when possible, and I keep this option in mind when assignments are due and around exam periods.

TA Office Hours

Your TAs will also likely have their own office hours, which they can handle in an individual or group setting. The TAs I have worked with generally like to have a set queue that students must sign up on for help, and the TAs go through each student one at a time. The queue can either be on paper or a white board, or there are also online queues, e.g., queuestatus.com.

As discussed in Chapter 9, you should plan on either training your TAs on how to conduct office hours effectively, or at least have a discussion with them about your expectations. For example, TAs should avoid answering questions in a way that does work the students are expected to do – i.e., they shouldn't be writing code for students, or giving them help that undermines what you want the students to accomplish on their own. You should also prepare your TAs to handle large numbers of students, if that is a possibility in your course. In large courses, students and TAs can get frustrated with long office hours queues and short amounts of time getting help, and you need to manage both the students' and the TAs' expectations. This is not always an easy conversation to have, especially with large classes and not enough resources. Students should know that you are doing the best you can with the TA resources available, and you should encourage them to reach out to department and school administrators who are in a position to provide more resources to your course.

INDIVIDUAL MEETINGS WITH STUDENTS

Students will ask to meet with you outside your scheduled office hours, and it is your decision whether to have those meetings or not. You may also decide to have an *open door* policy, where students can simply stop by to talk to you when you are in your office. Beware that an open door policy can lead to students taking up time that you would rather be spending on preparing for class or other important duties. Of course, closing your office door when you don't have time to talk is an option.

When students ask to meet with me, I point them to an online appointment calendar that I set up so they can find a meeting time. I set aside a couple of hours per week on my calendar for these sorts of meetings, and sometimes it is empty, and sometimes it is full. The busiest times on my calendar are when I am meeting with advisees, which happens *en masse* when students are working on their schedules for the following term. My meeting times are 20 minutes each, and I limit the students to signing up for a single meeting except in circumstances where I think the meeting needs to be longer. It is rare that a meeting needs more than twenty minutes, in my experience.

Students will often ask to meet outside of office hours if they are struggling in your class and need guidance on how to get back on track. I would urge you to prioritize those meetings, as it gives you an excellent opportunity to help students who may be at a critical point in your course.

I almost always ask students to sign up for individual meetings when they ask me for letters of recommendation, even if I know them relatively well. See below for details about writing recommendations.

ADVISING COMPUTER SCIENCE MAJORS

As a faculty member, you may be required to have academic advisees in their major. Their major is usually Computer Science, although sometimes it can be a related field (Stanford has the *Symbolic Systems* major, for instance, and faculty in CS can advise those students as well). If you are a teaching-track faculty member, the advisees will usually be undergraduates or Master's students. If you are in a research position, you may also have Ph.D. student advisees. This section will focus on undergraduate student advising, although much of it translates well to Master's level students. If you are a secondary school teacher, your students likely have guidance counselors who handle their academic advising, but there are schools that have faculty members advise students as well, and this section may be of interest to you.

Agreeing to be an Advisor

Depending on your school, potential advisees may be directly assigned to you, and/or students may ask you to be their advisor. In the former case, your school likely has a system to distribute potential advisees among the faculty, and there may be a limit to the number of students assigned in this way. In the latter case, many students may ask you to be their advisor, particularly if you teach introductory courses, which are often large and where you are one of the first CS instructors that students meet. New faculty members often readily agree to be an advisor, but be careful that you do not accept too many advisees all at once. See the section below about handling your advising load.

Keep in mind that as a new faculty member, you probably do not know that much about advising at your school (unless you at-

tended the school yourself, and even then, you were on the receiving end of advising, not the advisor). It will take time to learn the
nuances of the academic pipeline and requirements at the school,
including:

1. What are the core classes (if any) for the major?

2. What courses are recommended for my future goals?

3. What requirements are there for non-computer science
   courses? (e.g., foreign language, humanities electives, ethics
   courses, etc.)

4. How many credits / units are needed to graduate, or to apply to certain graduate programs (e.g., a 5th-year Master's
   program at your school)?

5. What forms need to be signed, and when?

6. Is it possible to change majors?

7. Are there courses I shouldn't take concurrently (i.e., because
   they are both extremely challenging)?

The list above is certainly not all-inclusive, and your advisees
will ask you hundreds of different questions, some of which you
will be able to answer (with experience), and some that you will
have to research the answer to yourself. Once you get your first
advisee or advisees, ask around to see which other faculty members are known to be good advisors, and seek them out. Ask if
you can sit in on one of their initial meetings with a new advisee,
and when you do join the meeting, take notes. Also, ask for their
advice about advising students at your school in general – every school has its own requirements, and often you never know
about those requirements unless someone tells you about them
(e.g., you may be required to meet with advisees once per term).
It is also a great idea to get to know the administrative team for
your department, as they have seen hundreds or thousands of

students about academic requirements, and they are probably the ones you should go to first if you don't know the answer to a student question. Additionally, your school or department may have an advising manual, or (even better) advisor training. Use those resources to their fullest if they exist.

When a student asks you to be their advisor and you are considering saying yes, you should schedule a meeting with the student to discuss their decision to choose their major, and to discuss their academic plan and their plans post-college. I ask the students to set up a twenty-minute meeting with me through my online appointments calendar.

Depending on your school, students may be very early in their collegiate career or mid-way through before they declare their major. In some cases, students decide to declare their major late (junior year is generally fairly late), or they decide to change their major late, and you should be prepared to discuss options with both categories of students.

Also dependent on where you teach is the procedure for students declaring their major. At many schools, once students are accepted into the school, they can choose any major, and switching is often easy as well, as long as students are on track to finish the major requirements. At other schools, becoming a major is limited by internal school (Engineering -vs- Liberal Arts, for instance), and students may have to be admitted into the major through a competitive process based on their grades or even when they apply in high school. You should understand the requirements before agreeing to be a student's advisor.

Questions and Direction for your New or Potential Advisees

When you meet with your new or potential advisee for the first time, you should have a set of questions to ask, and an initial set of guidance to give them. I set up twenty-minute meetings and the meeting goes by very quickly as I try to cover a lot of material. Declaring a major is a big step for many students, and you should ensure that you talk them through the ramifications (mostly positive) of declaring their major, and you should make them aware of follow-on steps.

After congratulating them on their decision to choose a major, I talk to my potential advisees about the following list of topics during our initial meeting. They may not know the answer to all of the questions, and they may not have even considered some of the topics (e.g., post-college plans) at this point, particularly if they are in their first year of college. That is okay, but making them aware of things they will eventually need to consider is important even during your first meeting.

1. *Why do you want to be a computer science major?* Most students can answer this question relatively easily, and their answer gives you a good idea about their motivations in general. Students will often say that they have enjoyed their computer science courses, and they think being a software engineer or a programmer would be fun. Others love the math and problem-solving aspect of the major, etc. Some, frankly, see that computer science majors make decent salaries, and that is a primary motivation.

2. *Are you a first-generation college student?* This can be a critical question for students who are the first generation in their family to attend college. Students whose parents have college degrees are more likely to be able to navigate the major process, although this certainly isn't always true. However, first-gen students may need more specific guidance about certain aspects of college, majoring, etc., and knowing this about them early on is helpful. I always congratulate first-gen students, noting that their family is probably very proud of them. The first-gen students I have known are almost always particularly motivated, and I very much enjoy advising them.

3. *What is your post-college goal after graduating as a CS major? Have you considered graduate school, industry, or another path?* This may seem premature, but I like to get the question out early. Some students haven't even begun to think about this yet, and that is okay. However, this will provide a foundation to discuss their collegiate path, and if they do have ideas about it, it is best to talk about them early. Students who are considering graduate school need to know that their grades are going to potentially be more important than otherwise, and that undergraduate research can be critical, as well (see below for questions about graduate school).

4. *What classes have you already taken in the major?* First year students probably have not taken many courses yet, so this gives you a good opportunity to discuss the major and what courses will be required. I normally follow up this question with one about the courses they are planning for the following term, as well (though that can come later in the conversation). More advanced students have probably taken more classes, and have a better idea of their course path. However, some advanced students are getting into the major late and have *not* taken many courses, so putting together a schedule that allows them to graduate on time can be challenging.

5. *Have you thought about what concentration (if applicable) you want to pursue in the major, and what elective courses you want to take?* This type of question depends on where you teach, but there are going to be certain major requirements that your advisee should be aware of. See below for more information about scheduling classes.

6. *Have you considered graduate school for either a Master's or a Ph.D.?* Again, this is a question that many students may not have considered, but it is worth bringing it up early. Students may want to start considering doing research, or taking specific classes if they want to eventually attend grad-

uate school. Some schools have a 5-year Master's program that is available for students to apply to, as well, and discussing this with advisees to make them aware of the option is important, as well.

7. *Are you planning to go abroad for a term while you are a student?* When students are planning out their course plan to complete their major, they will have to schedule around a term abroad. Many study-abroad programs do not have computer science courses that they can take for their major (although some do), so they need to be aware of the limitations. I almost always encourage students to spend a term abroad, as it can be a fun and enlightening experience. Almost all students can fit a term abroad into their schedules without hurting their ability to finish their major on time.[3]

8. *Have you put together a draft of your four-year plan yet?* Your school or department has documents that describe the major requirements, and you should point your student to those references. They should be broadly planning out their four-year plan as early as possible. They should include the major requirements (core), and any electives that will be necessary for a concentration, if that is needed. A spreadsheet is a good tool for the job, and some schools have example schedule templates they can use as a start. They don't have to plan it exactly, of course, but they should leave space for *CS Elective* or *School Requirement* as is necessary. You should offer to review their schedule with them after they put it together

9. *What are you planning to do for the upcoming summer?* This answer can depend on when during the school year you meet with your students. These days, students looking for

---

3 Pre-med students (some of whom do, indeed, study CS as their major), and double-majors have more trouble fitting all their coursework in on time if they study abroad.

summer internships often start looking as early as the Autumn before the summer – right at the beginning of the school year. This disadvantages Freshman, who many not even have taken a computer science course yet in order to start looking. However, most Freshman also don't need to get a summer internship after their first year, and I often encourage Freshman to avoid the stress of trying to get on this early in their collegiate career. I generally suggest that they take time during the summer to investigate something technical, even if they have a non-technical job. For example, I suggest that students learn a new programming language (*Haskell* is my new favorite to propose), or to learn how to program an app on their phone. Or, I suggest that they read an interesting book about computing, and I have recommended *Gödel, Escher, Bach, An Eternal Golden Braid*, by Douglas Hofstadter a number of times.

For students who are looking for summer internships, I give them pointers on how to go about finding companies (school job fairs are often the best avenues, though a targeted online search for companies that interest them sometimes works well, too), and what to look for in an internship. We discuss the differences between working for a large or a small company, and startups. I tell them that the benefits to working at a large company often include a robust internship program with high-quality projects, and well-defined mentoring. The downsides can include feeling like you are working on a tiny part of a huge project that doesn't feel particularly relevant. The benefits of working at a startup include being part of a vibrant, new company where you may be able to work on something very relevant to the company as a whole. The downside is that you may be given too much responsibility with little mentorship, and you may have been hired because you are cheap labor. I also caution the students to not simply jump at the first offer they are given, and to understand that almost all internships in CS are paid, and that unlike some of their fellow students in other majors, they should expect to be paid well for internships.

For students who are considering graduate school (particularly Ph.D. programs), I suggest that they strongly consider getting involved with research over the summer for at least one summer during college. If they end up doing worthwhile research, this can positively affect their graduate school admissions chances.

Overall, what students do over the summer can be important, both for future job prospects (or graduate school), and also to help inform them about what they might want to do after they graduate. I suggest that they try a variety of different opportunities, if possible.

10. *Is anything else on your mind?* I then talk to potential advisees about the mechanics of declaring their major, and some of the benefits of declaring (e.g., getting on the department mailing list, being eligible for specific majors-only opportunities, etc.). At Stanford, students can change majors, or change advisees without penalty, and I also discuss this option. I tell students that they are welcome to search for an advisor that does research on what they are particularly interested in, as well, and I tell them that it is easy to switch if that professor agrees to be their advisor eventually.

As a new faculty member at a school, you won't know the answers to some of your advisees' questions, particularly as they relate to specific requirements of the major. Be up front with them about this, and assure them that if they ask you a question you don't know how to answer, you will try to find someone who can answer the question. As you have more advisees and the longer you are at your school, the more details you will know about advising, and the more questions you will directly be able to answer. I will often suggest to students who ask me about taking particular courses to talk to other students who have taken the course directly for answers about whether it is a good course, etc. Their peers will be able to give them specific information that you won't be able to provide.

Ongoing Interaction with Advisees

You should strive to interact with your advisees at least once or twice a year, at a minimum. Your school may have a policy that students must meet with their advisor before choosing courses for a term, in which case you should meet with them during those times, at least. If you have many advisees (some advisors have fifty-plus advisees these days), you should schedule the meetings using a calendar. Keep in mind that individual meetings can, in aggregate, take *a lot* of time: for fifty advisees meeting for fifteen minutes each, that is over twelve hours of meetings! Finding twelve extra hours of time in a busy schedule over the course of a week or two is challenging, at best. Some schools allow group meetings, which also may be a time-saving possibility, at the expense of one-on-one time between you and your advisees.

Unless your school has other requirements for meeting students, you are free to meet with them on your own chosen schedule. Some students will want to meet, and others will be happy to simply know that you are available. My own strategy is as follows: at the end of each term, I download my advisees' grades, using a script I wrote to scrape the grades from our online system. Then, I use another script to write a template email to each student, which is stored in a single text file. I fill in the details of the emails based on the student's performance during the term (using the grades), and for those who are doing great, I complement them, and for those who had a rough term, I ask if there is anything I can do to help for the upcoming term. I also offer to meet with them in person. I would say that roughly one third of my advisees end up meeting based on those emails, which I send using a third script. Most of my other advisees reply to the email thanking me for reaching out, and decide not to meet.

Handling the Advising Load

Because computer science is a burgeoning field, and because CS faculties have a hard time growing as fast as the number of students who want to study CS grows, you may find yourself with more advisees than you think you can handle. I have had upwards of sixty or seventy advisees at a time, and it was certainly challenging to make sure I gave all of them enough personalized time.

In your first years of teaching, make sure you discuss your advising load with your department chair, and try to negotiate keeping a small number of advisees for at least a year or two. I would start the discussion with a preferred maximum at about ten new advisees each year. This could grow to about forty advisees, and then should stay steady at that level. Again, the number of advisees you will be required to have, or that you will end up having, will depend on your school and the method for assigning advisees.

As students get to know you, more and more will likely ask you to be their advisor (if your school allows assigning advisors that way). While it can be difficult to say "no" to a student, if your advising load is at your maximum, you should plan out a strategy to point the students to someone else. One way to do this gently is to say that your door is always open to chat, and it is actually to their benefit to get an advisor who they don't know yet, so that they will have another faculty member to interact with.

If you do find yourself overwhelmed with advisee meetings or you simply have too many advisees in general, consider setting up a forum that you moderate where your advisees can ask general questions that others might be able to answer. Not only does this help spread out the advising load a bit, but it also can provide a cohort-like feel to your advising group, which can be beneficial to your advisees. The forum can be as simple as a private Facebook group or invite-only Subreddit, or it can be a Piazza forum or other class forum that you re-purpose for your advising group. It could also be a simple email list, but that can quickly become overwhelming.

You want to be able to give your advisees good advice (of course), and having too many advisees can stretch your time too thin to effectively meet that goal. Use the tools that you have to manage your time, and, as mentioned above, try your best to limit the number of advisees you have until you have enough experience to grow your group effectively.

WRITING RECOMMENDATION LETTERS

As an instructor, you will have students ask for letters of recommendation often during the year. The brunt of the requests will happen on a school calendar schedule, as most letters of recommendation will be for further schooling, whether that is an undergraduate school application (if you are a high school teacher), or a graduate program. Letters are usually due in late Fall or early Winter (in North America), and you can expect to be busy writing the letters during those times. However, students ask for letters of recommendation for scholarships and fellowships, job applications, and other situations, and you may have to write letters that are due at any other time during the year.

If you think about the number of letters of recommendation you have asked for over the years, it is probably not a small number. You had to ask high school teachers for letters of recommendation for college, you had to ask your professors for graduate school letters, and you probably also had to ask for letters to land your current job. Whenever I get flustered by the sheer number of letters I have to write for my students, I think about how I have benefited from letters for me, and that perspective puts me in a positive mood to write top notch letters for my own students.

In this section, I will discuss writing letters for different situations, and for managing your time with many letters, as well. I have written many hundreds of letters in my teaching career, and for certain programs I have had to write upwards of thirty letters at a time. Managing this load while also writing meaningful letters can be challenging, and having a good strategy is key.

Handling recommendation letter requests

When a student (current or past) asks you for a letter of recommendation, you should plan on having a meeting with the student to discuss it. This is particularly important for students who you don't know that well. Perhaps they were a student that never came to office hours, or they rarely spoke in class, or they took the class many years ago and you barely remember them. Even for students that you do know well, setting up a meeting gives you an opportunity to ask them about what they are applying for, and whether they would like you to highlight something important about them. Letters that have impact say something specific about the student above and beyond the grade they got in your course. One of the least impactful letters is what is known as a *Did Well in Class* (DWIC) letter, where you simply comment on the fact that they did well in your class, and don't have much else to offer. The readers of a *DWIC* get little substance from it, and even if the student received an A+ in your class, the letter can actually do more harm than good.

Your meeting about the letter does not need to be long (and can happen over the phone or video), but these are the topics you should discuss:

1. *What are you applying for?* This should be apparent in the original correspondence from the student about the letter, but if it is a program or scholarship you don't already know about, try to find out about it from the student. It is even

better if there is a website that they can point you to about it.

2. *When is the letter due?* This is a critical piece of information. Most students graciously give you enough time to write a letter, which is at least a couple of weeks. But, I have had students ask for letters that are due within a week (and even the next day!), and if this is the case, you need to assess whether you have the time to write the letter. If you don't have time, apologize to the student, and say that you would not be able to write a sufficient letter in such a short time. Telling a student this is harder than you might think, as it means that they will have to scramble to find another letter writer. Your time is important, though, and don't accept the request if it would impact your schedule significantly.

3. *Who else is writing your letters?* Depending on what the student is applying for, this can be an important question. For example, if a student asks you to write a recommendation letter for a Ph.D. program, and you do not have any first-hand knowledge of their research, you should ensure that someone else writing a letter does. While it is often a good idea to have letters from a range of different people, some programs would rather have three letters from the field that the program is in. You (and the student) may not know this, but often program descriptions will indicate the types of letters that should be sent. Additionally, if you know that you will be the only person writing from a particular perspective, you will know to focus on the aspects relevant to that perspective.

4. *Is there anything you want me to focus on?* The student may or may not have an answer to this, but sometimes they do, and it is nice to know if they want you to write about a particular topic. This is also important if you don't remember enough about the student, and need more information. For

students applying to graduate school who have been my teaching assistants, they will often will ask me to focus on their teaching, with the understanding that their academic performance will be discussed by other letter writers. If the student wants you to write about something that you don't have much insight on, then either you need to find out more about that, or you need to tell the student that it isn't something you feel comfortable commenting on. It is not always easy to write about a student you don't know very well, as you may not have much information beyond what is in your gradebook.[4] Sometimes, you can reach out to the teaching assistant for their section (if there are sections in the course), but if you think you are going to struggle with what to write, make sure to get them to tell you something more about themselves for your letter.

What should I write?

It is impossible to be specific with this question, but you should aim to write a letter that tells whomever is reading it something about the student that they could not get from reading a transcript or resume. That said, I always ask my students to send me a resume and an unofficial transcript so I can know a bit more about them. This isn't mandatory, but it can round out the picture for you when you are writing the letter. You can see how they did in other courses to yours, and you can also see what they have done outside of their academics that might be important to discuss in the letter. Some students also send me some written thoughts expanding upon their accomplishments, and that has been extremely useful to inform a number of letters I've written. See figure Figure 8 for an example of a letter I wrote for a former student of mine (I have redacted identifying informa-

---

4 Keep your gradebooks from all your classes for at least five years, as you never know when a former student may ask for a recommendation!

tion). Although I did get to know the student in the course she took, and as an advisee, she and I had a comprehensive discussion about her accomplishments, and I included those in lieu of talking more about her coursework, which was outstanding and clearly demonstrated on her transcript.

You should mention the course or courses that a student took from you. In general it is a good idea to briefly describe the courses as well, with enough information that is apparent what the course was. If the course is known to be one of the more difficult courses in the curriculum, or if there is something unique about the course, mention that, as well.

Each letter is going to be different, and you will spend more time writing some letters than others. How much time you spend on a letter will depend on a number of factors. For some programs, it may be the case that a short letter to the point is all that is needed. This is often true for same-university Master's programs, where students transition from an undergraduate program into the Master's program at your school. Before you spend hours writing letters for such programs, talk to someone on the admissions committee (often it is a faculty member in your department) who can tell you whether they expect detailed letters or not.

Writing letters for your best students is often, but not always, easier than for students who may have struggled in your course. It may be that a student who aced your course did so without seeing you much outside of class, and you don't have as much non-DWIC type feedback. Again, this is a good chance to ask the student whether they would like something specific in the letter, which can give you more to discuss. If it is true that your only real impression of the student is that they did well in the course, then that is what you can talk about, but do keep in mind that it does not make for a particularly strong letter.

Writing letters for students who didn't do terrifically in your course can also be challenging. These are some of the letters that can take the most time to write, particularly if you feel that the student is better than their grade reflects. Perhaps they came to your office hours regularly, and you saw their determination on assignments first-hand. Maybe you saw them work in a lab with partners and they were always the one leading the discussion and problem-solving task. Or, maybe the student did a fantastic job on a final project which you can talk about. Maybe the student did well on assignments but really struggled on exams. You may know of a situation (e.g., an emergency medical situation) which may have also contributed to their less-than-stellar performance, and you can discuss that. All of the situations above merit inclusion in your letter, and can work to the student's benefit. However, one thing to absolutely avoid is to be untruthful in your letter. If a student got a B in your class, and you say, *[the student] was one of the top students in the course!*, it will ring hollow when looked at beside their transcript. That said, if you have a stringent grading policy, and a B is in fact an excellent grade, you should certainly mention that in your letter, to put some perspective on it.

If a student who did not do particularly well in your course asks you for a recommendation letter, they potentially do not have many other instructors to go to where they did better. Or, they think you have a better understanding of their academic situation, and they think a letter from you will be better than one from another instructor. Do those students the favor of taking time to write thorough letters, particularly if you do think it will help their applications.

Sometimes, a particular scholarship or program will ask you to write about specific qualities of the student (e.g., are they independent thinkers, or do they work well in a team environment). If you can follow those guidelines, do so, but don't limit yourself specifically to those prompts. It is important to follow the prompts to a certain extent for some more important applications, such as a Rhodes Scholarship, or an application to medical school. In cases like these, find out if there is an office at your school that handles those applications, and reach out to them to ask if they have suggestions for writing an exemplary letter. If there isn't an office at your school, do some research online and this may lead to good tips and suggestions.

How much time should I spend writing a letter?

As you have more and more students, you will find that the number of letters students ask you to write increases quite significantly. While it would be nice to take an hour to craft the perfect letter, you probably only have time to do this for a small subset of students. Letter-writing *does* take significant time, but if you can eventually get to a point where you write a decent letter in fifteen to twenty minutes, you will be in good shape. You should have a good template for your letters (on your school's letterhead), complete with heading and signature block already filled in. This will make starting each letter quick, even if the writing itself does take some time.

If you get many requests that are due around the same time, try your best not to procrastinate on writing them. From experience, it is no fun writing a dozen letters of recommendation the day they are all due. Spacing out the letter-writing allows you to have a clear head for each letter, and you won't get overwhelmed trying to rush through many letters in a row.

Formatting your letter

Your letter should be on your school's letterhead. Your school may have a general template for you to use with your favorite word processing application, and it is a good idea to search for this before trying to create your own. These days, almost all letters can be in PDF format, and will either be uploaded to an application website, or emailed directly to a point-of-contact. Make sure that the letter identifies the student you are writing about in the heading. You can electronically sign your letter, although it is nice to have an image of your real signature to paste into the document.

Stanford University   DEPARTMENT OF COMPUTER SCIENCE

November 20, 20--

Re: Recommendation for ------, Master's Program in Computer Science

To Whom it May Concern,

I am very pleased to write this recommendation for ------ for acceptance into your Master's of Computer Science program. I taught ------ in CS 106B (*Programming Abstractions*), which is the second course in the computer science core curriculum at Stanford, and serves as a Data Structures course that prepares students for future courses where they are expected to have an excellent programming background. ------ is also my advisee for her undergraduate CS major. She did exceedingly well in CS106B, but her accomplishments go above and beyond academics.

------ is a tremendously motivated student who has already distinguished herself in the computing and biomedical fields with a number of research projects. She has worked on research projects at the Stanford School of Medicine, the Stanford Department of Chemistry, and at ------, and her projects have been a mix of computational biology, biochemistry, and web programming. She also branched out from the research last summer to work at ------ on the ------ team.

In addition to her technical skills, ------ has a passion for increasing female interest and involvement in computer science and technology, and this is primarily why she is such an outstanding candidate for the VMWare scholarship. She holds a leadership position for *Girls Teaching Girls to Code*, a Stanford-run organization that is dedicated to teaching Bay Area high school girls to program, and she was the high school liaison from ------. In the leadership role, she has directed mentors and she has run the group's code camp, influencing hundreds of collegiate and high school women in the process. When ------ was in high school, she founded a middle school STEM outreach program that targets students who have not had formal STEM training and introduces them to science through science bowls and and science fairs. She has received funding to continue the work, as well.

------ epitomizes the type of engaged, creative, and forward-thinking student that motivates women to become interested in and to excel in computing (and STEM in general), and she also provides an exemplary model for such students with her own excellence in education and research.

Academically, ------ has done well in the CS program, and she will continue to excel in your Master's program. She is an excellent candidate and has my full support for admission.

Sincerely,

Chris Gregg, Ph.D.
Lecturer, Computer Science

Department of Computer Science
Gates Computer Science Building, Stanford, CA 94305 | 857.234.0211 F 650.123.4567

Figure 8: Example of a Master's Program letter.

Most often, you should limit your letter to a single page, but this is not a hard rule, especially if the student is applying to a prominent program or for an important scholarship. If you have enough important content that you think bolster's the student's chances for the application, include it. Just be wary that letter-readers appreciate concise prose and don't want to read eloquent text that goes on too long. Some scholarships may require a particular form or format, and follow those guidelines to the best of your ability. If an application asks that you limit your letter to a certain number of pages or word count, follow that guidance.

In all cases when writing your letter, proof-read it at least twice before sending it. You want to write a professional letter, and professional letters should not have spelling or grammatical mistakes. Minor mistakes are not critical, but you should try your best to avoid them. If you feel it is necessary, ask someone else to look over your letters, as well.

Figure 8 shows an example letter that demonstrates reasonable formatting.

WHAT TO DO IF...

What if a student keeps emailing me about writing the letter before it is due?

Students understandably get nervous as the deadline for a letter approaches. Most application websites will tell a student whether their letters have been submitted or not, and if they see yours still outstanding, they may email you to remind you about it. Most of the time, a simple, *Thank you! I will have it written by the deadline* is sufficient to allay their fears. I have never had to write this response more than once.

What if I don't want to write a letter for a particular student?

There are a few situations where you may not feel comfortable writing a letter for a student. If you don't think you can write a decent letter for them, and you don't want to write an unflattering letter, then you should be upfront with the student so they can ask someone else. For students who did poorly in your class and want a recommendation, you should be honest with them that you will need to discuss that they did not do well. I have told a student, "I will have to say that you received a C in the course, and as you know that is not a terrific grade." I have also had students who I have caught cheating in a course ask (amazingly) for a letter of recommendation, and I have told them that I did want to write a letter for that reason.[5]

Some instructors will write unflattering letters if they think it is called for, but I would advise against it, if only because it does tend to be cruel. In my opinion, it is better to tell a student that you won't write a letter than to write a derogatory letter (or even a simply mediocre letter). When a student asks you for a recommendation letter, it is almost certainly because the student thinks you will write a positive letter that will be beneficial, and if you don't want to write a beneficial letter, it is better to tell the student that up front.

What if I miss the deadline for writing a letter?

While it goes without saying that you should try not to miss a deadline, sometimes this happens. The good news is that if you are within a couple of days, most recommendation sites have a grace period and you will still be able to submit the letter. This is not universal, and you should not rely on it, but it is often true. If the recommendation site has already blocked submission, do whatever you can to contact the school or group in charge of the

---

5 The student in question got the point.

application and try to get a letter to them that will be read. Most programs do not penalize a student if their letter-writers do not meet a deadline, but you do owe it to your students to do your best to have the letters in on time. In any case, do not be surprised if a student frantically emails you after the deadline, though, and if that happens apologize and get the letter in immediately.

What if a student wants me to send them a copy of my letter?

In most cases, recommendation letters you write should be private, and should be sent directly to the organizations that requests them. In some cases, a student may ask that letters be sent directly to them for inclusion in an application package. It is up to you whether you want to send the letter or not, and you can ask that they provide you with the contact information to send it yourself. If a student insists, you can either acquiesce and send them a copy, or you can tell them that you would rather not write a letter in that case. This can lead to an awkward conversation, but it is up to you whether you want to share the letter or not. I usually send the letter, as I don't normally have anything to hide in the letters, but I also do not recall being asked to send a letter to a student that I would not be comfortable with them reading.

In some cases, you might want to proactively send a letter to a student. For example, if you know that the student struggles with self-esteem issues, and you have written a glowing letter, feel free to send it to them, as they might appreciate knowing that you would say such nice things about them. In other cases, you may want the student to see if you followed their suggestions for what they asked you to write about, but this is rare.

What if the student does not check the box on the application that says, "I waive my right to see this letter"?

In the United States, the Family Educational Rights and Privacy Act of 1974 (FERPA) protects the rights of students to see their educational materials, and this includes recommendation letters. Therefore, many applications for college and graduate school ask students to waive their right to see the recommendation letters, on the idea that a letter is going to be more honest if it is confidential between the letter-writer and the admissions committee. However, even if a student does not waive the right, they are only allowed access to their records after they are accepted to, and enroll at, a particular school. Almost all students do waive this right, although occasionally a student will not. It is certainly up to you whether you want to decline to write a letter based on this, but it is a fairly minor issue, and I have never declined to write a letter in such a case. What you should definitely avoid is writing your letter with this in mind – write what you want to say regardless of whether the student has waived their right to see the letter eventually.

Should I ask (or let) my student draft their letter for me?

There are some instructors who ask that their students draft their recommendation letters for them. It saves them time, and it also ensures that the letter says what the students want it to say. While those sound like reasonable reasons, I would argue that it undermines the point of letters of recommendation in general. It is not really the truth to say that you wrote a recommendation letter if it was actually the student who wrote it, even if you edited the letter and added your own touch. Furthermore, it puts the student in the position of trying to write in your voice and give your perception, and that isn't fair to the student, whether they agree to the idea or not. Asking the students to provide you some idea of what they might want you to talk about (as discussed above), is reasonable.

Should I accept gifts after writing a letter?

Accepting gifts from students in general is an ethical question that you must answer for yourself. Obviously, you should never accept any gift prior to writing a letter, as this is easily construed as bribery and it also may color your honesty in writing a letter.

There may be rules in your school about accepting gifts, and those rules may forbid accepting any gifts, or put a maximum monetary value on gifts you can receive. Be sure to understand any rules that exist before deciding what to do yourself. Some instructors politely turn down all gifts as a matter of course, and this is a fine option, though it may risk a *faux pas* with students from cultures where gift-giving as thanks is deeply ingrained. Other instructors believe that accepting a card along with a small token of thanks (e.g, an inexpensive gift or a low-denomination gift certificate) is reasonable, and turning away such a token would potentially insult a student who is trying to show you gratitude. Some instructors will never accept gifts for current students, but do accept gifts for graduating students, or students who would otherwise never be in another of their classes. If you do decide to accept a gift, be thankful in return, and know that the student is grateful to you for taking time to write them a letter.

Should I tailor my letters to each school individually?

Sometimes a student is applying to many schools simultaneously, and asks that you send a recommendation letter to each school. You do not have to write multiple letters, and the one letter you write should be generic enough to work at any school. One exception would be if a school asks specifically for you to highlight some particular aspect of the student, and you don't think it fits into a generic letter. Another exception might be if you have a particular connection to a school (e.g., if it is for your own school's program, or if you are an alumnus of the school you are writing the letter to), you might want to take the time to personalize some of the individual letters.

FINAL THOUGHTS

You will interact with students outside of class more frequently than you think. Whether it is during office hours, or to discuss a letter of recommendation, or to talk about how the student can improve in your course, be welcoming, and treat the student and their questions with respect. You are a role model for your students, and you should consider your meetings with them an important part of your teaching. Writing recommendation letters for students can be time consuming, but it is also an important part of your students' academic and post-academic careers.

15

PRIORITIZING YOUR TIME, AND WHEN TO JUST SAY NO

MUCH OF THIS BOOK HAS discussed time management, and I have stressed that during your first year of teaching you will be stretched for time almost continually. It is no secret that preparing to teach, and teaching itself, is time consuming, and preparation time is magnified tremendously in your first year because everything is new. Therefore, you will certainly come upon situations during your first year teaching that you will have to make a choice about what to spend your time on, and sometimes making that choice is challenging. In this chapter, I'll discuss some strategies for making those choices, and I will also talk about when you should be assertive and *Just Say No* to requests for your time.

HOW TO PRIORITIZE YOUR TIME

There are twenty-four hours in a day, and that's all you get. In those hours, you need to take care of yourself (eat, drink, sleep, bathe, pay bills, have fun, etc.), you need to attend to any family members who rely on you, and, of course, you need to do your job as a teacher. This last category involves planning, teaching, grading, working with TAs, meeting with students and other faculty, writing recommendation letters, potentially doing research, and reflecting on your teaching, as well. Finding the time for all of this is difficult, and it can be stressful. You need to prioritize your time, and making decisions about what is most important and necessary can be hard.

When prioritizing your time, you actually need to think about your own personal needs first. If you don't get enough sleep, or you aren't eating well, you'll wear down faster, and this will, ultimately and perhaps surprisingly, give you less time to work on the other tasks you need to accomplish. Additionally, if you aren't thinking of yourself first, you risk putting your mental health in jeopardy, and this can lead to burnout, and even worse, to a potential mental health breakdown. In either case, you will negatively affect your time management if you don't take care of yourself first. Putting your work above your own needs isn't worth the risks.

The above paragraph notwithstanding, you may find yourself sleep-deprived during your first year of teaching. You should try to set aside enough time for rest, but there are going to be times when you have to spend a few more hours working on a lesson plan, or grading assignments, and sleep will have to wait. If this does happen, do your best to catch up on a weekend, or find a time to fit in a nap. You will thank yourself for it.

While you are ensuring that your own base needs are met, you do need to prioritize your work. You aren't always going to make the same choices in every situation, but you should put together a decent hierarchy of what must be done through what can wait. Prioritizing your time based on what you think is best for your students is a decent place to start. That means that assignment and lecture preparation are critical, because they fall in a tight schedule. You can't easily move assignment dates too much, and your lecture times are fixed. Returning grades reasonably quickly is also important, as students should know how they are doing in your course, particularly if they want to improve. If you return all the grades near the end of the term, students won't have time to make any changes, and that is not fair to them. Sometimes you can prioritize certain grading over others (e.g., grading exams before lab reports).

You will have other hard deadlines that you need to meet, such as grade reporting deadlines and recommendation letter deadlines. You can only postpone attending to these tasks for so long before the deadline is upon you, so they do need to eventually take priority.

As discussed in Chapter 9, you need to manage your teaching assistants if you have them. It is important, particularly at the beginning of the term, to prioritize their training and to ensure that they are ready to teach or grade. You should have a regularly scheduled meeting with your TAs, as well, and you should not cancel these meetings unless absolutely necessary.

Meetings with students can be a big time commitment, and you should have some flexibility with scheduling these meetings. You should prioritize meetings with current students who have an important topic to discuss, such as improving in the course, or if they have a personal emergency they want to discuss. You can be more flexible with meetings with advisees or other students, and scheduling these around other deadlines is usually easier.

You may have duties or committee meetings to attend, and if you have to miss a meeting once in a while, that is probably fine (though don't make a habit of it). Other faculty members understand the time crunch, and most recognize the extra amount of time that new teachers spend planning, as well.

If you are conducting education research, hopefully most of the data collecting is happening as the course is progressing, and you should plan on doing most of your analysis when you don't have other pressing duties. You may be shooting to have a paper written by a particular deadline, but if the time crunch becomes too great, know that there will always be future conferences to submit your paper to.

It is important to have a good calendar to keep track of your commitments. Every time you get something with a deadline, put it on the calendar, and check your calendar often. A calendar program that sends reminders is useful, although it can get frustrating snoozing all of the reminders when they pop up. I find it useful to have *TODO* lists to prioritize my time, and it is a bonus to feel the sense of accomplishment when you finally finish all of the items on a particular list[1]. You should try to find a way to keep track of your priorities, and stick to it.

WHEN TO JUST SAY NO

Because you will have so much to do in your first year of teaching, you will have limited (at best) time to take on new responsibilities. There will, however, be a potentially endless stream of requests for your time that you might feel obligated to accept, and in some cases, the correct thing to do is to decline those requests. You may get asked to serve on committees (sometimes you are place on committees as part of your job obligations), you may be asked to attend meetings about curriculum, to help with interviewing prospective new hires, or to help plan a department event. You might be asked to proofread a colleague's paper, or to help brainstorm ideas for a new course. You will be asked by students to go to some of their extracurricular events (e.g., sports, plays, concerts, etc.), or to attend a school or dorm-sponsored meal. Students might also ask for non-office hours help on assignments or even for something from another course.

Your primary responsibility as a teacher is to teach, and to perform all of the teaching-related duties covered in this book. If you get a request to do something extra, you should feel no guilt in turning down the request if you don't think you have the time for it. This is not always easy, particularly if the person making the request is your boss or department chair. Your best bet in this case is to be honest about your stance (that you don't have time), and to be diplomatic about it. Apologize, and thank your boss for thinking of you. If your boss insists that you accept, then it was not really a request in the first place, and you may not have a

---

1 I rarely get through all of my *TODO* items on any particular list, unfortunately! But, the few times I have, it is a big sense of accomplishment.

choice in the matter.[2] Most department chairs recognize that new teachers are extra busy, so you may have better luck turning down the request than you might think.

It is also sometimes difficult to turn down student requests. After all, you want the students to flourish, and it is flattering to be asked by a student for help, or to attend an event of theirs. However, if you assess that you don't have time to accept the request, reject it nicely and with tact, and do not feel guilty about it. You may be able to schedule something after the term ends, or at some more suitable time, as well, and if you think that is possible, ask the student to do so. In the case of missing an event or performance, you could ask them to find a different event to ask you to attend in the future.

As mentioned in the previous section, one your most important time prioritizations should be to yourself, for your own needs. This may include turning down social requests, as well, particularly in the interest of getting a bit of rest. Teaching itself is exhausting, which means that you may feel you actually need more sleep than you would when you aren't in the middle of a term. One of the best pieces of advice I received when I was a new teacher was to avoid agreeing to going out to socialize on Friday nights. You'll be exhausted from your week of teaching, and there is nothing more satisfying than simply going home for that well-needed nap. That is not to say that you should turn down all social events. On the contrary, a drink with friends after a exhausting week might be exactly what you need to unwind. You just might be too tired for a late Friday night gathering.

---

2 If you think the duty is beyond the scope of your job, and you are in a union, you could talk to your union representative about it. Again, though: remain diplomatic during any conversations with your boss.

WHAT TO DO IF...

What if I get burned out?

Getting burned out during your first year teaching is a very real concern. You want to avoid this to the best of your ability, and good time management can go a long way towards this goal. If you do find yourself burning out, here are some suggestions that you can try that may help:

1. *Plan a "rejuvenation" day for yourself.* This may seem counterintuitive if you are swamped with work, but if you are getting burned out, you need to interrupt the burnout cycle in some way. Schedule a day in the near future where you promise that you will turn off all your electronic devices, and avoid any work whatsoever. Pamper yourself, and do your best to forget about the work, just for the day. You can do this on a weekend day, or, you can take what is known in the business as an *Emotional Health Day*, where you take a day off, cancel everything, and mentally decompress. Yes, this means canceling class (or getting a substitute), and as long as this isn't a regular occurrence, don't feel guilty about it. As I said in the previous section, your mental health must come first, or you eventually won't be able to do your job at all.

2. *Find a guest lecturer for the day.* It is amazing how much you can benefit from a single day off of teaching and planning to teach. Much like a rejuvenation day, you will feel a release of pressure where you can (if you want) catch up on other work, or you can simply relax a bit. Students appreciate having a guest for the day, and if you can find someone with expertise in the topic scheduled for the day, that is perfect. The guest lecturer could be another instructor, or someone you know from another school, or someone in industry. It can also be a TA who you know would like to teach a full

class (many do). You do have to plan this with enough time for your guest to prepare (with at least a week or two notice), and while you don't have to attend the class yourself, you probably should. Again, don't underestimate how much relief it will be to have a single day off from planning and teaching.

3. *Find a therapist.* This may seem like overkill, but having someone to talk to in a clinical sense is a terrific way to work on burnout. In the U.S., almost all medical health insurance plans allow for a small number of visits to a psychologist or therapist for no more than the cost of a co-pay, and a few visits might be enough to get you out of your rut.

4. *Commiserate with colleagues.* There is nothing wrong with reaching out to a colleague to vent about your workload, although you don't want to come off as whining (they are likely very busy, too!). It is nice to have someone who knows the struggles of a first year teacher to talk to, and it can be cathartic. You may also get specific advice to help out, too.

5. *Reduce some time-consuming part of your course.* This may seem drastic, but making a change to your course mid-term is often doable. If you had planned seven assignments for the term, and you know you won't have time to create all of them, simply take away one assignment, and either extend the due date on some of the other assignments. An added benefit is that many, if not all, of your students will actually appreciate the gesture, as they are busy, too, and will welcome the relief. You can frame it as giving everyone a break in the course, and no one will be wiser that your ulterior motive was to reduce your own overworked self.

What if I miss a critical deadline?

Sometimes your workload can get so overwhelming that you miss a deadline. There are actually very few critical deadlines in academia, and as long as you catch the mistake relatively quickly, you can probably make up for it. As mentioned in Chapter 14, missing a recommendation deadline is not usually critical, and most academic deadlines are somewhat flexible if you apologize and fix the problem when you find out about it. As an example, at many universities, submitting grades for graduating seniors is an important deadline, and sometimes comes before grades for other students are due. If you miss this deadline, the registrar might email you with a plea to submit your senior grades immediately, but you won't be stopping a student from graduating if you comply when you get the email. Remember: schools are unlikely to penalize a student for a minor faculty mistake. You do want to avoid making missing deadlines a habit, but if one happens occasionally, it is not the end of your career.

What if I promised students something but can't make the deadline I set?

This is similar to the last question, in the sense that it is probably not critical. If you promised your students something (e.g., getting their grades back by a certain date) but miss the deadline, own up to it, and be honest with the students, and then re-prioritize your work to meet the promise as soon as you can. Honesty is the key here: you have to let the students know you are responsible, and will do your best to make it right by them. If that means pushing a deadline for the students out on an assignment, for example, you should be willing to do that as well.

What if I accepted a request but realize later I don't have the time for it?

This is unfortunate, but again, you need to be honest with the person who made the request, and apologize for your mistake. Sometimes it is too late for someone else to take over, in which case you really should re-prioritize to do the work yourself. If it means a sleepless night or two, then it will serve as a good reminder in the future for you to remember that you can say *no* to some requests.

What if my teaching suffers because I have too much to do?

In your first year of teaching, there may be times where you feel that your instruction, assignments, or other student-facing work is not up to the standard you would like it to be. Don't be too hard on yourself, as this happens to virtually everyone in their first year of teaching. Again, re-prioritize as necessary to satisfy your own teaching goals, and do the best you can. Use the experience to do better next term, and learn from the mistakes. In my first year teaching at Tufts University, I misjudged my time and gave out a rushed assignment that had coding mistakes, and that had instructions that were grossly unclear. The main reason was that I had not given myself enough time to plan the assignment, and it went out without being properly vetted. The students had a difficult time with the assignment, and many rightly blamed me for it. I received a number of derogatory comments in the end-of-term evaluations about that one assignment. But, I recovered for follow-on assignments, and I have made sure to never put myself into that position again.

FINAL THOUGHTS

You owe it to yourself to manage your time as effectively as you can during your first year (and future years) of teaching. Time management means prioritizing important duties and responsibilities, and to know when to say *no* to a request, but it also means taking time for your own needs so you don't get burned out. You may be surprised at how busy you are during your first year of teaching, but you can do it, and trying to get ahead of the time crunch is one of the most important suggestions I can offer as you embark on your teaching career.

EPILOGUE

EPILOGUE: HAVE FUN!

I HOPE THAT HAVING FINISHED THIS BOOK, you realize that I love teaching in general, and that I love teaching computer science specifically[1]. Teaching can be a wonderful and fulfilling profession, with the upsides vastly outnumbering the downsides. That said, it may not always feel that way. In this book I have tried to comprehensively outline the responsibilities you will have in your teaching career, and I have not sugar-coated the challenging parts of the job. Your first year teaching is going to be demanding, and you should be prepared for that, and you must plan well. I have known many teachers over the years that have *not* been prepared for the rigors of their first year, and in more than one case they gave up on the profession after a tiring and frustrating experience. What I hope is that when you start to get exhausted, and you feel thwarted by the lack of hours in the day you realize that these experiences are part of the job, but are an even bigger part of the job during your first year. In that respect, *you can do this!* Your first year teaching can feel like a trial by fire, and one of the reasons I wrote this book is to give you the firefighting tools you'll need to battle that blaze without getting burned.

Warnings aside, I also sincerely hope that you do enjoy teaching during your first year, and that for every challenging situation that arises, you have a dozen amazing student interactions, and a dozen more times where you are as excited as the first day you took your first computer science course, and the first day you realized that you wanted to teach computer science. You are going to meet some amazing students and colleagues, and you are going to enjoy piloting your students through their own journey though your courses.

---

1 I also love teaching high school physics, too!

Be proud of finishing your first year! Also be proud of finishing your first lecture, your first assignment, your first exam, and every other *first* you have – they are all important, and each one marks a milestone in your year. Each one brings its own challenges, but after completing something once, you now have experience that you can use to improve it next time. Hopefully most of those firsts will also turn out great, and as you reflect on the experience, you'll realize that your hard work and planning paid off. For those that didn't go as planned, remember to write down what you think you can improve, and go back to your notes the next time. Your *second* year teaching will be better than the first, I guarantee it.

In the twenty years I have been teaching, I have learned something significant during every course I have taught. My teaching today is different in many ways than it was during my own first year of teaching, certainly. I have adopted new methods and I have retired methods that don't work as well as I had hoped. As I said in Chapter 11, observing other teachers has been a critical part of my own teaching, and I hope you also have the opportunity to observe as many other teachers you can, both during your first year and beyond. Seeing how others practice our craft diffuses good practice throughout the teaching field, and when other teachers observe you, the diffusion continues.

So: *Have Fun* during your first year of teaching. You are embarking on an exciting journey of your own, and even if half way through the term you wonder what you have gotten yourself into[2], you will make it to the end of your first year, and it will be triumphant. Congratulations in advance, and when you make it through your first year, send me a note, so that I can congratulate you personally.

---

2 Feel free to re-read Chapter 1!

APPENDICES

TEACHING ONLINE

In 2020, THE COVID-19 PANDEMIC CAUSED many of the world's teachers to take their courses online. Most were not prepared to do so, and had little time to prepare. In many of those cases, this led to incredible frustration from the teachers and their students. The goal for this appendix is to provide some framework for teaching a computer science course online to what would otherwise be taught to traditional students in a classroom or lecture hall.

Online teaching is not new, nor is teaching computer science online. There are excellent models for certain types of online learning. For example, Coursera provides *Massive Open Online Courses (MOOCs)*, and Kahn Academy provides course-like videos and tutorials for students. Many universities also held online courses before COVID-19, and continue to do so as a matter of routine. However, COVID-19 forced *all* courses to go online at many schools, and unless an instructor was already teaching online, converting their courses to an online format may have been challenging, and the resulting course might not be as refined as it could have been without more time to plan.

In this appendix, I will outline some steps you can take to convert a course that you already teach into an online course, with some best practices I have learned during the COVID-19 pandemic in my own courses. Some aspects of computer science coursework are relatively easy to transition – assignments, for example, can often be used in exactly the same form as they would in an in-person course, as students are expected to work on them independently, and this doesn't change in an online offering. Other aspects are more difficult to transition. Certainly, lecturing is different online than it is in person. Although Zoom or other online video-conference platforms offer a medium for you to lecture to your students, questions from students are often more difficult to take, and there is much less interpersonal feedback over video. Students are also less likely to ask questions than if they were in a regular classroom or lecture hall. Examinations are also necessarily different: proctoring an exam without students in the same room is completely different, as is the ability to control what resources your students are using to take the exam.

PREPARATION

When schools started converting to online teaching during the COVID-19 pandemic, many teachers did not have much time to prepare their classes to work in an online format. If you do have time to prepare, you will want to think about what parts of your course can work without much (or any) change, and what parts you will have to overhaul significantly. You should first find out if there are any limitations or changes that your school has instituted for online courses. For example, your school may have changed the schedule, where the term is shorter or longer than a regular term. Or, your school may have limited how or when exams can be given. If your school has, for instance directed that there will not be a final exam period as there normally is, you will have to plan for something different than a traditional final exam. Your school may also insist that all lectures are recorded, and that students should be able to watch the videos at their convenience. This may inform your schedule for assessments, particularly if you have an assignment that expects students to have seen the lecture. If some may not see it for a day or two after you deliver it, you may have to move assignment dates to compensate.

After confirming the parameters around which you need to re-plan your course, you should start setting out your calendar, as described in Chapter 6. Your calendar serves as scaffolding for the course, and you will build the rest of the course around the calendar. Be as precise as you can about dates: at the very least rough out your assignment and assessment dates as early as possible. Start filling in lecture topics, as well, with the understanding that you may have to add or remove a small number of lectures if the school's calendar has been modified.

In your early planning stages, you should consider the overall format of your course, and think about ways that you can make it a better experience for online students. Perhaps you want to think about a flipped classroom approach, where you have lecture videos that students watch on their own time, and you spend the actual lecture time in a less formal setting where you answer questions, or go over more detailed examples. I will discuss more about lectures below, but you if you do decide on a flipped model, you may also want to consider canceling some of the live lectures each week so students will have more time to watch the other material. When thinking about the format of the course, you can also consider modifying how you grade assignments, or how you handle assignment deadlines. With the COVID-19 pandemic, many instructors tried to limit their students' stress levels by being more lenient with assignment deadlines, or by allowing students to re-do work. If you are planning for an online course that isn't being held because of a particular situation (like a pandemic), making these kinds of changes might not be necessary. With whatever changes you make, however, you should consider how it will change your grading or assessment schedule. For example, allowing students to re-do work means that someone will need to grade the new work, and you will have to budget time for that.

In your preparation phase, get to know the new tools that you will have to use for the online course. If you are using a video meeting software (e.g., Zoom), you should look at the features, and try them out. For example, Zoom has two different types of meetings, a regular meeting and a *webinar* format, which is designed for large meetings (>100 students). The regular meeting has video for all participants and you can put participants into *breakout rooms* for small discussions. There is also a chat window for comments, but (at the time of this writing) no formal question and answer window. The webinar only allows video for the host and so-called *panelists*, but viewers (i.e., your students) will not have video that you can see. Webinars do have a useful question and answer window, but does not support break-out rooms. So, your planning should include becoming familiar with the type of video meetings you can have, and you should make any decisions about how you are going to use them. You should also practice with them. For example, putting students into breakout rooms has a couple of steps, and practicing those ahead of time is wise. Also make sure that you understand how to record on whatever platform you use. It would be unfortunate if you had to re-do a lecture for recording because it didn't record the first time. You should also make sure that you are posting your videos in an approved way – this is usually through your schools LMS system. Posting on sites like YouTube or Vimeo may be a possibility, but you must check with your school to see if there are any limitations (e.g., the videos must not be public, or they must be password protected, or they must have closed-captions, etc.).

Also make sure you test any screen-sharing that you will be using (for slides, videos, etc.) during class. You should recruit someone to help test the screen sharing, to ensure that it is working correctly. For example, if you want to play a video on Zoom, you need to ensure that sound is being broadcast from your computer to your class, and there is also a Zoom-specific checkbox that says, "Optimize for a full-screen video clip." This makes videos show better to your class, but it also often blurs text on slides. So, you would want to practice sharing your screen for videos, and then sharing your screen for slides.

You need to decide how (and if) you are going to "write on the board" in your lectures, if you generally do that in real life. Some instructors decide not to write at all, and just talk over static slides. Others like to use a tablet such as the iPad / Apple Pencil combination, so they can draw on top of their slides. I prefer an attached screen that has a pen, and software that allows me to draw over anything on the screen.[1] Again, make sure you practice with the technology so that when you use it you aren't fumbling around with the hardware or software.

If you are going to be on camera for lectures (either recorded or live), you should invest in a decent microphone and some good lighting. You should ask your department to at least partially fund these items. For sound, you can use a lapel microphone that clips onto your shirt under your chin, or you can use a standalone microphone. You can also get an earbuds / microphone combination, but you should look at the reviews to ensure that they will be good enough for your lectures. For light, make sure that you have some light on your face, and a well-lit room may be all that you need. But, a good ring light can also help to brighten up your face.

LECTURING ONLINE IN REAL TIME

Lecturing to a screen is significantly different that lecturing in person. Some teachers find it difficult to do, as you don't get feedback in the same way you do in class, and you aren't standing up in front of anyone (in most cases, you aren't standing at all![2]). When you are lecturing to a screen, it sometimes feels very much like you are talking to nobody in particular, especially if you are lecturing in a format where student videos are turned off. You need to mentally adjust your pacing to address this, and you may want to stop more frequently for questions.

When preparing your lectures for online delivery, you will have to think about how you want students to participate in the lecture. Do you want them to use the *raise hands* icon and wait for you to call them? Do you want them to put questions in a chat window, or to use a dedicated question/answer part of the video platform

---

1 I use a Wacom Cintiq 16 and Deskscribble software on my Apple Mac computer.
2 That said, I have colleagues who insist on standing to deliver their lectures on video, and some use a real whiteboard. If you decide to do this, make sure you test your recording ability to ensure that everything is in frame and clear.

(if it exists)? You may want them to ask questions on an external forum, which may have more flexibility regarding how the questions get asked. One problem with almost all of these methods is that it means you must pay attention to the part of your screen where the questions (or raised hands) will appear, then address the questions. This can be disruptive to your own flow. One way to mitigate this is to have a TA fielding questions during class, and typing the answers. If the TA thinks that a question is something you should address out loud, the TA can interrupt you to suggest that you answer it.

One observation I have made about students in live online lectures is that they are quite happy to ask many questions by typing them, but much more reluctant to ask a question on video (more so that in a regular classroom, certainly). This means that you will likely get more questions than in an in-person lecture, but they will be typed and require you to read them. This is another good reason to enlist the help of a TA, so that they can field the greater number of questions in real-time.

Enticing students to ask questions, or to participate in general, in an online lecture can be challenging. Some students just do not like speaking on video, knowing that everyone else in the class is staring at them on their computer. One idea to increase participation is to allow students to ask a question with their video off, leading to less stress for students who are worried about being on screen. Another idea is to be sure to give plenty of time for questions. I like to spend at least ten minutes after class fielding questions, and more students tend to ask questions during that time period. I actually leave the recording going to capture those questions, though I know some instructors turn off the video before answering questions after lecture.

If you decide you want students to talk among themselves during your lecture, you will need to use a breakout room strategy, where you place or allow students to go into private chat rooms to discuss the topic under consideration (e.g., how to solve an algorithm, or the answer to a coding question). You can jump into the breakout rooms, as well, to see how students are doing. I will admit that I am not a big fan of breakout rooms, simply because it takes a non-trivial amount of time to manage them, and I have also heard from many students that they do not find them particularly helpful. A quick *think-pair-share* question during an in-person lecture can take 50% longer to run in an online class, simply because of the logistics. But it is an option if you want to pursue it.

One thing to keep in mind when delivering online lectures is to break your lecture into digestible parts of between five and fifteen minutes a piece. Watching a lecture online can lead to fatigue if the instructor talks for long stretches, and it is easy to get distracted when you are in front of a computer in general. It also makes it easier for those watching a recording to know when a good place is to pause.

As always, practice your lectures ahead of time, particularly at the beginning of the term. Work on timing and managing your screen, in particular. If you can enlist the help of someone to watch some of your practice, they can give you feedback on what works and doesn't work. It is also a good idea to get feedback from the students about what they think is working well and what isn't working well, and then try and tailor your remaining lectures based on the feedback.

When it finally comes time to give your lecture online, try to be as relaxed as you would for any other lecture. It may be difficult to do this at first, as you are on a different medium, and you might be nervous that you haven't prepared well, or that you will make a mistake. Actually, it is true that you likely *will* make some mistakes, but this is also true for in-person lectures, as well. If you are recording the lectures then yes, you will have a more permanent record of those mistakes, but just like in an in-person lecture, you should try not to be overly concerned about it. If you make a mistake that you think should be addressed, then you can do it in the next class, just like you would in an in-person lecture.

RECORDING LECTURES AHEAD OF TIME

You may decide to record lectures, or other videos for your students. You may want to do this if you have a flipped classroom model, or if you simply want to provide the students with more content. Keep in mind that recording lectures can take a significant amount of time. When you record a video, there is a big temptation to make it perfect, and this can lead to spending (too) many hours working on your videos. As described above, you don't have a chance to fix mistakes in a live lecture, whereas when you are recording a lecture, you could stop the recording and re-shoot when you make a mistake. Unless you re-film the entire lecture or part of the lecture you are recording, you will then have to use video editing software to combine the clips, and again, this can take time[3].

My first suggestion when recording videos is to keep recording, even if you make a mistake. Unless the mistake is so major that you feel you *must* re-shoot it, just move on. If you want to use video editing software to put some text over the video where you made the mistake to correct it, that's fine, but you probably don't have time to continuously stop and re-shoot parts just because they aren't absolutely perfect.

My second suggestion when recording videos is to try and keep each one relatively short (5-15 minutes). You can assign students multiple videos per week, and with each one short it is easy to re-shoot (if necessary). Your students will also appreciate bite-sized videos, too – it provides a good place to take a break, and there less video fatigue when they watch a series of shorter videos to make up an entire lecture.

One very nice thing about recording videos is that you can re-use them in future terms. It may take a long time to produce the videos, but as long as you don't have any specific informa-

---

3 Not to mention that learning video editing software takes a significant amount of time, too.

tion about the current term, you can easily re-use them in future classes.

If you do decide to record videos and assign the students to watch them, you should come up with a plan for ensuring that they are indeed watching them. One of my colleagues, Nick Troccoli, assigns very short post-video multiple choice quizzes that students must complete after watching a series of short content videos. The quizzes are not worth a large number of points, and they are easy to grade. But, they are a decent forcing function to make sure that students are looking at the videos.

If you are having students watch content videos, you can devote your normal lecture time to answering questions, or working on longer examples. Given the amount of time watching the lectures takes, you should also consider making these live sessions optional for the students. I have found that those that do attend the sessions get a lot out of them. If you record those sessions, as well, then all of your students can benefit from them.

ASSIGNMENTS

Assignments for an online computer science course don't necessarily have to be any different than your assignments during an in-person term. If you allow students to pair-program for their assignments, then you may need to think about how they can realistically share code to work on the project, as partners will likely not be co-located. There are various tools dedicated to remote pair-programming, such as codetogether.com. Otherwise, you can almost certainly use assignments that are the same or very similar to the ones that you would use in any other term.

One consideration you may have to address is that your office hours (for you and your TAs) will be strictly online, and for students who get a significant amount of help for assignments during office hours, the difference may be important. If they cannot get as much help (or the help they get is not as useful) from office hours, then they may not do as well. This can also, unfortunately, lead to students looking at external resources for help (e.g., on-line, or from friends or classmates), which may be against your honor code policy. See the next section for ideas on how to make office hours efficient.

OFFICE HOURS

One of the most significant and challenging differences between an in-person course and an online course is with office hours, and with TA helper hours. If your students are used to going to office hours on campus, they will have to adjust to online office hours, in whatever form you and your TAs end up holding them.

Predicting whether online office hours will be more crowded than in-person office hours is not easy, though you and your TAs should be prepared to manage an increased number of students to the best of your ability. Because online office hours do not ne-cessitate your students actually going anywhere, it is likely that you will see more students than you would in an equivalent in-person setting. If you know that you will have students in various time zones, you should also try and accommodate that to some extent. If you also have TAs in different time zones, setting their schedules accordingly will help, as well.

Your Office Hours

You can use whatever technology you feel most comfortable with for your office hours, and it is probably easiest to use the same video software you use for your lectures (e.g., Zoom, or WebEx, etc.). The students will be used to the system, as will you be. There are, however, various software packages that have been developed recently that are specifically designed for office hours or for stu-dent help sessions, and if you have time you can take a look at some of those packages.

As discussed in Chapter 14, you can hold one-on-one office hours or group office hours. With software such as Zoom, you can bring students into a one-on-one breakout room as the other students wait in the main room, or you can use the *waiting room* functionality, where students do not see any other students and just wait for you to let them in. My preference is to let all students into the main room and then either bring them one at a time into a breakout room, or simply help students in the main room. I do not like to simply have students wait for long times in the waiting room, as it is not as welcoming. If all the students are in the main room, then you can foster a situation where they can discuss ideas among themselves, and this can lead to better student understanding, as well.

One excellent feature of programs such as Zoom is screen sharing, where you can let students share their screen with you as if you were with them in person. If you help students directly with their code, this allows you to directly help them with their code, and you can also annotate the screen (i.e., you can draw on their screen with your mouse or a pen) if you need to show them something, or point them to a particular place in their code or in a debugger (for instance). It is particularly easy to annotate the screen if you have a drawing tablet, iPad, or other device that uses a pen. You may also be able to completely take over your student's screen and their mouse, although I have not found that to be necessary except in rare situations (for example, if you need to help them debug a software installation).

One nice benefit of holding your office hours in an group form where all students are on screen simultaneously is that other students can learn from your conversations with particular students. Students who have similar questions benefit from this open discussion, and it sometimes cuts down on the time you have to spend with individuals. You do have to be somewhat careful with screen sharing, as the other students can see each others' screens, as well, and this could lead to honor code violations if they copy code or answers. I have not found this to be a problem in my online courses, but if you want to look at student screens privately, you can jump into a breakout room.

I have found that managing online office hours is more challenging than in-person office hours. As with in-person office hours, you should keep track of the order in which students arrive, so that you can meet with them in that order. I have not found a way to do this using the video presentation software, so I simply keep track in a document as I let them into the room, and I check them off as I get to each one.[4] If students are waiting for you when office hours start (so you don't know the order in which they arrived), you should just take them randomly. In that case, I usually just populate my document with the names in random order and then let them all in at once. Then, I tell them the order, so they know roughly how long they will have to wait. When new students arrive, I put them on the list, let them in, and tell them approximately how many students are ahead of them.

During office hours, after I see each student once, I will encourage them to stay online and I will try and get back to them. Some students do stay online, and others will drop off, but it usually works out that I get back to all of the students if they are still having trouble. However, as with in-person office hours, you may find that you have too many students for the allotted time, and it is difficult to get to all of them. I make it a priority to try and get to each student at least once during my office hours, and I will extend the office hours if I can to accomplish this. If you find that you routinely have too many students to handle during office hours, consider adding more office hours, or bringing in a TA to help with the load. If neither of those is an option, then you need to decrease the amount of time with each student, which is not always easy to do. But, do your best to manage the student load so that you can talk to each student.

---

4 You can use queuing software, such as Queuestatus, if you'd like, too.

Your TA Helper Hours

If you have TAs for your course, you should have them hold on-line office hours for at least the same amount of hours that they would for an in-person course. If you have multiple TAs that will be working concurrently, it is ideal if you can use a scheduling system to put the students into a queue. Each TA will then be able to dequeue the next student, and the throughput of students can be optimal. There are online queue systems that you can investigate, such as https://queuestatus.com. Your school may also have an in-house queuing system that you can use, as well.

TAs will have to get used to online office hours, and there will be some overhead to working with students online. Transitioning between students can take some time, and if your TAs will be sharing the students screen to help with code, this adds more time to the interaction. As mentioned above, you may also find that online office hours need to serve more students than in-person office hours did, simply because the barrier to "go to" office hours is lower. If you and your TAs find this to be the case, it is critical that you work with your TAs to manage the load effectively, or you risk both burning out your TAs and frustrating the students who may feel that they are not getting enough help. Management can include limiting the amount of time each student gets with a TA, adding more TA hours (which is not always possible), or creating separate queues for different types of questions (e.g., code help -vs- conceptual questions). You can also have TAs hold group office hours where they help students with general questions but do not work with students on individual code.

As always, making sure that your TAs are properly trained for working with students is vitally important. For an online course, your training will be different than for an in-person course, and it should include thinking about how to handle too many students, how to effectively use the software, and how to efficiently help students so that the queue does not stall, or become too long.

EXAMINATIONS

You will need to carefully plan your quiz, test, or exam assessments for your online course. If your in-person course would normally have in-class assessments that you proctor, you won't be able to proctor them in the same way (if at all) for your online course. You may be under certain restrictions from your school on the format, timing, or allowable resources. At Stanford, for example, all online quizzes and exams cannot be closed book, with the rationale that closed book exams that are not proctored puts an undue burden on students to uphold the honor code. However, instructors can impose rules such as "you cannot post questions online about the exam problems, nor can you search for specific solutions to exam problems." As another example, Stanford instructors cannot force students to limit the time they spend on a take-home exam (e.g., "you are only allowed to work on the exam for two hours"), for the same honor code reasons. However, using electronic means to timestamp the exams does allow an instructor to impose a limit. You should clarify any policies your own school may have before administering an assessment.

If you proctor your in-person examinations, you will likely have to modify your exams or expectations so they will work without the need for a proctor. There are software packages that can monitor student test-taking with the student's laptop camera (including eye-tracking!), audio, and other means to attempt to catch cheating, and some schools are using these tools. While these tools can be effective, you should weigh potential privacy concerns your students might have before using them, and of course you should ensure that your school (and even local laws) allow them.

There is also software that you can use to administer exams that times the students and provides a relatively secure system for taking the exam on their computers, but would not be considered anti-privacy. One example is the *Bluebook* software as discussed in Chapter 5. Please email the author for more information.

One concern about giving exams during online courses is the timing of when the students take the tests. If you expect students to attend the class live, you may be able to schedule the exam during a regular class time, and all of your students can take the test at the same time. This can work well for high school courses, for example. But, for many classes, it will be hard to schedule all of your students to take exams simultaneously, particularly if they are in different time zones. If students take an exam at different times, there is a likelihood that some students who take the exam before others will discuss the exam with those taking it later, compromising the exam. One way to remedy this is to modify the exam to give different questions to different students. However, this can increase grading time, and it can also be difficult to ensure the fairness of all questions across all students. If your exam is numerical, there is software that can randomize the question values, but students can still give away the type of problem to others.

If your exams consist of students writing code, you can consider using one of the tools discussed in Chapter 5 (e.g., MOSS) to check student code against each other to look for significant overlap (and a good chance for cheating). This assumes you have the exams in digital format, and it also assumes that the exam questions will lead to significantly different answers.

Alternatives to examinations

Because of the nature of online classes with respect to exams and also because of the potential for cheating, you may want to think about alternatives to traditional examinations.[5] Testing isn't always the best way to assess your students. As with any assessment, you want to be able to differentiate the students who can demonstrate proficiency with the course material, from those that

---

5 You may want to think about alternatives to exams for an in-person course, as well!

do not. You ideally want a decent range of grades, as well. Exams tend to have both of these features, so finding alternate types of assignments that do both can be challenging. See Chapter 7 for a detailed look at alternatives to exams. In particular, see the Subsection *Do you need to have exams?*.

SECTIONS AND TEACHING ASSISTANTS

If you hold regular TA-taught recitation sections for in-person courses, and you want to continue to offer them for online courses, you will need to plan out the logistics carefully. You should consider whether you want to make the sections mandatory or optional, and you need to ensure that your TAs understand the format for section and that they understand any differences between in-person sections and online sections. If sections are normally TA-led where the TA delivers lecture-like material to students, or goes over problems on a board, etc., then the transition could be as simple as converting to an online video conferencing system like Zoom. If, however, the TA usually facilitates students in pairs or groups, then you need to plan how that will occur. The TAs could use breakout rooms in Zoom or another similar system, but they should plan on some additional overhead in terms of the amount of time it takes to set up and transition between rooms during section.

If you decide to make sections mandatory, and particularly if you have students in different time zones, you should do your best to ensure that there are enough sections available for students to enroll in a section that is at a reasonable time. This is not always possible, of course, but if there is time to poll the students to find their geographic location, then you may be able to plan better. You may also have TAs in different time zones, as well, so this may be beneficial for your section scheduling.

During the term, check in frequently with your TAs to see how sections are going. Has there been good attendance and participation? Have students been happy with breakout rooms? Do the

TAs have suggestions to make sections smoother? As always, if you get good suggestions, do your best to make changes, if possible.

GRADING

Grading for an online course does not have to be significantly different than for an in-person course, although it may be difficult to schedule grading parties with your TAs. Depending on *why* you are holding an online course, you may want to reconsider how you grade students' work. During the COVID-19 pandemic, students were often more stressed than in a normal term, and it made sense to me and my teaching colleagues to be considerate of the students' needs when grading. For example, we accepted late work with very little (if any) push-back. Students did not (to my knowledge) abuse this. We also tried to give students more time for certain assignments, which led to higher grades overall. This did not affect how we graded the assignments, but it ultimately affected the grades themselves.

COMBATING "ZOOM FATIGUE"

Taking a class online necessarily means that you, your TAs, and your students will be sitting in front of a computer for even longer than you normally do. This also includes participating in many online video sessions, which can quickly become tiresome. You will have multiple online meetings to attend (with students, TAs, other faculty, etc.), and you will have less direct interaction with people in general, much less with your students. So-called "Zoom Fatigue" can quickly set in, and you, your TAs, and your students may start resenting having to attend one more online meeting. This is particularly true if you are teaching multiple online courses at the same time, and if your students are taking multiple online courses.

As your course progresses, try to proactively limit the amount of extra online time you expect from your TAs and students. Make TA meetings as succinct as you can, and schedule them for as short a block of time as you can. Likewise for any ancillary meetings or for videos that you want your students to attend or watch. It might sound like a great idea to put together extra videos to provide more support, but students may start to resent the fact that they have more to do for the course, even if it is optional. If you teach live lectures and they are more than fifty minutes, take a break in the middle to let your students relax their eyes for a few minutes. Also, don't be too surprised if your students don't catch everything you say (this is true for any lecture in general, truthfully), because it is more difficult to pay attention to a video or an online presenter than when in a live lecture.

Finally: although it is cliché, make sure that you close your computer for some scheduled down-time outside of meals and sleep. Don't try to attend every meeting if you can help it (though don't miss the important ones), and try to exercise at least a bit every day, even if it is just a quick walk outside.

WHAT TO DO IF...

What if my students don't want to show their video?

With the advent of teaching live to students online who have video cameras on their computers, it would seem like the best idea would be to encourage your students to turn on their videos to get the best experience for them and for you. Some students don't want to turn on their videos, for various (and mostly) legitimate reasons. While it might seem like students are trying to *appear* like they are paying attention by being connected but really just tuning out, be careful not to assume this. They may very well be paying as close attention as anyone else attending the class. Students may not be comfortable showing their home surroundings, or perhaps their Internet access is too slow to reliably stream their own video. They may be working in cramped conditions with others around, or they may not want to show their home environment for reasons that are not your business. Keep in mind that in an in-person classroom, the students are paying attention to you, and they are only actively facing *you*. They aren't directly facing their peers, and they can easily look around to see if anyone is observing them if they wish. Online, however, everyone's video is shown to all participants, and no one has any idea if someone else is observing them, or not. This is not a normal situation for a student.

Encouraging students to show their video is reasonable, but be careful not to put too much weight on it, and it would be a good idea to be clear that it is not mandatory. Your school may have certain requirements for students to show their video, but if they do not, I would strongly urge you to let the students who are not comfortable with their video just attend by audio only (or through watching the recording). You should also address this with your TAs if they have section: yes, it can be awkward for them to teach to a mostly blank screen, but that is one of the challenging aspects of teaching online. If you require participation in lecture or section, you should also allow your students to do so through audio (or even typed text, if necessary).

What if something goes wrong during lecture?

It will! During a lecture in my first online class during the COVID-19 pandemic, I accidentally knocked over my computer and monitor, and the whole setup went crashing to the floor. Luckily nothing broke, but it took me thirty seconds or so to re-position everything, and to get over the shock of it. I looked at the recording after the course, and it was quite comical. But, once I composed myself, I made a quick joke about it, and then moved on, and no one ever mentioned it again.

Your students will forgive you if you have technological challenges while teaching – they understand that this is part of working with technology in general. If your computer crashes (virtually, not just onto the floor!), or if there are Internet disruptions, you should try to reconnect as quickly as possible, and try not to get too stressed about it. If for some reason you cannot get back online, your students will eventually realize what happened, and you can triage the situation after the fact, by reconvening, or by recording a lecture. Likewise if something else breaks, such as the pen for your tablet, do your best to continue without the tool.

What if my students have technological challenges attending class, or completing assignments?

This is a challenge for some students. Their Internet may be sub-par, or they may have older equipment that cannot handle high speed video conferencing, or the software that they need to use. You can try to work with your school's administration to mitigate some of these issues, and there may also be other organizations that can help out with upgraded technology (e.g., getting a student a new computer). Do your best to work with any affected students as best you can, and if the issues are not the students' fault, you should consider treating it as an accommodation and give leeway when you can. Furthermore, be aware that if they are having technological trouble in your class and they are also taking other online courses, they are likely having similar issues in the other classes, too. I have given students incomplete grades (where they can complete the class after the term ends) in situations where their technology has broken or was not up to the challenge of the online course.

What if my students watch the lecture recordings at 2x speed?

Many video players allow students to watch class recordings at increased speeds. You presumably pace your lectures reasonably well for real-time watching, but students who want to get through the lectures faster can be lured into watching them at speeds from 1.25 times faster all the way up to two times normal speed. It goes without saying that watching sped-up videos is likely to be detrimental to your students' assimilation of the course material. Unfortunately, there isn't much you can do about it, except to acknowledge that it is likely happening for a subset of your students. Some platforms allow you to limit faster-than-normal speeds, and you can see if you have the ability to do this. However, students know the technology is possible, and will find a way if they really want to do it.

So: you can encourage them to watch the videos at normal speeds. You can also encourage "lecture watching parties" where students watch the recordings together (virtually) so they can discuss the lectures. I have colleagues who have had lecture-watching parties that included a TA to answer questions live. But, the bottom line is that you probably cannot do too much to limit students from watching the videos at faster speeds, and the burden is on them to watch at a speed that allows them to learn the material.

What if my office hours are too busy?

Because the barrier to "go to office hours" is lower for online courses, you may find that your office hours are busier than they would be for an online course. You can try to encourage students to go to other less-busy office hours if they can, and you may also be able to arrange to have a TA help out with your office hours. You can also consider holding more office hours to spread out the load. Finally, you could try to have a rationing system where you prioritize helping students who have not been to office hours too often. Unfortunately, many students who come to office hours frequently are also the ones who need them more, so this may not be a worthwhile strategy.

What if my class size gets much bigger for my online course?

At Stanford during the COVID-19 pandemic, we found that many computer science courses had significantly increased enrollments (sometimes as much as 100% increases). This may be because students have the idea that computer science courses are easier to transition to in an online format, or it could be that students wanted to take challenging courses online[6], because they think it will be more manageable. As with any other enrollment increase, you should involve your administration as needed to try and get more resources (e.g., more TAs). Once you know your enrollments, you can also brainstorm how to manage the increased workload. This may include reducing the number of assignments (to allow for longer grading times), or changing the format of exams to be easier to grade. You may also have to change office hours formats to be able to handle the increase in attendance. None of these changes are ideal, but you need to manage them as best you can.

FINAL THOUGHTS

Teaching an online class can be stressful, particularly if you are doing it for the first time. You will make some mistakes, and as always, learn from the mistakes for the next time around. Teaching online can be an excellent experience, though, and you should be willing to try new ideas, and to make changes when things are going as smoothly as you had hoped they would.

As discussed in Chapter 12, you should elicit feedback from your students often, especially if you are teaching an online course for the first time. Ask them what is working and what isn't working, and make changes if you can. If you aren't able to make changes, open a dialogue with your students about your reasons

---

6 During the first term, we also had a school-wide Pass/Fail option for all courses, so this could have increased enrollment, as well. But, enrollments also stayed large in follow-on, non-Pass/Fail terms.

for keeping things the way they are. In general, allow constructive feedback at every opportunity, and act on it when you can.

If your colleagues are also teaching online courses in the same term that you are, reach out to them to discuss their strategies and ideas, and share your own. During the COVID-19 pandemic, it was extremely helpful to have colleagues to talk to about modifying my courses to be online, and there are many decisions that my co-instructors and I made that were based on suggestions and feedback from colleagues.